FILM 68/69

An Anthology by the
National Society
of Film Critics

edited by

HOLLIS ALPERT

and

ANDREW SARRIS

Simon and Schuster   New York

The reviews and articles in this book originally appeared, for the most part, in the publications for which the contributors regularly write. Thanks are hereby given by the contributors as follows:

Hollis Alpert, reviews of *Shame, 2001: A Space Odyssey, Joanna, Bullitt, Wild 90, The Birthday Party*, and the article, "The Graduate Makes Out," reprinted by permission of *Saturday Review*, Copyright 1968, 1969, Saturday Review, Inc.

Harold Clurman, reviews of *The Birthday Party* and *The Killing of Sister George*, reprinted by permission of *The Nation*, Copyright 1969, The Nation, Inc.

Penelope Gilliatt, reviews of *The Green Berets, Les Carabiniers, 2001: A Space Odyssey, Hunger, Young Törless* and *Targets*, reprinted by permission of *The New Yorker*, Copyright © 1968, The New Yorker Magazine, Inc.

Philip T. Hartung, reviews of *For Love of Ivy, Dark of the Sun, Planet of the Apes, War and Peace, The Boston Strangler, The Lion in Winter* and *Romeo and Juliet*, reprinted by permission of *Commonweal*, Copyright 1968, Commonweal Publishing Co., Inc.

Pauline Kael, reviews of *The Fox, La Chinoise, China Is Near* and *Weekend*, reprinted by permission of *The New Yorker*, Copyright © 1968, The New Yorker Magazine, Inc.

Stefan Kanfer, reviews of *No Way to Treat a Lady, The Thomas Crown Affair, Candy*, and the articles, "The Student Movie-Makers" and "The Late Show as History," reprinted by permission from *Time*, The Weekly Newsmagazine, Copyright 1968, Time, Inc.

Stanley Kauffmann, reviews of *The Charge of the Light Brigade, Up Tight, Tell Me Lies, The Anderson Platoon, Inside North Vietnam, Yellow Submarine, Beyond the Law, Fist in His Pocket, Warrendale*, and *War and Peace*, reprinted by permission of the *New Republic* © 1968, Harrison-Blaine of New Jersey, Inc.

CONTENTS

FOREWORD / Stanley Kauffmann   11
INTRODUCTION   13
   ① The Anthology / Hollis Alpert   13
   2. The Awards / Andrew Sarris   16

I. THE YEAR'S FILMS

1. VISIONS   23

Shame / John Simon, Hollis Alpert, Wilfrid Sheed   23
Weekend / Pauline Kael, Andrew Sarris   32
Belle de Jour / Andrew Sarris   43
Rosemary's Baby / Andrew Sarris   49
2001: A Space Odyssey / Penelope Gilliatt, Hollis Alpert,
   Joseph Morgenstern   53
Planet of the Apes / Philip T. Hartung   63

2. RUMBLINGS OF REVOLT   65

La Chinoise / Pauline Kael, Andrew Sarris   65
China Is Near / Pauline Kael, Andrew Sarris   75
Up Tight / Stanley Kauffmann   83
For Love of Ivy and *Dark of the Sun* / Philip T. Hartung   87

7

3. MEN AT WAR   89

The Charge of the Light Brigade / Stanley Kauffmann,
    John Simon   89
Les Carabiniers / Penelope Gilliatt   94
A Face of War / Richard Schickel   98
Tell Me Lies, The Anderson Platoon, and
    Inside North Vietnam / Stanley Kauffmann   100
The Green Berets / Penelope Gilliatt   103

4. MEN AND WOMEN   107

Petulia / Richard Schickel, Wilfrid Sheed   107
The Thomas Crown Affair / Wilfrid Sheed, Stefan Kanfer   110
Joanna / Hollis Alpert, Joseph Morgenstern   113
Rachel, Rachel / Arthur Knight, Richard Schickel   116
Zita / John Simon   120
Faces / Andrew Sarris, Arthur Schlesinger, Jr.   122

5. THE ARTIST AS ANTI-HERO   127

Hunger / Penelope Gilliatt   127
Hour of the Wolf / John Simon, Richard Schickel   130
Charlie Bubbles / Andrew Sarris, Richard Schickel   136

6. COMEDY AND SATIRE   142

The Odd Couple and others / Wilfrid Sheed   142
The Producers / Arthur Schlesinger, Jr.   147
I Love You, Alice B. Toklas / Arthur Knight   148
Candy / Stefan Kanfer   149
Barbarella / John Simon   150

7. MUSICALS   152

Yellow Submarine / Stanley Kauffmann, John Simon   152
You Are What You Eat / Wilfrid Sheed   154
Star! / Arthur Schlesinger, Jr.   156
Finian's Rainbow / Arthur Knight   157
Oliver! / Joseph Morgenstern   159

8. VIOLENT GENRES 162

The Bride Wore Black / Andrew Sarris 162
Bullitt / Hollis Alpert 165
Targets / Penelope Gilliatt 166
Wild 90 / Hollis Alpert 168
Beyond the Law / Stanley Kauffmann 170
Will Penny / Arthur Knight 172
Wild in the Streets / Joseph Morgenstern, Wilfrid Sheed 173

9. CLINICAL CASES 176

Pretty Poison / Joseph Morgenstern 176
Fist in His Pocket / Stanley Kauffmann 178
Young Törless / Penelope Gilliatt 179
Charly / Arthur Knight 181
The Boston Strangler / Philip T. Hartung, Wilfrid Sheed 182
No Way to Treat a Lady and Rod Steiger / Stefan Kanfer 185
Warrendale / Joseph Morgenstern, Stanley Kauffmann 188

10. ADAPTATIONS 194

The Fox / Pauline Kael 194
The Lion in Winter / Philip T. Hartung,
    Arthur Schlesinger, Jr., John Simon 200
Romeo and Juliet / Philip T. Hartung, John Simon 206
The Killing of Sister George / Harold Clurman 210
The Birthday Party / Harold Clurman, Wilfrid Sheed,
    Hollis Alpert 211
War and Peace / Philip T. Hartung, Stanley Kauffmann,
    Richard Schickel 216
The Heart Is a Lonely Hunter / Richard Schickel 223
The Fixer / Richard Schickel, Arthur Schlesinger, Jr. 225
The Sea Gull / Arthur Schlesinger, Jr., John Simon 228

II. REFLECTIONS

The Graduate Makes Out / Hollis Alpert 235
Burton and Taylor Must Go / Wilfrid Sheed 242

The Student Movie-Makers / Stefan Kanfer   247
The Late Show as History / Stefan Kanfer   252
L'Affaire Langlois / Arthur Knight   257
Oscar Wiles / Andrew Sarris   261

ABOUT THE CONTRIBUTORS   267

INDEX   269

FOREWORD

First, a note of acknowledgment. The reception of the first volume in this series surpassed our hopes, let alone our expectations. The society, which turns all proceeds to society purposes, is very grateful.

In the foreword to that volume, I explained those purposes. That was when we were new. What to say now? I remember a brochure I once got from a just-opened Miami Beach hotel named (let's assume) the Beachview, in which everything about the place was called brand-new. A year later when I got their next brochure, I wondered what they could possibly say. I opened that second brochure and read: "In the old Beachview tradition . . ."

In the old NSFC tradition, we offer this second volume, with thanks and greetings.

STANLEY KAUFFMANN, *Chairman,*
National Society of Film Critics

INTRODUCTION

1. THE ANTHOLOGY

It was not so long ago that films could enter the market-place unaffected to any important degree by critical reaction, whether approving or disapproving. It was a Hollywood maxim, in fact, that critics didn't mean anything; the audience was there for the films it wanted to see. It was assumed, too, that the audience could be manipulated into a receptive mood through publicity, star appeal, tried and proven subject matter. Pictures either were "pre-sold" or could be given "the hard sell." Most critics were just as content to have it so, for it was not the critic's function to sustain or boost the medium financially. In the broadest sense, his function had to do with aesthetic assessment, insofar as this was possible with a medium so often devoted to the most crass of considerations.

In recent years, however, the situation not only has changed, but shows increasing signs of reversal. First it was the so-called "art-house" kind of film that benefited noticeably from favorable reviews. But even then it was the importer and distributor of foreign films who was put in the position of having to worry about reviews. His hard cash was on the line if his own judgment was not borne out by reviewers for *The New York Times* and other important daily and weekly publications. New York, without question, has become the testing ground for the imported film (and the modest domestic film of quality); good reviews usually mean good box office in the city; and distribution throughout the country becomes more easily gained thereafter.

13

But, from the American industry point of view, the critic still operated from what was thought to be a tower of non-commercial purity. Sure, it was fine to have him on one's side, if only for purposes of ego gratification, but the public still knew what it wanted, could still be led by the nose, and film-makers hit by unfavorable notices could still cry all the way to the bank. There were said to be two kinds of movies: the commercial picture and the "critic's picture."

What has become apparent in the last year or two is that even this distinction seems to be blurring. Not in toto, obviously. John Wayne and *The Green Berets* can still shoot their way to box-office victory through a hail of critical crossfire. Violence- and sex-oriented movies can still be sold on the basis of their ingredients—how much more so, though, when critics find the violence artistically meaningful, the eroticism honest! If one were paranoiacally inclined, one might almost suspect a conspiracy between the critic and a large part of the audience. Those films that are "liked" do much better, on the whole, than those that are not. The situation has not yet reached the extreme of the "hit or flop" condition of the Broadway-based theater, but it is certainly beginning to be reminiscent of it. During the past year several of the most expensive and star-studded films released by major companies failed at the box office after receiving lackluster critical welcomes. Not even the sacrosanct Julie Andrews could carry *Star!* to a happy box-office ending. The redoubtable Burton-Taylor combination was of little help to films such as *The Comedians* and *Boom.*

Does this new state of affairs mean, then, that the film critic has reached a position of power comparable to that of the *New York Times* theater critic? Or has the audience for motion pictures changed and grown mentally to a surprising degree? The critics represented in this second annual volume would probably agree that it is the second possibility that is the more likely. Films these days are more likely to be talked about, to be the subject of social conversation, than new plays both on and off Broadway. The critical consensus is, in a sense, the published record of informed opinion about new movies. That informed opinion is broadly based. The enthusiasm of the new generations for film is matched by that of an older crowd that has discovered movies and takes them seriously.

The movies themselves have a lot to do with it, of course. Not that they are so much better than older movies, but the cinema form does continue to reveal its potential, it continues to excite and stimulate, and it continues to grow freer. Because of its recently found freedom to treat frankly of virtually all subjects, it is now very much a symptomatic art of our times. It may be of interest to mention that while literary critics debate with each other over "the death of the novel," no one has so much as mentioned the death of the movies. Not, anyway, since talkies supplanted the silent film.

Thus, if this anthology of critical and essayistic pieces by film critics has some primary value—besides being a record of published reviews of the more significant movies released in 1968 in the United States—it is as a demonstration of the kind of lively discussion that films make possible. The critics herein, though they are members of a "society" of film critics, by no means agree with each other. Often enough, their views of the same film are poles apart. But if not all of these critics take themselves with total seriousness, they all take films seriously and deem them worthy of high standards of criticism. This in itself says something about films and what they are becoming.

But it says something about the film audience too. Film critics don't address themselves to a vacuum. Many of these critics have large, not to say mass, readerships. They are not writing down to or over the heads of their audiences. This is straight-on discussion, in other words. This, then, is the real power of the critic: not that he can influence a film financially, but that he can speak directly to and with the audience for films. Even the twelve-year-olds the movie industry was once said to address itself to have grown wiser, if not older. Some of these new generations are terrifyingly sophisticated.

The audience for films is not all young, but lately it has become predominantly so, and it wants to know more and understand more about films. It discusses not only films, but film critics. Critic-baiting, in fact, may become another national sport. Fair enough: the street ought to run both ways. Criticism is a basically healthy activity, no matter at what or whom it is directed. This, at least, is one attitude shared in common by the contributors to this volume. The editors have attempted to provide a balanced and representative selection of reviews, along with a fair representation of the work of individual critics. A few may be said to be slightly under-represented, but this is either because the exigencies of editorial considerations cause them to write briefly or because, for one reason or another, they were not able to have a full year's output. Harold Clurman, for example, began his film reviewing late in the year. As little editing as possible has been done, but now and then a segment relating to a particular film has been lifted out of the context of a larger piece. A good many of our fellow contributors flower out now and then into critical and reportorial essays. This has happened so frequently during the past year that it was felt a special section of these essays might add to the flavor of the book, and add more perspective to what transpired cinematically during the course of the year.

HOLLIS ALPERT

2. THE AWARDS

The National Society of Film Critics' awards for 1968 were determined in each competitive category on the second ballot, no candidate having won a majority on the first. Hence, each critic was asked to vote for three candidates in each category (the first choice worth three points, the second two, the third one), a simple plurality establishing the winner. *Shame* (sixteen points) won as best picture, followed by *Faces* (thirteen) and *Weekend* (eleven). The voting, in order of each member's preference, breaks down as follows: Hollis Alpert: *2001: A Space Odyssey, Rosemary's Baby, Belle de Jour.* Harold Clurman: *Shame, Faces, Love Affair.* Philip T. Hartung: *Rachel, Rachel, Nazarin, Shame.* Pauline Kael: *Weekend, Shame,* no third choice. Stefan Kanfer: *Shame, Faces, Weekend.* Stanley Kauffmann: *Love Affair, Weekend, Faces.* Arthur Knight: *The Lion in Winter, The Fifth Horseman Is Fear, The Fixer.* Joseph Morgenstern: *Weekend, Shame, Love Affair.* Andrew Sarris: *Belle de Jour, China Is Near, La Chinoise.* Richard Schickel: *Faces, Belle de Jour, Weekend.* Arthur Schlesinger, Jr.:

2001, *Shame, Faces.* Wilfrid Sheed: *Faces, China Is Near, Bullitt.*
John Simon: *Shame, China Is Near, The Fifth Horseman Is Fear.*
Ingmar Bergman (*Shame, Hour of the Wolf*) won as best direc-
tor, with seventeen points, over Jean-Luc Godard (*Weekend, La
Chinoise, Les Carabiniers*), twelve, and Marco Bellocchio (*China
Is Near, Fist in His Pocket*), ten. Alpert: Peter Yates (*Bullitt*),
Luis Buñuel (*Belle de Jour*), Michael Sarne (*Joanna*). Clurman:
Bellocchio, Bergman, John Cassavetes (*Faces*). Hartung: Carol
Reed (*Oliver!*), Bergman, Buñuel (*Nazarin*). Kael: Godard, Berg-
man, Bellocchio. Kanfer: Bergman, Cassavetes, Yates. Kauffmann:
Dušan Makavejev (*Love Affair*), Godard, Richard Lester (*Petu-
lia*). Knight: Yates, Roman Polanski (*Rosemary's Baby*), John
Frankenheimer (*The Fixer*). Morgenstern: Godard, Bergman,
Makavejev. Sarris: Buñuel, Godard, Bellocchio. Schickel: Buñuel,
Cassavetes, Godard. Schlesinger: Bergman, Stanley Kubrick
(*2001*), Godard. Sheed: Bellocchio, Cassavetes, Yates. Simon:
Bergman, Bellocchio, Robert Enrico (*Zita*).

Per Oscarsson (*Hunger*) was chosen best actor, with sixteen
points to nine each for George C. Scott (*Petulia*) and Alan Arkin
(*The Heart Is a Lonely Hunter*). Alpert: Trevor Howard (*The
Charge of the Light Brigade*), Miroslav Mahaček (*The Fifth
Horseman Is Fear*), Oscarsson. Clurman: Max von Sydow
(*Shame*), Arkin, Peter Sellers (*I Love You, Alice B. Toklas*). Har-
tung: Ron Moody (*Oliver!*), Alan Bates (*The Fixer*), Oscarsson.
Kael: Oscarsson, Gian Maria Volontè (*We Still Kill the Old Way,
The Violent Four*), Steve McQueen (*Bullitt*). Kanfer: Oscarsson,
Mahaček, McQueen. Kauffmann: Oscarsson, Nicol Williamson
(*Inadmissible Evidence, The Bofors Gun*), Robert Shaw (*The
Birthday Party*). Knight: Moody, Cliff Robertson (*Charly*), Wal-
ter Matthau (*The Odd Couple*). Morgenstern: Oscarsson, Arkin,
no third choice. Sarris: George C. Scott (*Petulia*), Glauco Mauri
(*China Is Near*), Matthau (*The Secret Life of an American
Wife*). Schickel: Scott, Sellers, Arkin. Schlesinger: Scott, Oscars-
son, Matthau (*The Odd Couple*). Sheed: von Sydow (*Shame,
Hour of the Wolf*), Williamson (*The Bofors Gun*), Arkin.
Simon: Arkin, Mahaček, von Sydow (*Shame*).

Liv Ullmann (*Shame*) completed the Scandinavian sweep with
twenty-one points to thirteen each for Lynn Carlin (*Faces*) and
Joanne Woodward (*Rachel, Rachel*). Alpert: Maggie Smith (*Hot
Millions*), Mia Farrow (*Rosemary's Baby*), Carol White (*Poor

Cow). Clurman: Ullmann, Carlin, Farrow. Hartung: Ullmann, Woodward, Katharine Hepburn (*The Lion in Winter*). Kael: Barbra Streisand (*Funny Girl*), Ullmann, Vanessa Redgrave (*The Sea Gull*). Kanfer: Ullmann, Woodward, Carlin. Kauffmann: Ullmann, Woodward, Anne Heywood (*The Fox*). Knight: Hepburn, Woodward, Joanna Shimkus, (*Zita*). Morgenstern: Streisand, Ullmann, Woodward. Sarris: Carlin, Redgrave, Tuesday Weld (*Pretty Poison*). Schickel: Carlin, Weld, Catherine Deneuve (*Belle de Jour*). Schlesinger: Redgrave, Ullmann, no third choice. Sheed: Woodward, Carlin, Beryl Reid (*The Killing of Sister George*). Simon: Ullmann, Carlin, Woodward.

Seymour Cassel (*Faces*) won the best-supporting-actor award, with eleven points to nine for Dirk Bogarde (*The Fixer*) and seven for Sydney Tafler (*The Birthday Party*). Alpert: Jeremy Kemp (*The Strange Affair*), Cassel, Tafler. Clurman: Tafler, Harry Andrews (*The Sea Gull*), Cassel. Hartung: Bogarde, Andrews, Kemp. Kael: Ossie Davis (*The Scalphunters*), Joseph Wiseman (*The Night They Raided Minsky's*), Glauco Mauri (*China Is Near*). Kanfer: Bogarde, Gene Wilder (*The Producers*), Michel Bouquet (*The Bride Wore Black*). Kauffmann: Trevor Howard (*The Charge of the Light Brigade*), John Gielgud (*Brigade*), Bogarde. Knight: Norman Wisdom (*Minsky's*), Timothy Dalton (*The Lion in Winter*), Tafler. Morgenstern: Cassel, Tafler, Wiseman. Sarris: Bouquet, Richard Chamberlain (*Petulia*), Tafler. Schickel: Cassell, Bogarde, Davis. Schlesinger: Jack Albertson (*The Subject Was Roses*), Andrews, Gielgud. Sheed: Ian Holm (*The Bofors Gun, The Fixer*), Cassel, Howard. Simon: Paul Crauchet (*Zita*), Bouquet, Kemp.

Billie Whitelaw (*Charlie Bubbles*) won the best-supporting-actress award, with sixteen points to fourteen for Geneviève Page (*Belle de Jour*) and eleven for Paola Pitagora (*Fist in His Pocket*). Alpert: Page, Irene Papas (*We Still Kill the Old Way*), Joyce Van Patten (*I Love You, Alice B. Toklas*). Clurman: Pitagora, Van Patten, Page. Hartung: Kate Harrington (*Rachel, Rachel*), Whitelaw, Page. Kael: Pitagora, Van Patten, Papas. Kanfer: Shirley Knight (*Petulia*), Page, Pitagora. Kauffmann: Whitelaw, Knight, Pitagora. Knight: Ruth Gordon (*Rosemary's Baby*), Van Patten, Joanna Shimkus (*Boom!*). Morgenstern: Pitagora, Van Patten, Page. Sarris: Whitelaw, Page, Kathleen Widdoes (*The Sea Gull*). Schickel: Whitelaw, Knight, Van Patten. Schlesinger:

Papas, Whitelaw, Page. Sheed: Whitelaw, Elda Tattoli (*China Is Near*), Dandy Nichols (*The Birthday Party*). Simon: Page, Kim Hunter (*Planet of the Apes*), Harrington.

John Cassavetes (*Faces*) won the award for best screenplay, with twelve votes. Marco Bellocchio and Elda Tattoli (*China Is Near*) were tied with Ingmar Bergman (*Shame*) at eight points each. Alpert: Charles Wood (*The Charge of the Light Brigade*), Zbyněk Brynych and Ester Krumbachová (*The Fifth Horseman Is Fear*), Bellocchio and Tattoli. Clurman: Bellocchio and Tattoli; Miloš Forman, Ivan Passer, Jaroslav Papušek (*The Fireman's Ball*), Dušan Makavejev (*Love Affair*). Hartung: Cassavetes, Stanley Kubrick and Arthur C. Clarke (*2001: A Space Odyssey*), James Goldman (*The Lion in Winter*). Kael: Jean-Luc Godard (*Weekend, La Chinoise*), Bergman, Bellocchio and Tattoli. Kanfer: Bergman, Cassavetes, Brynych. Kauffmann: Makavejev, Brian de Palma and Charles Hirsch (*Greetings!*), Wood. Knight: Stewart Stern (*Rachel, Rachel*), Goldman, Lawrence B. Marcus (*Petulia*). Morgenstern: Makavejev, Godard (*Weekend*), Brynych. Sarris: Harold Pinter (*The Birthday Party*), Godard (*La Chinoise*), Mel Brooks (*The Producers*). Schickel: Marcus, Cassavetes, Kubrick and Clarke. Schlesinger: Cassevetes, Kubrick and Clarke, Herbert Sargeant (*Bye, Bye Braverman*). Sheed: Bellocchio and Tattoli, Bellocchio (*China Is Near, Fist in His Pocket*), Cassavetes, Hirsch and de Palma. Simon: Bergman, Stern, Brynych.

William A. Fraker (*Bullitt*) was voted best cinematographer with twelve points to eight for Sven Nykvist (*Shame*) and seven for Geoffrey Unsworth (*2001: A Space Odyssey*). Stanley Kauffmann abstained from the voting on the grounds that there were too many worthy candidates. Alpert: Fraker, Pasquale de Santis (*Romeo and Juliet*), Walter Lassally (*Joanna*). Clurman: Nykvist, Jean Boffety (*Zita*), Jan Troell (*Here Is Your Life*). Hartung: Unsworth, de Santis, Jack Cardiff (*Girl on a Motorcycle*). Kael: Nykvist, Haskell Wexler (*The Thomas Crown Affair*), no third choice. Kanfer: Raoul Coutard (*La Chinoise, Weekend, Les Carabiniers*), Nykvist, Unsworth. Knight: Fraker (*Bullitt*), Fraker (*Rosemary's Baby*), Fraker (*The Fox*). Morgenstern: Jan Kališ (*The Fifth Horseman Is Fear*), Oswald Morris (*Oliver!*), Andrew Laszlo (*Minsky's*). Sarris: Coutard (*La Chinoise*), Coutard (*Weekend*), Coutard (*Les Carabiniers*). Schickel: Unsworth, Nick Roeg (*Petulia*), no third choice. Schlesinger: Unsworth,

Roeg, David Watkin (*The Charge of the Light Brigade*). Sheed: Fraker, Cardiff, Roeg. Simon: Troell, Boffety, Cardiff.

Special awards of merit (by simple majority vote) were presented to Allan King's *Warrendale* and Eugene S. Jones's *A Face of War* for feature-length documentary, and to *Yellow Submarine* for feature-length animation.

ANDREW SARRIS

1966 AWARDS

Best Picture: *Blow-Up*
Best Director: Michelangelo Antonioni
Best Actor: Michael Caine (*Alfie*)
Best Actress: Sylvie (*The Shameless Old Lady*)

1967 AWARDS

Best Picture: *Persona*
Best Director: Ingmar Bergman
Best Actor: Rod Steiger (*In the Heat of the Night*)
Best Actress: Bibi Andersson (*Persona*)
Best Supporting Actor: Gene Hackman (*Bonnie and Clyde*)
Best Supporting Actress: Majorie Rhodes (*The Family Way*)
Best Screenplay: David Newman and Robert Benton (*Bonnie and Clyde*)
Best Cinematography: Haskell Wexler (*In the Heat of the Night*)

I:

THE YEAR'S FILMS

I
VISIONS

SHAME

JOHN SIMON

Ingmar Bergman's *Shame* is a war film almost not about war. It is about the *condition humaine,* for which war serves as metaphor. Eva and Jan Rosenberg, married seven years and childless, are former philharmonic musicians. A civil war has been rampaging through the country for years. They now live in an island cottage with an orchard and a greenhouse and sell fruit for a living. A bad heart—this too will prove partly metaphorical—has kept Jan out of the army. The couple have all but accepted war as the natural state of affairs. They hear its percussion, observe troop movements, but are left alone. It is an incomprehensible war, particularly to artists. Only when Jan has a toothache does he wonder if the dentist is still there; inscrutable and devouring, war is tolerated as long as it leaves thee and me reasonably unscathed.

It is a Friday morning, with the everyday irritations and petty sloppinesses encroached on by strange signs. Jan relates a dream he has had: they were back in the symphony orchestra, playing the slow movement of the Fourth Brandenburg Concerto (remember the significance of Bach on the radio in *The Silence* and *Persona?*) —that *was* peace. Jan has a bothersome tooth but exaggerates the pain; he is too lazy to shave. Eva has to do the accounts and get the car ready. Church bells are heard ringing—mysteriously for a Friday. The phone also rings, but whenever Eva picks up the receiver no voice answers.

Some tanks go by. Eva and Jan fetch the lingonberries they are to deliver to the mayor. Jan bumbles and they have a tiff. Recon-

23

ciled, they finally drive off. The camera has been hovering close to them: a few medium-long shots, but mostly close-ups, some of them extreme. Often a two-shot is held for a very long time, like the one over Jan's shoulder, our gaze riveted on Eva's radiant aliveness.

The station wagon rolls out into the landscape and into a long shot of great and disquieting beauty. Not only does the car glisten ominously, the whole landscape has a strident, metallic quality, as if you could cut yourself on the light it reflects. The couple stop by a nervily splashing stream to get a fish for dinner from Filip, the grizzled fisherman. The sound of the river is one of the very few natural ones that we shall hear on the sound track; mostly there will be sounds of war, or silence—never background music. Filip warns Eva about approaching enemy movements. The Rosenbergs' radio has once again not been functioning; Jan, the escapist, thinks it is better so. He also thought, as he watched Eva get the fish, how much he loved her, how beautiful she was. She laughs and exclaims, "Only from a distance."

On the ferry to the mainland they meet the mayor and his wife, off to see their soldier son. All around them armament, bustle, tension. The lingonberries will be deposited with the maid; but the four of them must get together again one of these evenings to play chamber music. Bergman uses the device of shooting a head in very tight close-up, but leaving just enough space around the edges of the frame for suggestions of surrounding upheaval to form an agitated halo. On the mainland, the Rosenbergs have received enough money to treat themselves to a bottle of wine. They go to Lobelius the antiquarian—the graciousness of wine is now sold along with other antiques. Lobelius has been called up; his baggy uniform is pathetic, as are his relationship with his housekeeper and his pitiful hope of getting an administrative job because of a bad leg.

The interior of the shop is tenebrous, yet here Sven Nykvist, Bergman's camera wizard, deploys some of his greatest artistry. The images become extremely sharp, glossy, ripe with chiaroscuro—as we remember them in the dinner-party scene in *Smiles of a Summer Night*. Lobelius shows his friends his most precious object, a little twosome of Meissen figurines making actual, tinkling music. All three watch and listen raptly. In this piece of eighteenth-century porcelain the past comes alive; so, too, as they sample the

German wine they are about to buy, the affability of yesteryear returns. Eva gently pats a stray curl on Jan's temple. The camera follows her gesture and pans around the room, picking out statues, pictures, clocks—an anthology of bygone well-being. When we come back to the Rosenbergs, they sit side by side, transfigured. Parting from Lobelius is halting, awkward, full of stabbing silences.

Back at the cottage, an idyllic outdoor dinner of fish and wine. The couple, tête-à-tête, are lovers again; they talk of having children after the war. Eva worries about her husband's potency in the most fondly fumbling way. Touchy though he is, Jan is in such a good mood nothing can unsettle him. Why not make babies right now, he suggests, and adds that he is no determinist. Stumped by that word, she replies, "I don't give a damn what you are, as long as you clean the sink." That is woman's practical wisdom. As they withdraw to make love, the man's hand is seen in extreme close-up picking a daisy from the table vase for his lady. More than a gesture of love, it is a pious offering to the goddess of the hearth.

Later that evening terrible things happen. A patrol warns the Rosenbergs about enemy parachutists. Air-to-ground battle. A man parachutes into a tree of the forest that surrounds the cottage. Eva rushes to help him, Jan is being cowardly. But the paratrooper in the tree is dying. His comrades now surround the cottage. Instead of killing the couple, they film an interview with Eva, asking her tough, confusing political questions, to which she gives honest but apolitical answers. When it is Jan's turn, he collapses. The patrol that came to warn them now counterattacks, and the invaders are drawn away.

That night Eva lies down close to the distraught Jan and tries to warm him with her creature heat. A close-up shows their faces, hers slightly above and behind his, filling the screen. It is a kind of *Pietà*. In the morning, they frenziedly load a few belongings into the car and head for the sea. Jan again proves his incompetence. He suggests they take some of the chickens along for food; can he cut off their heads, Eva asks. No, but he can shoot them with his rifle. He proceeds to miss one at point-blank range. "Oh God, I'm tired," Eva groans in disgust. (People who question Bergman's sense of comedy should have their noses rubbed in this scene.)

They drive through a landscape of death, reminiscent of the plague-ridden countryside through which the knight and squire of *The Seventh Seal* rode. The dead lie in horrible, undignified postures and groupings—death has caught them *in flagrante* with life, in desperate dalliance with survival. A tracking shot (the car) moves relentlessly forward, and the Guernican images it captures are tossed aside as quickly as they are picked up. Yet, for being almost subliminal, these visions are more infernal: they explode not on the screen but, like delayed-action bombs, in your mind.

Through a wooded landscape full of forest fires to a sea that is blocked off by abandoned and destroyed armament—and, suddenly, the corpses of children. Eva runs out of the car to bend over a little girl sprawled out like a discarded doll. There is a close-up of Eva's face against an ashen sky, her eyes torn open by grief. This woman will not have children, ever. She tells Jan to drive back home. It is not clear whether they return to survive or to perish with their house.

After a night of bombardment during which her whiter hand clasps his darker one for comfort, Eva and Jan rise to survey the damage. In one of the most haunting sequences of the film, the two stand incredulous before the devastation around them. In the background, the forest is burning: hideous balls of fire are climbing up slender, virginal birches and ravishing them. But also—irony or hope?—there is bird song; clear, liquid bird song on the sound track. And the sound of water dripping from a faucet. Perhaps life *can* go on. Later, in a darkened interior, Jan removes his precious viola from its case. In a beautiful, perhaps too deliberately composed, shot with chiaroscuro worthy of Georges de La Tour, the two heads bend over the instrument and, with it for hypotenuse, form a triangle. He tells her the story of Pampini, who made this viola and died of the cholera or something—Jan does not remember. Art survives disaster; but what of the artist?

This somewhat self-conscious scene is redeemed by a beautifully humane one. An attempt of the Rosenbergs to make love is foiled by Jan's getting a cramp in his leg. That night, when Eva asks Jan to join her in her bed, his childlike alacrity makes clear that he is seeking her, and she receiving him, as a mother, not as a wife.

The next few sequences are too dense, too rich to be cited in detail. The Rosenbergs, along with many other people suspected of collaboration, are herded into the headquarters of the island authorities, who have repulsed the invaders. There are marvelous shots of the Rosenbergs' heads bobbing up and down on a sea of driven humanity. The couple are roughly questioned about the film they made for the enemy: another voice has been dubbed in for Eva's, and it spouts collaborationist propaganda. Other people are treated worse than they, though Jan insists that during a brief separation from Eva he was brutally beaten.

They are now surrounded by the victims of interrogation. Some are badly hurt, one is a corpse. The horror is magnified by the fact that this is a converted schoolhouse; at dreadful moments the camera catches innocent children's drawings on the walls or scraps of disused learning on a blackboard. A cynical doctor ministers to them lackadaisically. Amid all this, Eva blurts out the second dream in the film. She feels as if she were in a dream, not hers but someone else's (Pascal's God's, we presume), and wonders "What happens when that person wakes up and is ashamed?"

There is a ghastly mock-execution scene, more frightening than a real one, but Mayor (or Colonel) Jacobi, who is in command here, spares his friends the Rosenbergs. In his office, Jacobi explains that he knows their innocence and that they were hauled in only to set an example to others; his instructions were not to hurt them, and he assumes they were obeyed. Jan eagerly confirms this. Eva gives him a quick, withering look, which Bergman's camera brilliantly keeps in the middle distance, showing it from Jacobi's observant point of view. They leave. Jacobi is revealed as not only shrewd but also tired, defeated: in extreme close-up, his cane pulls an antiquated heater closer to his chilly self, as he tries in vain to concentrate on his newspaper. Noises of trucks carrying off the condemned streak across the sound track.

The Rosenbergs live in relative comfort now; Jacobi supplies them with various amenities. We see him come to visit, bringing Eva a family heirloom and Jan a first edition of a Dvořák trio he hopes they will all play someday. As they sit around the table, he becomes momentarily sinister. "The sacred freedom of art," he snorts, thunderously bringing down his cane on the table; and then: "The sacred slackness of art!" The Rosenbergs are embarrassed by his presence; Filip the fisherman has warned them against this nexus.

Jan dozes off. In the bedroom, Jacobi, who has become her lover, hands Eva a large sum of money, his life's savings. She refuses it, and it remains on the bed as Eva leads Jacobi to the greenhouse where, she says, they must conduct their clandestine intercourse. There we see Jacobi's head in Eva's lap, just as Jan's had been in an earlier scene. He took the gauleiter's job only out of fear of active combat, Jacobi explains. He too is pitiable.

At dawn, Jan wakes up, lights upon the money and perplexedly pockets it. Then he sees Eva and Jacobi emerge from the greenhouse. The scene is brilliantly staged. He pads halfway up the stairs and sits down. The camera shoots through the balustrade, disclosing only his legs and feet encased in thick, silly-looking socks; we hear his reiterated "Eva!" among thin, puling sobs. He rises, staggers against the wall, and we see his chest, in a ludicrous pajama top, grievously heaving.

Jacobi is captured outside the cottage by Filip, who is a partisan leader, and his men. For a large ransom—they need funds—they'll let him go. Jacobi asks for a loan of the money he just gave Eva; Jan disclaims any knowledge of it. The cottage is viciously ransacked; even the rare viola and the seemingly invulnerable chickens are now destroyed. Finally the place is burned down. Filip hands Jan a gun; to prove his political cleanness, he must execute Jacobi. Recoiling at first, Jan warms to the task and kills with gusto—in a scene unsurpassable for controlled terror. Jacobi's body is carted off, with cans of food and other loot piled on top of it. Jan hands Eva the money. Again she just looks at him. When, later, she becomes hysterical, he slaps her; this only makes her cry harder.

They walk through a landscape of scorched tree skeletons even more horrible than the previous one with dead bodies: Nature itself seems to have been exterminated. A young deserter surprises them in the greenhouse; he has a gun, but drops it from fatigue and hunger. Eva feeds him, and his head too comes to rest buried in her lap. Eva—woman, wife, mother; all men, like unicorns, press their horny heads against her womb. But war has transformed Jan from a pacific coward into a belligerent one; he kills the boy for his boots and for the place he has reserved on a rowboat leaving for the mainland. Eva refuses to follow Jan. "Easier if you stay!" he retorts —and then she does trail after him like a frightened dog. She, the once pure and strong one, has capitulated; to save her life, she loses her soul. As they make off, the camera briefly catches in the background a pitifully small black funeral procession heading for a half-ruined church.

In exchange for Jacobi's money, Filip, who is sailing the boat, takes on Eva and Jan with the other refugees. The motor breaks down; food and water run out. One night, as the others sleep, Filip gives Jan, the only watcher, a leaden, fellow-in-guilt look and quietly slips overboard. Vacant sky and sea keep reappearing as a baleful refrain between shots of this derelict boatload struggling to survive. One morning they have run aground on what proves to be a floating island of dead men in full fighting gear and life belts. The boat creaks as if in pain. Only with utmost effort can it be extricated from this shoal of clinging dead.

Another dawn. Extreme long shot of the boat adrift. Then close-up of Eva's and Jan's adjacent heads, as in a sequence long before. She tells a dream she has had. She was carrying her little daughter through a strange town; suddenly she notices a panoply of roses spilling over a garden wall. Beautiful—but an airplane comes and sets the roses on fire. And it's still not awful, because it is so beautiful. Hugging her child close, Eva realizes she must remember something someone said—but she has forgotten what. End of film.

The third dream is the key. What Eva has forgotten is the two previous dreams: Jan's memories of Bach and her own righteous indignation against a cruel God. Everything has become absorbed by the naked, ignoble hunger for this horrible but still lovely life. It does not matter whether she and Jan survive; those to whom the condition of total war has become the human condition are dead anyway. Liv Ullmann, Max von Sydow, and Gunnar Björnstrand portray the principals. Like their supporting cast, they are superb.

If I have related plot and technical highlights in such detail, it is for a reason. *Shame* is so tightly packed that you can fully appreciate it only on second seeing. This review hopes to make it possible for you to start, as it were, with a second viewing.

HOLLIS ALPERT

If, on the surface, Ingmar Bergman's *Shame* appears to be clearer, more direct in its meaning than many of his previous films, dealing as it does with war and its effects on two uninvolved people, this impression doesn't last long. The clue comes from Bergman himself, who, some time ago, stated that he made his films for a Scandinavian audience and a Scandinavian market: any acceptance elsewhere was a bonus, so to speak. So, to take the film as a personal statement on war and to apply that statement universally is to overlook Bergman's deep roots—physically and psychically—in his homeland. Bergman has always been a Swedish artist; this orientation is necessary to him; and it helps explain why he never leaves home to make a film elsewhere.

Curiously, Sweden, a peace-loving nation, is possessed of a sense of guilt. I have noticed it during trips to Sweden, and on meeting Swedish intellectuals. It has to do with the nation's noninvolvement during the great World Wars; while blood soaked the earth of its neighbors, Sweden remained inviolate. It took in a few refugees, it still takes in some war protestors. But I felt (and I must admit this is only an impression) that a good many Swedes have a sense of discomfort about their material comfort. And because of this I doubt that the real force of Bergman's *Shame* can be felt by anyone but Swedes and their Scandinavian neighbors. For this reason, I haven't been quite able to understand all the praise that has been showered on the film by Americans, unless it's because they equate the two harried characters with the peasants of Vietnam. Bergman is of course aware of Vietnam. But he is more aware of Sweden.

Note, then, that the Rosenbergs, a retired musical couple, live on an island. (In an ideologically warring world, Sweden is an island.) Elsewhere, on the mainland, there is a war, perhaps a civil war, but obviously a war in which two ideologies (not really specified) are clashing in the most brutal of terms. The time has been set forward to 1971, and now the island too is an arena of war. The Rosenbergs are sensitive, humane, cultivating on the one hand their at times neurotic attachment to each other, and growing berries as a means of livelihood. But on any issue outside of the love of nature, art, their home, amenities such as good food, good wine, good talk they take no position. When captured by paratroopers, they quite honestly disclaim any loyalty toward one side or the other. But their very disclaimer is used against them, twisted for propaganda purposes. The point is that there is no such thing as noninvolvement. It doesn't work. And the more they attempt to protect their insularity, the more their shame deepens and the more degraded they become. Detachment becomes the ultimate shame.

In its implications *Shame*, it seems to me, is not merely on one clear level. I rather suspect that, first of all, Bergman is addressing himself directly to his compatriots, and expressing a guilt that is all-pervasive in his country. And there is another mystique at work, too, having something to do with the supposedly salutary effects of a bloodletting. This, after all, was the preferred method of treating illness for ignorant centuries. I found the film unsettling—strong, brooding—but pervaded with an air of resignation. A nightmare vision, to be sure, but one with no awakening. Anything but a man espousing war, Bergman seems to be saying that one day his country may pay a terrible price for its peace. To simply dismiss the film as a masterpiece is to ignore everything significant about it.

WILFRID SHEED

A while back, Ingmar Bergman compared his craft to that of a single craftsman working on one small section of a cathedral. And although he is still the only man at work on this particular cathedral, he plugs along in this spirit, not seduced into shooting up private shrines, pleasure domes, encrusted outhouses, but hammering methodically at his door.

To an American, this seems a perverse self-limitation. Other directors are flying to Texas, signing up the Beatles, building their own rocket installations. Overreaching yourself is the one mark of genius we understand. Yet Bergman is neither limited nor timid. Every film is a dare, a bet with the devil; and at the end, he is said to be as depleted as an exorcist. What marks him off from others is his fanatical sense of vocation, of submission to his material and hence refusal to show off. "The only thing to do in art is the next thing possible," said T. S. Eliot, a fellow medieval character. And this for Bergman does not include signing up Brigitte Bardot or crapping around Hong Kong.

His latest movie, *Shame*, is his biggest venture into public, political life. (*The Silence* was that, too, but through a mirror, like the Lady of Shalott. This time he stares us in the eye.) His theme is the demoralizing effects of war on personal relationships. The walls come down which have kept the people in place and they are released like house animals to scavenge the fields. A man sees his property burn; next thing, he is killing another man for his boots. We have been told about this before, but never with such visual logic. The disintegrating people and the disintegrating environment keep perfect time.

Unfortunately, in going for public, political effects, Bergman has slightly underdone the personal for once. His hero (Max von Sydow) is, by B's standards, something of a caricature. He is the same weak, self-absorbed artist that was last seen in *The Hour of the Wolf*, but this time viewed coldly and from the outside. Bergman hands him a violin, not one of his own tools, and then treats even this as a greedy boy's fetish rather than a glory. This is a hard, self-lacerating view of the artist, of a kind one associates with puritan Marxist converts. But I think it is done this way to save time.

Bergman leaves a good deal unsaid even in this, his most explicit movie. The scenes between husband and wife are semaphores of hatred that either we pick up or we don't. Bergman has gone so far in human horror and understanding that he can't keep turning back to explain. He does not make films for children. To the untrained eye, it looks as if the fiddler and his dame were in bad shape to begin with and didn't need a war to make things worse. But if you can read the nuances on gargoyles' faces, you will observe that they are in a lower part of hell by the end, and that they are now in it for good.

Weekend in Hell (WEEKEND)

PAULINE KAEL

Only the title of Jean-Luc Godard's new film is casual and innocent; *Weekend* is the most powerful mystical movie since *The Seventh Seal* and *Fires on the Plain* and passages of Kurosawa. We are hardly aware of the magnitude of the author-director's concept until after we are caught up in the comedy of horror, which keeps going further and becoming more nearly inescapable, like *Journey to the End of the Night*. The danger for satirists (and perhaps especially for visionary satirists) is that they don't always trust their art. They don't know how brilliantly they're making their points; they become mad with impatience and disgust, and throw off their art as if it were a hindrance to direct communication, and they begin to preach. When Godard is viciously funny, he's on top of things, and he scores and scores, and illuminates as he scores. When he becomes didactic, we can see that he really doesn't know any more about what should be done than the rest of us. But then he goes beyond didacticism into areas where, though he is as confused and divided as we are, his fervor and rage are so imaginatively justified that they are truly apocalyptic. It is in the further reaches —in the appalling, ambivalent revolutionary vision—that *Weekend* is a great, original work.

Weekend begins with a callous disrespect for life which is just a slight stylization of civilized living now; it's as if the consumers of *The Married Woman* had become more adulterous, more nakedly mercenary, and touchier. The people in *Weekend* have weapons and use them at the slightest provocation, and it seems perfectly logical that they should get into their cars and bang into each other and start piling up on the roads. By the time the bourgeois couple (Mireille Darc and Jean Yanne) start off on their weekend trip— to get money out of her mother—we have been prepared for almost anything by the wife's description of a sex orgy that moved from bedroom to kitchen and went so far she doesn't know for sure if it really happened, and by a couple of car collisions and the violence with which people responded to having their cars injured. And then the larger orgy begins, with a traffic jam that is a prelude to highways littered with burning cars and corpses. As long as Godard stays with cars as the symbol of bourgeois materialism, the movie is superbly controlled; the barbarousness of these bourgeois —their greed and the self-love they project onto their possessions— is exact and funny. But the movie goes much further—sometimes majestically, sometimes with brilliantly surreal details that suggest a closer affinity between Godard (who is of Swiss-Protestant background) and Buñuel than might have been expected, sometimes with methods and ideas that miss, even though the intentions are interesting. The couple wreck their car, and as they wander the highways, lost among battered cars and bleeding dead, they have a series of picaresque adventures, encountering figures from literature and from films, until they meet a new race of hippie guerrillas— revolutionary cannibals raping and feeding on the bourgeoisie. It is both the next step and a new beginning.

The movie has extraordinary sections: the sequence of the wife's erotic confession, with only very small camera adjustments slightly changing what we see; a long virtuoso sequence that is all one tracking shot of the cars stalled on the highway and the activities of the motorists, with the car horns sounding triumphantly, like trumpets in Purcell—a masterly demonstration of how film technique can itself become the source of wit—until we get to the accident that is the start of the congestion, and the principals drive by and out of frame; a discussion seen through the windshield of a moving car when the couple are grilled by an "exterminating angel" who promises them miracles but refuses to give them anything when he finds out what they want (a big sports Mercedes, naturally blond hair, a weekend with James Bond).

But not all the big scenes work. There is a respite in the story, a musicale sequence (which might be one of the cultural programs outlined in *La Chinoise*) in which a pianist plays Mozart in a farmyard while a few peasants and farm laborers listen or walk by. We are so alerted to the technical feat of this sequence (another single shot, this one a 360-degree tracking pan around the pianist, taking in the action in the area, and then returning to the pianist and circling *again*, catching the same actions at their next stage) that the actions caught seem too mechanical. And the meaning of the sequence is too ideological and too ambiguous (like much of *Les Carabiniers*); Godard may possibly believe that art must be taken to the peasants, but more likely he's satirizing the function and the place of art, of himself along with Mozart. This might be clearer if it were not for another, and worse, ideological sequence— a big symbolic garbage truck manned by a Negro and an Algerian, who empty the refuse of our civilization and make speeches directly at us. The more "direct" Godard is, the more fuzzy and obscure he is. Who can assimilate and evaluate this chunk of theory thrown at us in the middle of a movie? Probably most of us blank out on it. And there is the embarrassment of the Thirties again because artists are not as well equipped to instruct us in political decisions as, in the intensity of their concern, they may suppose. Though the movie slackens during this agitprop, the horrors soon begin to rise again, and they get higher and higher. Some of this doesn't work, either: Godard has been showing us life going wild and depraved into nightmare, beyond totem and taboo, but his method has been comic and Brechtian. Characters become corpses, and the actors reappear as new characters. We are reminded that the two principals are moving through the landscape of a movie; the fields are unrealistically green, and the blood on faces and bodies is thinly painted and patterned (like the blood on the peasant prostitute's face in *La Chinoise*), and when the heroine kills her mother, the mother's blood splashes over a skinned rabbit like cans of paint being spilled. But then Godard shoves at our unwilling eyes the throat-cutting of a pig and the decapitation of a goose. Now, when people are killed in a movie, even when the killing is *not* stylized, it's generally O.K., because we know it's a fake, but when animals are slaughtered we are watching life being taken away. No doubt Godard intends this to shock us out of "aesthetic" responses, just as his agitprop preaching is intended to affect us directly, but I think he miscalculates. I look away from scenes like this, as I assume many others do. Is he forcing us to confront the knowledge that there are things we don't want to look at? But we knew that. Instead of drawing us into his conception, he throws us out of the movie. And, because we know how movies are made, we instinctively recognize that his method of jolting us is fraudulent; he, the movie director, has ordered that slaughter to get a reaction from us, and so we have a right to be angry with him. Whatever our civilization is responsible for, that sow up there is his, not ours.

The excellent score, by Antoine Duhamel, is ominous and dramatic; the pulse of the music helps to carry us through some of the weaker passages (such as the witless movie jokes, and the prattling of the figures from literature, who are feeble and seem fairly arch—rather like the book people in Truffaut's *Fahrenheit 451*—though Emily Brontë has a good, flaming finish). The astonishing thing is that, with all these weaknesses, the nightmarish anger that seems to cry out for a revolution of total destruction and the visionary lyricism are so strong they hold the movie together; they transcend the perfectly achieved satire. The most hideously flawed of all Godard's movies, it has more depth than anything he's done before. Although by the end his conscious meanings and attitudes are not at all clear, the vision that rises in the course of the film is so surreally powerful that one accepts it, as one accepts a lunar landscape by Bosch or a torment by Grünewald. *Weekend* is Godard's vision of Hell, and it ranks with the visions of the greatest.

Weekend is the fifteenth of Godard's feature films, which began with *Breathless* in 1959, and he has also made sections of several omnibus films. At thirty-seven, he is in something of the position in the world of film that James Joyce was at a considerably later age in the world of literature; that is, he has paralyzed other film-makers by shaking their confidence (as Joyce did to writers), without ever reaching a large public. He will probably never have a popular, international success; he packs film-festival halls, but there is hardly enough audience left over to fill small theaters for a few weeks. His experimentation irritates casual moviegoers, but those who are more than casual can see that what may have appeared to be experimentation for its own sake in a movie like *Contempt* is validated by the way he uses the techniques in *Weekend*. It's possible to hate half or two thirds of what Godard does—or find it incomprehensible—and still be shattered by his brilliance.

Again like Joyce, Godard seems to be a great but terminal figure. The most gifted younger directors and student film-makers all over the world recognize his liberation of the movies; they know that he has opened up a new kind of movie-making, that he has brought a new sensibility into film, and that, like Joyce, he is both kinds of master—both innovator and artist. But when they try to follow him they can't beat him at his own game, and they can't (it appears) take what he has done into something else; he's so incredibly fast he always gets there first. He has obviously opened doors, but when others try to go through they're trapped. He has already made the best use of his innovations, which come out of his need for them and may be integral only to his material. It's the strength of his own sensibility that gives his techniques excitement. In other hands, his techniques are just mannerisms; other directors who try them resemble a schoolboy walking like his father. Godard has already imposed his way of seeing on us: we look at cities, at billboards and brand names, at a girl's hair differently because of him. And when others pick up the artifacts of his way of seeing, we murmur, "Godard," and they are sunk. At each new film festival, one can see the different things that are lifted from him; sometimes one can almost hear the directors saying to themselves, "I know I shouldn't do that, it's too much like Godard, but I've just got to try it." They can't resist, and so they do what Godard himself has already gone past, and the young film-makers look out of date before they've got started; and their corpses are beginning to litter the festivals. For if Godard can't save himself how can he save them? If he is driven, like his self-destructive heroes, to go to the limits and beyond, to pursue a non-reflective art as though fear-

ful of a pause, to take all risks and burn himself out, it's partly
because his imitators are without this drive—this monomaniac's
logic that carries him beyond logic to mysticism—that his liberation of film technique and content becomes mere facility when
they attempt to follow him. Michelangelo is said to have observed,
"He who walks behind others will never advance." Jean Renoir has
been a different kind of movie influence; with his masterly simplicity and unobtrusive visual style, he has helped people to find
their own way. You don't have to walk behind Renoir, because he
opens an infinite number of ways to go. But when it comes to
Godard you can only follow and be destroyed. Other film-makers
see the rashness and speed and flamboyance of his complexity;
they're conscious of it all the time, and they love it, and, of course,
they're right to love it. But they can't walk behind him. They've
got to find other ways, because he's burned up the ground.

Andrew Sarris

Weekend consolidates Jean-Luc Godard's position as the
most disconcerting of all contemporary directors, a veritable paragon of paradoxes, violent and yet vulnerable, the most elegant stylist and the most vulgar polemicist, the most remorseful classicist
and the most relentless modernist, the man of the moment and the
artist for the ages. When I bore witness to Weekend at the Berlin
Film Festival back in June, Godard seemed to be tuned in to the
youthful frequency of the future. He lost me somewhere between
the garbage truck of the Third World and the slaughtered pig of
the new breed, but I did feel the film unwinding with all the clat-
tering contemporaneity of a ticker tape, and the reading for Western civilization was down, down, and out. Seeing Weekend again
in a chill Nixonish November in New York, I am struck more by
Godard's melancholy than by his message. As much as Godard indulges in the rhetoric of rebellion, his deepest feelings seem to be
situated before the revolution. He was born, he implies, too soon
and too late, too soon to forget the sweetness of the past and too
late to perpetuate that same sweetness, particularly in the remembered realm of movies with subjects not yet swallowed up by the
subjective. Gösta Berling calling Johnny Guitar, Godard's puppets
prattle into their walkie-talkies. Potemkin calling Prisoner of the

Desert (the French title for John Ford's *The Searchers*). And there are still meaningful responses from the alumni federation of the first row of the Paris Cinémathèque. Johnny Guitar to Gösta Berling. Prisoner of the Desert to Potemkin. Communication confirmed. But for how much longer? Can there be as much fun in the future with Jean-Luc Godard calling Bernardo Bertolucci and Bernardo Bertolucci calling Alexander Kluge and Alexander Kluge calling Andy Warhol atop the last scrap heap of waste in the West? (We must try not to anticipate Antonioni's pilgrimage to Zabriskie Point.) Godard seems to want it both ways as the prime prophet of the first-person film and the lead mourner of the third-person movie. Indeed, Godard has been bemoaning the death of movies ever since *Breathless*, a period of almost a full decade, long enough to turn the tears of a meaningful prophet into the tears of a professional mourner. With *Weekend* Jean-Luc has been to the wailing wall once too often. Godard's weeping over the past is now merely one of his regular routines, a means of rationalizing his own increasing fragmentation in terms of the alleged chaos of his time. Hence, the opening credits of *Weekend* proclaim that what we are about to witness is more a relic of our reality than an interpretation of that reality. Godard's whimsically apocalyptic context for his films enables him to peruse daily newspapers as if they were ancient tablets, and why not? Who is to say that future millennia might not be more intrigued by the casual observation that Frenchmen had become so Americanized by 1967 that they were driving Japanese cars than by any of the anti-memoirs of Malraux. Godard's compulsive tendency to juggle cultural references from brassiere-ad copy to Brecht leaves him vulnerable to the charge of intellectual superficiality, a charge balanced off by the simple fact that Godard, like the subject of brassiere-ad copy, looks better than he reads, and a visual flair still counts for something even in the most modern cinema.

Godard's strengths and weaknesses are immediately apparent in the opening shots of *Weekend*. Husband, wife, and wife's lover-analyst sit on a leafy terrace. Phone rings and intrigues commence. Wife is cheating on husband and husband on wife, talk of poisons and inheritances, lust and avarice on the Jeeter Lester level of characterization, barnyard animal dramaturgy out of the nastiest comic-strip capitalism imaginable. But Raoul Coutard's fully textured, subtly shadowed color cinematography undercuts the calculating crudity of the dialogue. The dissociation of the visual from the verbal is no accident, however. Within the same sequence, Godard demonstrates the formal mastery of his material. The three bourgeois characters look down from their balcony at a street accident culminating in a violent brawl between the two drivers. Godard stages the brawl from such an insistently overhead viewpoint that he creates a metaphor for bourgeois detachment from social turmoil. The verticality of the viewpoint is sustained long enough to remind the educated moviegoer of a similar metaphor in Luis Buñuel's and Salvador Dali's more overtly surrealist classic, *Un Chien Andalou*. Whereas Buñuel and Dali treated apparent moral indifference as actual metaphysical liberation, Godard treats idle curiosity as immoral complicity. The difference between Buñuel-Dali and Godard is therefore the difference between irony and allegory. Furthermore, Godard's brawl is staged so elaborately that its violence is more rhetorical than real, more for the sake of a voyeuristic spectacle than for the release of psychic tensions. Hence, and this is true throughout *Weekend*, Godard's violence is more cerebral than visceral.

The bourgeois couple impersonated by Mireille Darc and Jean Yanne are less the involved subjects of *Weekend* than its detached objects. Never before has Godard been so far outside a pair of protagonists. Never before has he shown so little concern for their fate and so few close-ups of their features. After my first viewing of *Weekend*, I could barely remember what Darc and Yanne looked like, a sure sign that the closest bond between Godard and his characters is one of contempt. Even the *voyous* of Jean-Paul Belmondo in *Breathless* and Claude Brasseur in *Band of Outsiders* have hitherto been infiltrated by Godard's sensibility. By contrast, the bourgeois yahoos of Darc and Yanne are repeatedly harangued by Godard from the outside. Far from being treated as the victims of bourgeois society, they emerge as its arch villains. Symptomatic of Godard's intransigent indifference toward this despised duo is that the death of the husband and the desecration of the wife transpire offscreen with the most callous casualness.

Nonetheless Mireille Darc does manage to dominate a curiously sacramental scene in which her flesh is offered up to a Godardian fantasy reminiscent of the bare-buttocked Bardolatry of *Contempt*. This is the scene in which Darc describes an orgy in extravagant detail to her lover-analyst. When I saw *Weekend* in Berlin, most of Darc's descriptive dialogue was inaudible on the sound track, as if Godard were holding back on the lurid details to create a more ritualistic effect. In the version now on view in New York, the Grove Press subtitles come over lewd and clear, and the effect is therefore more sensually insinuating.

Darc's confessional has been compared to Bibi Andersson's in *Persona*, the latter hailed by many critics as supremely erotic. (I have never understood whether the existence of eroticism was established by the empirical evidence of erection or by a logical analysis of visual and verbal expression. Admittedly even Wittgenstein would wander far afield in this region of research.) The erotic element in Andersson's account is not so much the actual experience she is describing as the emotional vulnerability that she exposes in telling the story to Liv Ullmann, she of the vampirish eyes and seductive proximity. Bergman's sense of camera space is fundamentally bas-relief, with an occasional interchange of foreground and background for his eloquently expressive faces. Space itself does not really function for him as a stylistic figure. By contrast, Godard has inherited Murnau's mysticism about space on the screen, and his use of the camera in *Weekend* is therefore more dynamic than Bergman's in *Persona*, particularly as regards their respective oblique sex scenes. If I would argue that Godard is more erotic than Bergman on this occasion, it would amount virtually to a paradox. Normally Bergman is much more erotic than Godard, and there is simply no contest between Bibi Andersson (especially in *Le Viol*) and Mireille Darc. The difference is in the marvelously ceremonial indecorum with which Godard stages Darc's confessional. Seated on a sacrificial table with her legs drawn up, down to her bra and panties, deliberately shifting her position with each new climax to her confession, talking in a singsong monotone that emphasizes her emotional detachment from her outrageous complicity in the most bizarre perversions, Mireille Darc awakens a fantasy response through Godard's reflective ritual, the same ritual that ultimately delivers her body to her ambivalent lover-analyst. If Bibi Andersson misses out on this fantasy response, it is because she is too encumbered by Bergman's psychological mysteries which generate too much suspense for erotic ritual.

Eroticism aside, *Weekend* is most likely to be remembered for the sustained tracking shot of a traffic tie-up extending for miles across the dull French landscape. The first time I saw *Weekend*, I was struck most forcibly by Godard's lack of comic inventiveness in the description of the delay. By the standards of classical slapstick —Chaplin, Keaton, Lloyd, and Laurel and Hardy, the latter particularly for *Two Tars*—Godard runs out of inspiration about a third of the way along, or at about the time he repeats the gag about the two motorists playing chess. I wasn't impressed even when Godard sought to implicate the audience in the discovery of the bloody bodies that, once discovered and passed, enabled our stalled motorists to speed away with a lyrical vavoom to liberty and grace. Still, I recognized that old familiar feeling of survival of the fittest (or luckiest) on the open road. I just happened to be one or two beats ahead of Godard in anticipating his moralistic tag shot, and so I wrote off the scene as failed shaggy-dog story. This time around in New York, I was struck more by the insanely insistent honking of horns for minutes upon minutes until the bloody bodies became a blessed relief even to this forewarned spectator. Again, the morbid beauty of the camera movement convinced me that this was indeed no time for comedy or even satire. There was something too deterministic about that inexorably moving camera across the intransigently neutral landscape. Mere litterateurs can never appreciate the intoxicating quality of a meaningful camera movement as it obliterates the formal boundaries of the picture frame. Toward the end of the film, Godard stages an orgiastic Ode to the Ocean performed by cannibalistic French hippies, but the scene doesn't really work, because Godard doesn't seem to feel the ode very deeply, nor the communal mysticism the ode is supposed to express. Also, there is much more of the "oceanic" feeling Romain Rolland described to Sigmund Freud in Godard's tracking shot of the traffic jam than in the Ode to the Ocean.

The high point of *Weekend* is the culmination of the second circular camera movement around a pastoral, even rural, agricultural, performance of Mozart's Piano Sonata, K. 576, by Paul Gégauff, one of Chabrol's wilder scriptwriters. Gégauff's argument, perhaps Godard's also, is that so-called serious modern music has less to offer the modern listener than do such genuinely Mozartian descendants as the Beatles and the Rolling Stones. Godard would seem to be establishing a different critical line for music (his avocation) than for cinema (his vocation). It doesn't matter. Godard is interesting less for his attitude toward ideas than for his aptness for images together with the feelings these images express. Godard's concert is the most beautiful expression of the rapport between art and nature I have ever seen on the screen. The beauty may be attributable to the fact that Godard is somewhat ill at ease with both nature and art, and thus emotionally responsive to both.

Apart from its admirable set pieces, *Weekend* tends to disintegrate into witless bourgeois-baiting and coy Pirandellianism. Godard has destroyed the notion of beginning, middle, and end by shooting everything in existential sequence, so that his films do not so much end as stop. The disadvantage of this approach even for Godard is becoming increasingly apparent. Godard seldom has any kick left for the last lap. His best scenes are likely to be in the middle or the beginning or whatever day of shooting he felt up to it. By contrast, a brash entertainer like Fellini always saves something extra for his endings so that his audience can go dancing or crying out of the theater to Nino Rota's moodily Chaplinesque melodies. Fellini's instinct for showmanship is sounder and more appealing than Godard's instinct for audience alienation through calculating abruptness. But there is always something that lingers in a Godard film, perhaps a disturbing ambivalence or a morbid streak of style, but most often a uniquely cinematic intelligence that verges on artistic brilliance by any standard. The way Godard is able to deliver an impromptu essay on the point of view of an unmanipulated stone makes up for any number of embarrassingly inside "asides" like the embarrassing tramp character, right out of Bresson's *Mouchette*, who proceeds to rape Mireille Darc out of sight in a deep hole and then rises out of the hole and glances at his victim's husband as the camera moves with his glance past the husband to a meaningless distance down the road, solely to give time for Mireille Darc to climb out of the hole and rejoin her husband all in one shot, and that the most gratuitous in the history of the cinema. And yet there is the orgy and the traffic jam and the rock and the concert and, as always with Jean-Luc Godard, the promise of a fascinating future.

BELLE DE JOUR

ANDREW SARRIS

Luis Buñuel's *Belle de Jour* has evoked in many critiques that all-purpose adjective "beautiful." Catherine Deneuve is undeniably beautiful, never more so than in this context of Buñuelian perversity, and almost any meaningfully designed color film seems beautiful if only because the vast subconscious sea of the cinema is safely gelatinized within the frames of an academic painting. Describing a film as beautiful is unfortunately too often a device to end discussion, particularly nowadays when irrationality and hysteria have become institutionalized as life styles. *Elvira Madigan* is beautiful in the way flowery poems are poetical, not through functional expressiveness but through lyrical excessiveness. *Bonnie and Clyde* is beautiful when its luminously lyrical close-ups involve the audience with the killers, but the film is equally beautiful when its concluding slow-motion ballet of death and transfiguration takes the audience off the hook by distancing the characters back into legend and fantasy. The fact that the close-ups contradict the distancing is immaterial to the film's admirers. *Bonnie and Clyde* is beautiful, and consistency is the hobgoblin of little minds.

I would argue that *Belle de Jour* is indeed a beautiful film, but not because of any anesthetizing aesthetic of benevolently mindless lyricism. Nor is the film beautiful because its director's visual style transcends its sordid subject. The beauty of *Belle de Jour* is the beauty of artistic rigor and adaptable intelligence. Given what Buñuel is at sixty-seven and what he has done in forty years and twenty-seven projects of film-making and what and whom he had to work with and for, *Belle de Jour* reverberates with the cruel logic of formal necessity. From the opening shot of an open carriage approaching the camera at an oblique ground-level angle to the closing shot of an open carriage passing the camera at an oblique overhead angle, the film progresses inexorably upward, an ascent of assent, from the reverie of suppressed desires to the revelation of fulfilled fantasies. But whose desires and whose fantasies?

Buñuel's? His heroine's? Actually a bit of both. The exact proportion of subjective contemplation to objective correlative can best be calculated by comparing Joseph Kessel's basic anecdotal material with what appears on the screen.

In his preface to *Belle de Jour*, Kessel writes: "The subject of *Belle de Jour* is not Séverine's sensual aberration; it is her love for Pierre independent of that aberration, and it is the tragedy of that love." Kessel concludes his preface with a reprovingly rhetorical question for those critics who dismissed *Belle de Jour* as a piece of pathological observation: "Shall I be the only one to pity Séverine, and to love her?"

The "sensual aberration" of which Kessel writes undoubtedly seemed more shocking in 1929, when the first French edition was published, than it would seem in the current period of erotic escalation. Séverine Sérizy, happily married to a handsome young surgeon, goes to work in a house of ill-repute, actually less a house than an intimate apartment. The money involved is less the motivation than the pretext for her action. Pierre, her husband, provides for her material needs handsomely, but his respectfully temporizing caresses fail to satisfy her psychic need for brutal degradation, a need first awakened by a malodorous molester when she was a child of eight. To preserve a façade of marital respectability, Séverine works at her obsessive profession only afternoons from two to five, the mystery of her matinée schedule causing her to be christened Belle de Jour. Kessel's novel, like his heroine, is fatally divided between clinical observations on sexual psychology and novelistic contrivances to overcome the innate lethargy of a woman of leisure. Husson, a weary sensualist in her husband's circle of friends, is a particularly intricate contrivance in that he triggers much of the novel's intrigue. It is Husson who first alerts Séverine to her own frustrations by his unwelcome advances. It is he who inadvertently supplies her with the address of her sensual destiny, and who, discovering her double life, poses such a threat to her non–Belle-de-Jour existence that he precipitates, almost innocently, the final catastrophe.

Marcel, a gold-toothed gangster infatuated with Belle de Jour, provides a violently melodramatic climax to the novel, by agreeing to murder Husson to preserve Séverine's secret and Belle de Jour's respect. Irony is piled upon irony as Marcel's assault on Husson is deflected by Pierre, who is so grievously wounded that he is confined for life to helpless paralysis in a wheelchair. Marcel and Husson remain silent about Belle de Jour, thus enabling Séverine to escape a public scandal and even prosecution, but, perverse to the end, she confesses everything to Pierre, and is rewarded not with his forgiveness but with his stern silence.

Buñuel and his co-scenarist Jean-Claude Carrière retained most of the characters of the novel. Séverine goes to work for Madame Anais in both novel and film, and Belle de Jour's colleagues are Charlotte and Mathilde in both versions. The most striking variation between novel and film is in the elaborately structured dream apparatus of the film. Kessel's Séverine never dreams the concrete images of Buñuel's surreal reveries of feminine masochism. There are no floggings in the book as there are in the film, no binding of hands with ropes, no sealing of mouths, no splattering with mud. Kessel's Séverine never really dreams at all; she merely recollects the past and anticipates the future. If the novel had been filmed in the thirties or the forties by a French director trained in the Tradition of Quality, a Marcel Carné or Claude Autant-Lara perhaps, Séverine would probably have been played with many shimmering close-ups to dramatize the desperate conflict between her feelings and her senses. The background music would have been exquisitely sentimental. Except for the bells that signal the movement of the horse-drawn carriage, Buñuel uses no music whatsoever. No Simon and Garfunkel, no Beatles, no Donovan, not even the realistically based music of radios and record players. There is no radio or television in the modern world of Belle de Jour, but there is a Geisha Club credit card. Buñuel has stripped modernity of its specificity. Thus we are not bothered so much by the suspicion that horse-drawn carriages are not as likely to figure in the reveries of Séverine's (or Catherine Deneuve's) generation as in the memories of Buñuel's. The fact that Buñuel does not employ music in *Belle de Jour* is not significant as a matter of general aesthetic policy. Buñuel himself has derived ironic counterpoint from the musical backgrounds of such recent films as *Viridiana* and *Simon of the Desert*. He must have felt that he didn't need music to underscore the fundamental irony implicit in a woman with the face of an angel and the lusts of a devil. Still, *Belle de Jour* overcomes an awesome handicap of affect by disdaining the facile frissons of music.

Many of the script changes were dictated by the differences in the media. Pierre emerges through Jean Sorel as a much duller character than in the book, but it is difficult to see what any director can do with the character of the Noble Husband in such a grotesque context. The changes in Husson's character are more meaningful. Kessel's Husson was more mannered in his ennui, but he takes advantage of Séverine's degraded status as Belle de Jour to possess her body. Buñuel's Husson (Michel Piccoli) is more fastidious; he loses interest in Séverine at precisely the instant she becomes available to him as Belle de Jour. But it is Buñuel's Husson who tells Pierre of Belle de Jour after the accident; Kessel's Husson never seriously contemplated such a course of action before or after.

Kessel wants us to love Séverine by identifying with her; Buñuel wants us to understand Séverine by contemplating the nature of her obsession. Instead of indulging in Kessel's sentimental psychology by staring into Catherine Deneuve's eyes, Buñuel fragments Deneuve's body into its erotic constituents. His shots of feet, hands, legs, shoes, stockings, undergarments, etc., are the shots not only of a fetishist, but of a cubist, a director concerned simultaneously with the parts and their effect on the whole. Buñuel's graceful camera movements convey Deneuve to her sensual destiny through her black patent-leather shoes, and to her final reverie through her ringed fingers feeling their way along the furniture with the tactile tenderness of a mystical sensuality, Séverine's, Deneuve's or Buñuel's, it makes little difference.

The beauty of the filmed version of *Belle de Jour* arises from its implication of Buñuel is its vision of the world. It is Buñuel himself who is the most devoted patron of *chez* Madame Anais, and the most pathetic admirer of Catherine Deneuve's Séverine–Belle de Jour. Never before has Buñuel's view of the spectacle seemed so obliquely Ophulsian in its shy gaze from behind curtains, windows, and even peepholes. Buñuel's love of Séverine is greater than Kessel's, simply because Buñuel sees Belle de Jour as Séverine's liberator. The sensuality of *Belle de Jour* is not metaphorical like Genêt's in *The Balcony* or Albee's in *Everything in the Garden*. Most writers, even the most radical, treat prostitution as a symptom of a social malaise and not as a concrete manifestation of a universal impulse. Buñuel reminds us once again in *Belle de Jour* that he is one of the few men of the left not afflicted by puritanism and bourgeois notions of chastity and fidelity. The difference be-

tween Buñuel and, say, Genêt is not entirely a difference between a
man of images and a man of words. What distinguishes *Belle de
Jour* from most movies is the impression it gives of having been
seen in its director's mind long before it was shot. There is a pre-
conceived exactness to its images that will inevitably disconcert
middlebrow film critics, especially those who are highbrows in
other cultural sectors. It is only the specialist in film who can fully
appreciate the directness of Buñuel's image above and beyond the
novelistic nuances he sacrifices on the altars of shock and laughter.

The ending of *Belle de Jour* is tantalizingly open as narrative.
Husson has told Pierre about Belle de Jour, or at least we presume
so. Buñuel does not show the scene, and we are not obliged to
believe anything we do not see, but there is no particular reason to
believe that Husson has not carried out his stated intention.
Buñuel does not cast his audience adrift in a sea of ambiguity at
every opportunity; he is simply not that interested in dramatic suspense. Séverine enters Pierre's room, and for the first time in the
film Buñuel's technique obscures the flow of action. Buñuel breaks
up the spatial unity of the scene with alternative sights and sounds
to indicate a range of possibilities. Cut to Jean Sorel's tear-stained
face. Pierre Knows All and Feels Betrayed. Cut to his crumpled
upturned hand. Pierre Is Dead from the Shock of His Grief. Cut
on the sound track to the bells of a carriage, and to Sorel's voice
asking of Deneuve's pensive face what Séverine is thinking. Everything Turns Back to Fantasy.

Or does it? Some critics have suggested that Séverine has been
cured of her masochistic obsession by becoming Belle de Jour.
Hence the empty carriage at the end of the film. She will no longer
take *that* trip. One French critic has argued that the entire film is
a dream, but the big problem with such an argument is Buñuel's
visually explicit brand of surrealism. Earlier in the film, Husson
calls on Séverine at her home and is rudely rebuffed. Buñuel cuts
immediately to a shockingly "cute" Boy-Girl-profile two-shot of
Séverine and Husson at the ski lodge. As the camera pulls back, we
see Jean Sorel and Macha Meril at the same table. It must be a
dream, we assure ourselves, while Séverine and Husson slip out of
sight under the table to perform some unspeakable act of sacrilege
against bourgeois society. The table begins to bump up and down,
but the deserted partners, Sorel and Meril, are only mildly concerned. Buñuel has transported *Belle de Jour* back to *L'Âge d'or*,

but the effect of the scene is unsettling if we accept it as occurring in Séverine's mind. Here I think Buñuel slipped into a sadistic attitude of his own toward Pierre, since this is the only scene in the film in which Pierre is made to look completely ridiculous. The key to the scene, however, is not Séverine's characterization but Buñuel's satiric attitude toward Hollywood sentimentality. The profile shot more than the table-bumping gives the show away, but audiences would never "get" the joke without the table-bumping, and Buñuel does not disdain vulgarity as one of the strategies of surrealism.

Actually we are such Puritans that we talk of surrealism almost exclusively in the solemn terms of social defiance. Humor is only a means to an end, but not an end in itself. No, never? Well, hardly ever. And in Buñuel's case laughter serves to disinfect libertinism of its satanic aura. If we can laugh at the prissiness of perversion and the fastidiousness of fetishism, not with smug superiority, but with carnal complicity, we become too implicated to remain indifferent. Buñuel's masochist, unlike Genêt's in *The Balcony*, satisfies his devious lechery by stroking the thighs of his professionally cruel mistress. Buñuel's brothel is a brothel and not one of Genêt's microcosms, and Buñuel's sensuality turns in upon itself as an enclosed experience devoid of allegorical signification.

Similarly, the entire film turns in upon itself by ending with the same question with which it began: "Séverine, what are you thinking of?" And Séverine tells the truth in her fashion. She thinks of places and conveyances and trips and herds of Spanish bulls named Remorse except one named Expiation. At the end, she is still dreaming, and who is to say that the dream is any less real or vivid than the reality it accompanies? Certainly not Buñuel's probing but compassionate camera. There are several possible interpretations of Buñuel's ending, but the formal symmetry of the film makes the debate academic. Buñuel is ultimately ambiguous so as not to moralize about his subject. He wishes neither to punish Séverine nor to reward her. He prefers to contemplate the grace with which she accepts her fate, and Buñuel is nothing if not fatalistic. Even the hapless husband is granted a mystical premonition when he sees an empty wheelchair in the street. It is destined for him, and the concreteness of Buñuel's visual imagery is so intense that we feel that the wheelchair is as destined for Pierre as Pierre is destined for the wheelchair.

Buñuel's fatalism actually undercuts the suspense of the narrative to the extent that there is no intellectual pressure for a resolved ending. Between the fatalism and the formal symmetry, *Belle de Jour* seems completely articulated as a Buñuelian statement. We do not have to know what we are not meant to know, and Buñuel establishes a precedent within his film for the ambiguity of his ending. This precedent involves Madame Anaïs, after Séverine the most absorbing character in the film. Alone of all the characters, Madame Anaïs is the truth-seeker, and she is inevitably far from the mark. She misunderstands the motivations of Belle de Jour from the outset, and she misinterprets Belle de Jour's departure. Still, she is always staring at Belle de Jour as if it were possible to peel away layers of lacquered flesh to the raw impulses underneath. The scenes in which Geneviève Page's Madame Anaïs gazes with loving curiosity at Catherine Deneuve's Belle de Jour gleam with a psychological insight not customary with Buñuel, or, as rigorously empirical aestheticians would have it, the scenes gleam with the appearance of a psychological insight, the very beautiful appearance derived from two extraordinary screen incarnations.

The great irony of *Belle de Jour* is that a sixty-seven-year-old Spanish surrealist has set out to liberate humanity of its bourgeois sentimentality only to collide with the most sentimental generation of flowery feelings in human history.

ROSEMARY'S BABY

ANDREW SARRIS

Rosemary's Baby had been blessed with such extraordinary popularity from the printed page to the silver screen that it seems superfluous if not presumptuous for a critic to recommend the movie as good hot-weather-goose-pimply entertainment. Everybody read the book and now everybody's going to the movie, and book and movie are discussed interchangeably as media permutations of the same basic formula. Good luck and perfect timing have played a part in these proceedings. Certainly only luck can explain the fortuitous conjunction of a strong commercial property like Ira Levin's novel with a strong directorial personality like Roman Polanski without the novel being distorted or the director diluted. Indeed, Levin and Polanski actually reinforce each other, Levin being more a storyteller than a stylist and Polanski more a stylist than a storyteller. Even in *Rosemary's Baby* there are moments of excessive embellishment in the beginning when good old Elisha Cooke, Jr., is showing Mia Farrow and John Cassavetes through the Dakota Apartments. Polanski's camera seems a bit too jittery and his cutting a bit too jazzy and the over-all effect a bit too ostentatiously ominous. But then Levin's potent plot takes over, and Polanski seems to relax into a contemplative calm, with only occasional touches and asides to remind us of his impish irreverence.

By now the plot of *Rosemary's Baby* is familiar enough to analyze without spoiling anyone's fun. In an age of themes, Ira Levin has come up with a plot so effectively original that it is deserving more of a patent than of a copyright. The qualities of a good plot are simplicity, directness, and an oblique treatment of essentials. *Rosemary's Baby* can be synopsized in one sentence as the adventures of an actor's wife delivered to the devil and his worshipers by her ambitious husband so that she might bear the devil's baby, which she does. The beauty of the plot is that it virtually conceals its real subject. On the surface Rosemary's Baby seems merely a diabolical reversal of Mary's Baby, a reversal made even more flagrantly sacrilegious by Polanski's God-is-dead gaiety. A Catholic group has bitten on the bait by condemning the film, though probably more for the director's deftness with nudity than for his disrespect for the sacraments. Many critics have missed the point of the story because of their prejudice against melodrama as a meaningful dramatic form, a prejudice traditionally diagnosed as the anti-Hitchcock syndrome.

Rosemary's Baby is more than just a good yarn, however. Its power to terrify readers and viewers, particularly women, derives not from any disrespect toward the Deity nor from any literal fear of embodied evil. Ghosts, Holy or unholy, have ceased to haunt our dreams in their metaphysical majesty. The devil in *Rosemary's Baby* is reduced to an unimaginative rapist performing a ridiculous ritual. It could not be otherwise in an age that proclaims

God is dead. Without God, the devil is pure camp, and his follow-ers fugitives from a Charles Addams cartoon. What is frightening about Rosemary's condition is her suspicion that she is being used by other people for ulterior purposes. She has no family of her own to turn to, but must rely on a husband who seems insensitive to her pain, neighbors who seem suspiciously solicitous, a doctor whose manner seems more reassuring than his medicine, and a world that seems curiously indifferent to her plight. When she tells her story to a disinterested doctor, he dismisses it as pure paranoia, as most doctors would if a pregnant woman walked into their office and told them the plot of *Rosemary's Baby*. The disinterested doctor calls the witch doctor, and Rosemary is delivered to her satanic destiny. And then comes the final twist. After spitting in her hus-band's face, Rosemary approaches the rocker where her yellow-eyed baby is crying and by slowly rocking the infant to sleep acknowl-edges her maternal responsibility toward a being that is, after all, a baby and ultimately *her* baby.

Thus two universal fears run through *Rosemary's Baby*: the fear of pregnancy, particularly as it consumes personality, and the fear of a deformed offspring with all the attendant moral and emotional complications. Almost any film that dealt directly with these two fears would be unbearable to watch because of the matter-of-fact clinical horror involved. By dealing obliquely with these fears, the book and the movie penetrate deeper into the subconscious of the audience. It is when we least expect to identify with fictional char-acters that we identify most deeply. If Levin had been fully aware of the implications of what he had been writing, he would have been too self-conscious to write it. Conversely, Polanski, who is too aware of implications and overtones, could never have invented the plot of *Rosemary's Baby*. Hence the fruitful collaboration of in-stinct and intellect on this occasion.

Levin's lady-in-distress mannerisms are misleading in that they are designed merely as plot devices to tighten the tension during the period of pregnancy, a period during which even witches and warlocks lack the ability to accelerate events. At times the suspense of the story is more rhetorical than real, since we are always more curious about what Rosemary is trying to escape from (witchcraft) than what she is trying to escape to (the normal, neurotic everyday world). Consequently, Rosemary is infused with a feeling of help-lessness and Zen passivity that creates in the reader and viewer a mood of voluptuous self-pity. Where the story does succeed as melodrama is on the level of persecution trying to prove that it is not paranoia, and, of course, the best way for an artist to project his own paranoia is to describe real persecution. The great stories are acts of faith in the reality of feelings. The wondrousness of a story or a movie is a plea to the audience to be less skeptical about the possibilities of human experience.

No movie succeeds without a reasonable number of casting coups, and *Rosemary's Baby* is more fortunate than most in this regard. The biggest surprise is Mia Farrow as a Rosemary more ideal than anyone would have suspected after A *Dandy in Aspic*. Even her curiously pallid and awkward artificiality works to her advantage in a role for which it is desirable not to seem too credible to the outside world. Polanski is especially good in directing her physical movements of escape and evasion in a way that makes her plausibly but affectingly ineffective. And when she apologizes for her husband's rudeness by observing that even Laurence Olivier must be self-centered, her gaucherie is heartwarming to the point of heartbreak.

The supporting people are uniformly excellent, Ralph Bellamy being the outstanding revelation as the bearded witch doctor and yet typical of a cast that plays against the strangeness of the situation with a tenaciously tweedsy folksiness mixed with an air of perpetual preoccupation. Ruth Gordon, Sidney Blackmer, and Maurice Evans match Bellamy with an energetic seriousness that is amusing without ever being ridiculous. John Cassavetes is somewhat miscast as the actor husband, a part that would have been more appropriate for the narcissism Richard Chamberlain displayed so precisely in *Petulia*. Cassavetes is too intelligent and offbeat an actor to project self-absorption. Above all, he lacks the beautiful self-sacrifice mask of an actor capable of selling his wife to the devil for a good part. Cassavetes is simply more than his character calls for, but he too has his moments in an almost flawless entertainment.

2001: A SPACE ODYSSEY

Penelope Gilliatt

I think Stanley Kubrick's *2001: A Space Odyssey* is some sort of great film, and an unforgettable endeavor. Technically and imaginatively, what he put into it is staggering: five years of his life; his novel and screenplay, with Arthur C. Clarke; his production, his direction, his special effects; his humor and stamina and particular disquiet. The film is not only hideously funny—like *Dr. Strangelove*—about human speech and response at a point where they have begun to seem computerized, and where more and more people sound like recordings left on while the soul is out; it is also a uniquely poetic piece of sci-fi, made by a man who truly possesses the drives of both science and fiction.

Kubrick's tale of quest in the year 2001, which eventually takes us to the moon and Jupiter, begins on prehistoric Earth. Tapirs snuffle over the Valhalla landscape, and a leopard with broken-glass eyes guards the carcass of a zebra in the moonlight. Crowds of apes, scratching and ganging up, are disturbingly represented not by real animals, like the others, but by actors in costume. They are on the brink of evolving into men, and the overlap is horrible. Their stalking movements are already exactly ours: an old tramp's, drunk, at the end of his tether and fighting mad. Brute fear has been refined into the infinitely more painful human capacity for dread. The creatures are so nearly human that they have religious impulses. A slab that they suddenly come upon sends them into panicked reverence as they touch it, and the film emits a colossal sacred din of chanting. The shock of faith boots them forward a few thousand years, and one of the apes, squatting in front of a bed of bones, picks up his first weapon. In slow motion, the hairy arm swings up into an empty frame and then down again, and the smashed bones bounce into the air. What makes him do it? Curiosity? What makes people destroy anything, or throw away the known, or set off in spaceships? To see what Nothing feels like, driven by some bedrock instinct that it is time for something else? The last bone thrown in the air is matched, in the next cut, to a spaceship at the same angle. It is now 2001. The race has survived thirty-three years more without extinction, though not with any growth of spirit. There are no Negroes in this vision of America's space program; conversation with Russian scientists is brittle with mannerly terror, and the Chinese can still be dealt with only by pretending they're not there. But technological man has advanced no end. A space way station shaped like a Ferris wheel and housing a hotel called the Orbiter Hilton hangs off the pocked old cheek of Earth. The sound track, bless its sour heart, meanwhile thumps out "The Blue Danube," to confer a little of the courtliness of bygone years on space. The civilization that Kubrick sees coming has the brains of a nuclear physicist and the sensibility of an airline hostess smiling through an oxygen-mask demonstration.

Kubrick is a clever man. The grim joke is that life in 2001 is only faintly more gruesome in its details of sophisticated affluence than it is now. When we first meet William Sylvester as a space scientist, for instance, he is in transit to the moon via the Orbiter Hilton to investigate another of the mysterious slabs. The heroic man of intellect is given a nice meal on the way—a row of spacecraft foods to suck through straws out of little plastic cartons, each decorated with a picture of sweet corn or whatever, to tell him that sweet corn is what he is sucking. He is really going through very much the same ersatz form of the experience of being well looked after as the foreigner who arrives at an airport now with a couple of babies, reads in five or six languages on luggage carts that he is welcome, and then finds that he has to manage his luggage and the babies without actual help from a porter. The scientist of 2001 is only more inured. He takes the inanities of space personnel on the chin. "Did you have a pleasant flight?" Smile, smile. Another smile, possibly prefilmed, from a girl on a television monitor handling voice-print identification at Immigration. The Orbiter Hilton is decorated in fresh plumbing-white, with magenta armchairs shaped like pelvic bones scattered through it. Artificial gravity is provided by centrifugal force; inside the rotating Ferris wheel people have weight. The architecture gives the white floor of the Orbiter Hilton's conversation area quite a gradient, but no one lets slip a sign of humor about the slant. The citizens of 2001 have forgotten how to joke and resist, just as they have forgotten how to chat, speculate, grow intimate, or interest one another. But otherwise everything is splendid. They lack the mind for acknowledging that they have managed to diminish outer space into the ultimate in humdrum, or for dealing with the fact that they are spent and insufficient, like the apes.

The film is hypnotically entertaining, and funny without once being gaggy, but it is also rather harrowing. It is as eloquent about what is missing from the people of 2001 as about what is there. The characters seem isolated almost beyond endurance. Even in the most absurd scenes, there is often a fugitive melancholy—as astronauts solemnly watch themselves on homey BBC interviews seen millions of miles from Earth, for instance, or as they burn their fingers on their space meals, prepared with the utmost scientific care but a shade too hot to touch, or as they plod around a centrifuge to get some exercise, shadowboxing alone past white coffins where the rest of the crew hibernates in deep freeze. Separation from other people is total and unmentioned. Kubrick has no characters in the film who are sexually related, nor any close friends. Communication is stuffy and guarded, made at the level of men together on committees or of someone being interviewed. The space scientist telephones his daughter by television for her birthday, but he has nothing to say, and his wife is out; an astronaut on the nine-month mission to Jupiter gets a pre-recorded TV birthday message from his parents. That's the sum of intimacy. No enjoyment—only the mechanical celebration of the anniversaries of days when the race perpetuated itself. Again, another astronaut, played by Keir Dullea, takes a considerable risk to try to save a fellow spaceman, but you feel it hasn't anything to do with affection or with courage. He has simply been trained to save an expensive colleague by a society that has slaughtered instinct. Fortitude is a matter of programing, and companionship seems lost. There remains only longing, and this is buried under banality, for English has finally been booted to death. Even informally, people say "Will that suffice?" for "Will that do?" The computer on the Jupiter spaceship —a chatty, fussy genius called Hal, which has nice manners and a rather querulous need for reassurance about being wanted—talks more like a human being than any human being does in the picture. Hal runs the craft, watches over the rotating quota of men in deep freeze, and plays chess. He gives a lot of thought to how he strikes others, and sometimes carries on about himself like a mother fussing on the telephone to keep a bored grown child hanging on. At a low ebb and growing paranoid, he tells a hysterical lie about a faulty piece of equipment to recover the crew's respect, but a less emotional twin computer on Earth coolly picks him up on the judgment and degradingly defines it as a mistake. Hal, his mimic humanness perfected, detests the witnesses of his humiliation and restores his ego by vengeance. He manages to kill all the astronauts but Keir Dullea, including the hibernating crew members, who die in the most chillingly modern death scene imaginable: warning lights simply signal "Computer Malfunction," and sets of electrophysiological needles above the sleepers run amok on the graphs and then record the straight lines of extinction. The survivor of Hal's marauding self-justification, alone on the craft, has to battle his way into the computer's red-flashing brain, which is the size of your living room, to unscrew the high cerebral functions. Hal's sophisticated voice gradually slows and he loses his grip. All he can remember in the end is how to sing "Daisy"—which he was taught at the start of his training long ago—grinding down like an old phonograph. It is an upsetting image of human decay from command into senility. Kubrick makes it seem a lot worse than a berserk computer being controlled with a screwdriver.

The startling metaphysics of the picture are symbolized in the slabs. It is curious that we should all still be so subconsciously trained in apparently distant imagery. Even to atheists, the slabs wouldn't look simply like girders. They immediately have to do with Mosaic tablets or druidical stones. Four million years ago, says the story, an extraterrestrial intelligence existed. The slabs are its manifest sentinels. The one we first saw on prehistoric Earth is like the one discovered in 2001 on the moon. The lunar finding sends out an upper-harmonic shriek to Jupiter and puts the scientists on the trail of the forces of creation. The surviving astronaut goes on alone, and Jupiter's influence pulls him into a world where time and space are relative in ways beyond Einstein. Physically almost pulped, seeing visions of the planet's surface that are like chloroform nightmares and that sometimes turn into close-ups of his own agonized eyeball and eardrum, he then suddenly lands, and he is in a tranquilly furnished repro Louis-XVI room. The shot of it through the window of his space pod is one of the most heavily charged things in the whole picture, though its effect and its logic are hard to explain.

In the strange, fake room, which is movingly conventional, as if the most that the ill man's imagination can manage in conceiving a better world beyond the infinite is to recollect something he has once been taught to see as beautiful in a grand decorating magazine, time jumps and things disappear. The barely surviving astronaut sees an old grandee from the back, dining on the one decent meal in the film; and when the man turns around it is the astronaut himself in old age. The noise of the chair moving on the white marble in the silence is typical of the brilliantly selective sound track. The old man drops his wineglass, and then sees himself bald and dying on the bed, twenty or thirty years older still, with his hand up to another of the slabs, which has appeared in the room and stands more clearly than ever for the forces of change. Destruction and creation coexist in them. They are like Siva. The last shot of the man is totally transcendental, but in spite of my resistance to mysticism I found it stirring. It shows an X-ray-like image of the dead man's skull re-created as a baby, and approaching Earth. His eyes are enormous. He looks like a mutant. Perhaps he is the first of the needed new species.

It might seem a risky notion to drive sci-fi into magic. But, as with *Strangelove*, Kubrick has gone too far and made it the poetically just place to go. He and his collaborator have found a powerful idea to impel space conquerors whom puny times have robbed of much curiosity. The hunt for the remnant of a civilization that has been signaling the existence of its intelligence to the future for four million years, tirelessly stating the fact that it occurred, turns the shots of emptied, comic, ludicrously dehumanized men into something more poignant. There is a hidden parallel to the shot of the ape's arm swinging up into the empty frame with its first weapon, enthralled by the liberation of something new to do: I keep remembering the shot of the space scientist asleep in a craft with the "Weightless Conditions" sign turned on, his body fixed down by his safety belt while one arm floats free in the air.

Hollis Alpert

Now and then a movie project gets started that involves its makers in a greater outlay of time and energy than was at first envisaged; when the result finally emerges on the screen there is invariably the tendency to wonder if the effort was justified. I suspect this is going to happen in the case of Stanley Kubrick's 2001: A Space Odyssey. Kubrick's last film was the mordant and provoking Dr. Strangelove, released in 1964. We can assume that since then this youngish and remarkably gifted film-maker has been engaged on his cinematic visualization of the first human encounter with what sci-fi writers and addicts call extraterrestrial intelligence, and which some believers in flying saucers and related "sightings" regard firmly as reality.

Kubrick really isn't that type, however. He is obviously fascinated by current space hardware and projections of future developments in the field. He is also aware of the mathematical possibilities in favor of the supposition that some form of intelligent life exists elsewhere in the charted and uncharted reaches of the universe. And he is far too clever to couch his fantasy in the clichéd terms of Hollywood science fiction: monsters, and "things" of one horrible kind or another. He has also had the collaboration of one of the most intelligent writers of science fiction and science fact, Arthur C. Clarke. Between them they first drafted a novel (based on a Clarke short story) detailing the kind of space adventure Kubrick had in mind for his film, and from this they built the screenplay—which, by the way, has been kept under wraps during the long period of production.

An important part of Kubrick's plan was to develop new and improved special-effects techniques that would create the illusion of flight in space and that would give audiences the realistic feel of exploring our solar system. A space station, a huge double wheel, revolves at a calculated speed in space to give its occupants a gravitational weight similar to their accustomed one on earth. A space shuttle, run by that familiar firm, Pan American, carries its lone and important passenger to the station, and another vehicle takes him the rest of the way to a landing in an underground moon base. This kind of thing is beautiful, even breathtaking to watch, and somehow Kubrick's choice of an old-fashioned waltz, "The Blue Danube," to accompany the space acrobatics gives the right sense of innocent, almost naïve scientific adventure that is part of the story scheme at this point.

There is no doubt at all that Kubrick has notably advanced film technique when it comes to achieving perspective for this kind of trickery; how he has done it as yet remains a mystery. Also, for an early section of the film called "The Dawn of Man," he found a way, through the use of special lenses, transparencies, and mirrored screens, to enact on a sound stage scenes that would have otherwise required a long location sojourn in some desolate place of the world. Conceivably, if other directors are allowed to make use of similar methods, some of the more difficult kinds of location work can be drastically lessened or eliminated altogether—a development many in Hollywood would welcome.

But Kubrick and Clarke had more than mere space adventure in mind. They were concerned with the physical and metaphysical implications of an encounter with some otherworldly form of intelligence, if such were ever to occur. They have certainly been bold and imaginative—more so than any others who have played with the prospect in the film medium—but, as shown on the giant Cinerama screen, the awaited spectacle does come as something of a letdown. Somehow we expected more than we get, and, at the same time, Kubrick puzzles us both by what he does present and by how he presents it.

Intriguing indeed is the use of a monolith—a large slab—as the symbol of an extraterrestrial presence and the key to the story. The slab first appears before a colony of apelike creatures and becomes a sort of "gate" to the knowledge that will allow the development of man as we know him. In essence, the primitive grubbers discover how to make use of a weapon and become carnivorous and thus take the first step toward developing the ability to reach the moon some four million years later. Time 2001 A.D., and now another slab, four million years old, is found buried beneath the moon's surface, as though someone or something out there knew this would happen. The slab emits an ear-splitting signal which is tracked to the vicinity of Jupiter. Eventually (some two hours of film time later), a third slab is encountered by the lone surviving occupant of a spaceship about to orbit the distant planet. What happens next might cause some moviegoers to wonder if a solution of LSD has been wafted through the air-conditioning system, for the astronaut now, presumably, enters unknown dimensions of time and space not unlike a psychedelic tunnel in the heavens, and lands in—of all possible and impossible places—a kind of translucent Louis-Seize apartment.

The fourth slab appears before the aged astronaut as he lies dying in his splendid isolation, after which, in embryonic form, he floats back through space to twenty-first-century Earth and whatever destiny the viewer might want to imagine. It is this weirdly far-out finale that has a way of putting a strain on the longest section of the film—that dealing with the long Jupiter trip. Aboard are two active astronauts, three others in "hibernaculums," and an advanced computer that has been programed with human feelings and emotions. Hal, the computer, is there for company and control of the functions of the spacecraft. When Hal begins to make mistakes, as he puts it, matters get pretty sticky for Gary Lockwood and Keir Dullea, the two nonhibernating astronauts.

And for the audience too. Kubrick seems much too fascinated with his intricate and scrupulously detailed, even scientifically plausible space hardware. Those who dote on that sort of thing are going to share Kubrick's fascination. Others are going to wish for speedier space travel. Then, too, this almost mundanely technical section is poles apart from the wide-ranging fantastics of the final episodes. And, for all the beautiful models, the marvelous constructions, the sensational perspectives, the effort to equate scientific accuracy with imaginative projections, there is a gnawing lack of some genuinely human contact with the participants in the adventure. In fact, most human of all is Hal, the computer, and we feel more concerned with the electronic lobotomy performed on him than with anything that happens to the living and breathing actors. With all the sweep and spectacle, there is a pervading aridity. If people are going to behave like automatons, what happens to them isn't going to matter much, even if they become privy to metaphysical secrets.

Nevertheless, Kubrick has, in one big jump, discovered new possibilities for the screen image. He took on a large challenge, and has met it commendably. One quibble, though. There are still problems of distortion in that curving Cinerama screen—not of great concern when things are moving fast, but, on the longer takes, definitely an annoyance. Too bad Kubrick didn't overhaul the Cinerama system while tinkering with everything else.

JOSEPH MORGENSTERN

Most of the sporadic power and sly humor of 2001: A Space Odyssey derive from a contrast in scale. On the one hand we have the universe; that takes a pretty big hand. On the other we have man, a recently risen ex-ape in a dinky little rocket ship. Somewhere between earth and Jupiter, though, producer-director Stanley Kubrick gets confused about the proper scale of things himself. His potentially majestic myth about man's first encounter with a higher life form than his own dwindles into a whimsical space operetta, then frantically inflates itself again for a surreal climax in which the imagery is just obscure enough to be annoying, just precise enough to be banal.

The first of the film's four movements deals with man's prehistoric debut. It is as outrageous and entertaining as anything in *Planet of the Apes*, but much more engrossing. Cutting constantly between real apes and actors (or dancers) in unbelievably convincing anthropoid outfits, Kubrick establishes the fantasy base of his myth with the magical appearance of a monolithic slab in the apes' midst. They touch it, dance around it, worship it. The sequence ends with a scene in which one of our founding fathers picks up a large bone, beats a rival into ape-steak tartare with it and thus becomes the first animal on earth to use a tool. The man-ape gleefully hurls his tool of war into the air. It becomes a satellite in orbit around the moon. A single dissolve spans four million years.

With nearly equal flair the second movement takes up the story in the nearly present future. Man has made it to the moon and found another shiny slab buried beneath the surface. By this time the species is bright enough to surmise that the slab is some sort of trip-wire device planted by superior beings from Jupiter to warn that earthmen are running loose in the universe. Kubrick's special effects in this section border on the miraculous—lunar landscapes, spaceship interiors and exteriors that represent a quantum leap in quality over any sci-fi film ever made.

In a lyrical orbital roundelay, a rocket ship from earth takes up the same rotational rate as the space station it will enter. Once again, as in *Dr. Strangelove*, machines copulate in public places. This time, however, they do it to a Strauss waltz instead of "Try a Little Tenderness"—the smug, invariable, imperturbable swoops of "the Blue Danube" juxtaposed with the silent, indifferent sizzling of the cosmos.

Where *Strangelove* was a dazzling farce, 2001 bids fair at first to become a fine satire. We see that space has been conquered. We also see it has been commercialized and, within the limits of man's

tiny powers, domesticated. Weightless stewardesses wear weightless smiles, passengers diddle with glorified Automat meals, watch
karate on in-flight TV and never once glance out into the void to
catch a beam of virgin light from Betelgeuse or Aldebaran.

The third movement begins promisingly, too. America has sent a
spaceship to Jupiter. The men at the controls, Keir Dullea and
Gary Lockwood, are perfectly deadpan paradigms of your ideal astronaut: scarily smart, hair-raisingly humorless. The computer that
runs the ship and talks like an announcer at a lawn-tennis tourna-
ment admits to suffering from certain anxieties about the mission
(or, more ominously, pretends to suffer from them), but the men
are unflappable as a reefed mainsail.

Your own anxieties about 2001 may begin to surface during a
scene in which Lockwood trots around his slowly rotating crypt-
ship and shadowboxes to keep in shape. He trots and boxes, boxes
and trots until he has trotted the plot to a complete halt, and the
director's attempt to show the boredom of interplanetary flight becomes a crashing bore in its own right. Kubrick and his co-writer,
Arthur C. Clarke, still have some tricks up their sleeves before Jupiter: pretty op-art designs that flicker cryptically across the face of
the instrument display tubes, a witty discussion between Dullea
and Lockwood on the computer's integrity.

But the ship is becalmed for too long, with stately repetitions of
earlier special effects, a maddening sound of deep breathing on the
sound track, a beautiful but brief walk in space and then a long,
long stretch of very shaky comedy-melodrama in which the computer turns on its crew and carries on like an injured party in a homosexual spat. Dullea finally lobotomizes the thing and, in the absence of any plot advancement, this string of faintly familiar computer gags gets laughs. But they are deeply destructive to a film
that was poking fun itself, only a few reels ago, at man's childish
preoccupation with technological trivia.

On the outskirts of Jupiter 2001 runs into some interesting ab-
stractions that have been done more interestingly in many more
modest underground films that were not shot in seventy-millimeter
Super Panavision, then takes a magnificent flight across the face of
the planet: mauve and mocha mountains, swirling methane seas
and purple skies. But its surreal climax is a wholly inadequate response to the challenge it sets for itself, the revelation of a higher
form of life than our own. When Dullea, as the surviving astro-

naut, climbs out of his space ship he finds it and himself in a Louis XVI hotel suite. Original? Not very. Ray Bradbury did it years ago in a story about men finding an Indiana town on Mars, complete with people singing "Moonlight on the Wabash."

It is a trap, in a sense, with the victim's own memories as bait. The nightmare continues, portentously, pretentiously, as Dullea discovers the room's sole inhabitant to be himself. As he breathes his last breath another slab stands watching at the foot of his deathbed, and when he dies he turns into a cute little embryo Adam, staring into space from his womb. So the end is but the beginning, the last shall be first, and so on and so forth. But what was the slab? That's for Kubrick and Clarke to know and us to find out. Maybe God, or pure intelligence, maybe a Jovian as we perceive him with our primitive eyes and ears. Maybe it was a Jovian undertaker. Maybe it was a nephew of the New York Hilton.

PLANET OF THE APES

Philip T. Hartung

Returning to the idea that the proper study of mankind is man, movies are running the gamut this week from the sublime to the ridiculous. And much less ridiculous than one at first thinks is the science-fiction entry, *Planet of the Apes*. The earth-time year is 3968 A.D.—I think. I'm a little vague about this because the opening scene within an American space ship has astronaut-leader Charlton Heston recording and talking about their two-thousand-year trip through time and space in a scientific jargon a little too deep for the likes of me. The space ship crashes in a lake on a seemingly barren planet; Heston and two other men survive and then wander on and on over handsome, rocky, though lifeless, scenery. Then comes the shocker: the men are pursued by apes, who, it turns out, are the planet's top social order. These rather intelligent simians rule the planet and consider humans an inferior order, especially those primitive, animal-like men who run around in the woods and ruin the crops. The apes, however, fail to distinguish between the three astronauts and the mute senseless backwoodsmen. Needless to say, they give our boys a hard time; Heston is the only one to survive—after one of his pals dies and is stuffed for a diorama, and the other becomes the victim of an experimental lobotomy.

Although I have not read Desmond Morris' new book, *The Naked Ape*, I've read and heard so much about it that I kept thinking of it as I saw *Planet of the Apes*, especially during the scenes in which the simian scientists submit Heston to tests. It's pretty hard for man to retain any dignity when he's practically nude and on exhibition in a cage. But, fortunately for Heston, a chimpanzee woman doctor (Kim Hunter) and an archaeologist (Roddy McDowall) discover that Heston can speak, read and write; and they are anxious to keep him alive for further study. But very much against them is one of the state chieftains (Maurice Evans), who has ulterior motives in wanting to get rid of Heston. The woman doctor is very advanced and actually believes that it is possible that apes could have descended from that order of humans.

While *Planet of the Apes* has a first-rate cast and an outstanding production under Arthur P. Jacobs, the ape costumes and make-up, though excellent, keep us from recognizing the actors. Naked or in rags or chains, Heston gives a good performance throughout. Linda Harrison, as the mute girl thrown into his cage as a possible mate, is very pretty. But all I can say for Evans, McDowall and Kim Hunter is that they are in good voice. Voices are important. Director Franklin J. Schaffner manages to get a lot of action into his picture, but more vital are the arguments between apes and man, and, as presented in the screenplay by Michael Wilson and Rod Serling (from the novel by Pierre Boulle) they are fascinating. Man does not always come out best. Surprisingly enough, the film has some good humor, thanks, among other things to the script's putting clichés into the mouths of those apes who think they're so damn smart. The finale of *Planet of the Apes* will make your blood run cold. I can't remember when a science-fiction film like this socked you in the face at the end with a warning to mankind.

2

RUMBLINGS OF REVOLT

A *Minority Movie* (LA CHINOISE)

Pauline Kael

A few weeks ago, I was startled to see a big Pop poster of Che Guevara—startled not because students of earlier generations didn't have comparable martyrs and heroes but because they didn't consider their heroes part of popular culture, though their little brothers and sisters might have been expected to conceive of them in comic-strip terms. Jean-Luc Godard, who said on the sound track of a recent film, "One might almost say that to live in society today is something like living inside an enormous comic strip," has already made a movie about the incorporation of revolutionary heroes and ideas into Pop—*La Chinoise*. In the narration of an earlier movie, Godard defined his field as "the present, where the future is more present than the present." In *Masculine Feminine*, which was about "the children of Marx and Coca-Cola," a man about to burn himself up needed to borrow a match, and many people were irritated by the levity and absurdity of it—but the *Times* reported just such an incident this month. In the further adventures of those children, in *La Chinoise*, the heroine wants to blow up the Louvre; someone threw a stink bomb into a party at the Museum of Modern Art last week. We don't have time to catch up with the future that is here, and Godard is already making movie critiques of it—documentaries of the future in the present. His movies have become a volatile mixture of fictional narrative, reporting, essay, and absurdist interludes. His tempo is so fast that it is often difficult to keep up with the dialogue, let alone the punctuation of advertising art and allusions to history, literature, movies, and current events. There is little doubt that many of us react to movies in terms of how the tempo suits our own tempo. (As a child, I could never sit still through a Laurel-and-Hardy feature, and I have something of the same problem with most of Antonioni's recent work.) Since Godard's tempo is too fast for many people—perhaps most people—they have some ground for anger and confusion. But I think he is driven to ignore the difficulties that audiences may experience—not because he wants to assault them or to be deliberately "uncommercial," not out of pretentiousness or arrogance, but out of the nature of his material and his talent.

Though Godard is a social critic, using largely documentary material, he does not work in the expository manner of television documentaries but intuitively seizes new, rapidly changing elements and dramatizes them as directly as possible, projecting his feelings and interpretations into the material. He assumes in his audience an Americanized sensibility—that is, a quick comprehension of devices and conventions derived from American film style—and his temperamental affinity with American popular art probably seems particularly disreputable and trivial to those educated Americans who go to art-film houses for the European cultural ambiance. Antonioni's ponderously serious manner serves as a guarantee of quality; Godard is so restless and inquiring that he hardly develops his ideas at all. In a new picture he may leap back to rework a theme when he sees how to develop what was only partly clear before. His style is a form of shorthand, and this irritates even some people who one might assume are perfectly able to read it. We all know that an artist can't discover anything for himself—can't function as an *artist*—if he must make everything explicit in terms accessible to the widest possible audience. This is one of the big hurdles that defeat artists in Hollywood: they aren't allowed to assume that anybody knows anything, and they become discouraged and corrupt when they discover that studio thinking is not necessarily wrong in its estimate of the mass audience. Godard, like many American novelists, works in terms of an audience that is assumed to have the same background he has. And, of course, many people do—perhaps a majority of the people in the art-house audiences, though they're not used to making connections among fast references at the movies. No one complains about the quotation from Kafka's *Metamorphosis* in *The Producers*, or about Gene Wilder's being named Leo Bloom in the same film, or even about another character's being called Carmen Giya; this is considered cute "inside humor" when it's obviously done just for a laugh. But if, as in *La Chinoise*, some of the names are used as a shortcut to the characters' roles—Kirilov, for example, for the most desperately confused of the revolutionaries—people are sure to object, though this is done in novels all the time. There are many references that may be incomprehensible to some in the audience, but should Godard stop to explain who Rosa Luxemburg was or what Malraux stands for or why he brings in Sartre and Aragon or Artaud or Theater Year Zero or Daniel and Sinyavsky? Can't he assume that those who care about the kind of film he is making—those who are involved with the issues of his art—already share most of his frame of reference and are prepared to respond to someone's using it in movies, that they are no longer much involved with movies in the same old frame of reference, which doesn't permit dealing with the attitudes of, as in this case, radical youth? This is minority art not by desire but by necessity. Most innovative artists working in movies have tried to reach the mass audience and failed—failed to reach it as artists. Godard, who is perhaps a symptom of the abandonment of hope for a great popular art, works as artists do in less popular media—at his own highest level.

Inventive and visually gifted, Godard is also, and perhaps even primarily, literary in his approach, and his verbal humor presupposes an educated audience. In *La Chinoise* he uses words in more ways than any other film-maker: they're in the dialogue and on the walls, on book jackets and in headlines; they're recited, chanted, shouted, written, broken down; they're in commentaries, quotations, interviews, narration; they're in slogans and emblems and signs. Those who dislike verbal allusions will be irritated constantly, and those who want only straightforward action on the screen may be driven wild by his neo-Brechtian displacement devices (his voice on the sound track, a cut to Raoul Coutard at the camera) and by his almost novelistic love of digression—his inclusion of anecdotes and of speculations about movie art and of direct-to-the-camera interviews. And his doubts can be irritating in a medium that is customarily used for banal certainties. Not many movie directors regard their movies as a place to raise the questions that are troubling them. Sometimes Godard's questioning essays come apart like hasty puddings, and then his whole method falls open to question. He is also prone to the use of the *acte gratuit*, so common in philosophical French fiction of this century but rather maddening in films because such acts violate the basic premise of dramatic construction—that the author will show us what led to the crimes or deaths. Godard gives us quick finishes that are not resolutions of what has gone before.

Some of these factors are genuine deterrents to moviegoing, but Godard is, at the moment, the most important single force keeping the art of the film alive—that is to say, responsive to the modern world, moving, reaching out for new themes. The last year has been a relatively good year for American movies—there have been more pictures fit to look at than there were in the preceding few years, when Hollywood seemed to have become a desert: but, with the exception of *Bonnie and Clyde*, if you missed any or all of them you would hardly have missed a thing, because they are merely genre pieces brought up to date: thrillers, Westerns, or "strikingly new" films, which is to say films about adolescent rebellion that take over material, attitudes, and sensibility already commonplace to anybody who reads books or goes to plays. We can go to foreign films, and a romantic tragedy set in another period and culture, like *Elvira Madigan*, may be highly satisfying when we want to dream away and weep a little and look at lovely pictures—as we did at *Mayerling* in the Thirties. And a slick thriller or a Western may still be entertaining enough and basically, crudely satisfying when we are tired and just want to go sit and see some action. But what these late-Sixties versions of standard movies don't have is the excitement of contemporaneity, of using movies in new ways. Going to the movies, we sometimes forget—because it so rarely happens—that when movies are used in new ways there's an excitement about them much sharper than there is about the limited-entertainment genres. Godard's films—the good ones, that is —are funny, and they're funny in a new way: *La Chinoise* is a comic elegy on a group of modern revolutionary youth—naïve, forlorn little ideologues who live out a Pop version of *The Possessed*.

Godard once wrote, "I want to be able sometimes to make you feel far from the person when I do a close-up." We feel far from Véronique, the teen-age philosophy student of *La Chinoise*, all the time, and it's a scary sensation, because she is so much like every other girl on campus these days. As embodied by Anne Wiazemsky, the granddaughter of Mauriac who made her debut in Bresson's *Balthazar* and is now married to Godard, Véronique may be more of a representative of the new radical youth than any other movie has come up with. She is an engaged nihilist, an activist who wants to close the universities by acts of terrorism; she thinks that this will open the way for a new educational system, and that a few deaths don't matter. She is politically engaged, and yet this condition seems to go hand in hand with a peculiar, and possibly new, kind of detachment. She and the four other members of her Maoist group who share the apartment where most of the movie takes place seem detached from the life around them, from how they live, from feelings of any kind. In her soft, small voice, and with the unself-conscious, frightened, yet assured face of so many American college girls, Véronique makes rigid formulations about morals and philosophy; she has no resonance. The group live in a political wonderland of slogans lifted out of historical continuity; they prattle about correct programs and objective conditions and just, progressive wars and the Treaty of Brest-Litovsk. They have none of the strength or the doubts that come from experience. They are disparately together in their communal life; they could just as easily recombine in another grouping. Véronique is another version of Godard's unreachable, perfidious girl, but this unreachable ideologue, though as blankly affectless as the heroines of *Breathless* and *Masculine Feminine,* is not treacherous, nor is there any deep enough emotional involvement between the boys and the girls for deceit to be necessary or for betrayal or victimization to be possible. Sex is taken for granted, is so divorced from emotion that the members of the group seem almost post-sexual, which may be just about the same as pre-sexual. They study Marxism-Leninism and chant Chairman Mao's sayings from the little red book like nursery rhymes; they play with lethal toys, and—in that bizarre parroting of the Red Guard which is so common here, too— they attack not the economic system and the advertising culture that has produced them but the culture of the past and its institutions, and bourgeois "compromisers," and Russian-style Communists. Véronique wants to bomb the Sorbonne, the Louvre, the Comédie-Française; she murders a Soviet cultural emissary visiting Paris, a representative of the culture stifling the universities, who is selected almost at random to be the first in a series. The group's political life in the flat is a contained universe that almost seems to dematerialize the more familiar world, because it is such a separate, paper-thin universe. Their conspiratorial plots seem like games; they are too open and naïve to hide anything. They expel a member for "revisionism," and the little bespectacled boy goes to the foot of the table and consoles himself with bread and jam. Yet from the flat where they play-act revolution they go out and commit terrorist acts with the same affectless determination. Véronique kills the wrong man and is not fazed by it; she goes back and gets "the right one" as unemotionally as she might correct a mistake in an examination. Godard shows the horror, the beauty, and the absurdity of their thinking and their living, all at the same time.

La Chinoise is a satire of new political youth, but a satire from within, based on observation, and a satire that loves its targets more than it loves anything else—that, perhaps, can see beauty and hope only in its targets. But not much hope. In a section toward the end, the movie goes outside comedy. Godard introduces Francis Jeanson, an older man with political experience, a humane radical who *connects*. Jeanson tries to explain to Véronique that her terrorist actions will not have the consequences she envisions. She describes her tactics for closing the universities, and, gently but persistently, he raises the question "What next?" There is no question whose side Godard is on—that of the revolutionary children—but in showing their styles of action and of thought he has used his doubts, and his fears for them, to warn them. Though his purpose is didactic, the movie is so playful and quick-witted and affectionate that it's possible—indeed, likely—that audiences will be confused about Godard's "attitude."

How can the modern "possessed" be *funny?* The fusion of attitudes—seeing characters as charming and poetic and, at the same time, preposterous and absurd—is one of Godard's contributions to modern film. (Truffaut worked in almost the same mode in *Shoot the Piano Player*—the mode that in America led to *Bonnie and Clyde.*) Godard's attitude toward his characters is similar to Scott Fitzgerald's in that he loves beautiful, doomed youth, but his style is late-Sixties. If one examines books on modern movies, the stills generally look terrible—schlocky, dated, cluttered, and artificially lighted. Stills from Godard's films provide such a contrast that they can be spotted at once. In natural light, his figures are isolated and clearly defined in space against impersonal modern buildings with advertising posters or in rooms against white walls with unframed pictures from magazines. The look is of modern graphics, and that, of course, is why the stills reproduce so well. The ironic elegance of his hard-edge photographic compositions on screen is derived from graphics, comic strips, modern décor, and the two-dimensional television image. The frames in a Godard film are perfectly suited to fast comprehension—one can see everything in them at a glance—and to quick cutting. They can move with the speed of a comic strip, in which we also read the whole picture and the words at once. This visual style, which enables him to make a comedy out of politics and despair, has, however, often been misinterpreted as an attempt to achieve "pure form" on screen. Godard is not trying to create a separate world of abstract film that might be analogous to the arts of music and abstract painting, and it is a way not of explaining his movies but of explaining them away to say that they are works of art because they are going in the same direction as painting—as if every art reached its culmination when it was emptied of verbal meaning and of references to this world. Godard uses abstract design because he responds to the future in the present and because he is trying to show how human relationships are changing in this new world of advertising art, dehumanized housing, multiple forms of prostitution. He does not work in a studio; he selects locations that reveal how abstract modern urban living already is. He fills the screen with a picture of Brecht and the definition "Theater is a commentary on reality." He uses words as words—for what they mean (and he satirizes the characters in La Chinoise for using words abstractly). He is no more an abstractionist than the comic-strip artist, who also uses simplified compositions and bright primary colors as a visual-verbal shorthand technique. If the meaning is conveyed by a balloon containing the word "Splat!" you don't need to paint in the leaves on the branches of the trees or the herringbone design on the pants. And if modern life is seen in terms of the future, the leaves and the weave are already gone. The folly of viewing Godard's stripped-down-for-speed-and-wit visual style as if he were moving away from the impurities of meaning is that it is a way of canceling out everything that goes on in a movie like La Chinoise—of "appreciating" everything the "artist" does and not reacting to or understanding anything the person says.

For a moviemaker, Godard is almost incredibly intransigent. At this point, it would be easy for him to court popularity with the young audience (which is the only audience he has ever had, and he has had little of that one) by making his revolutionaries romantic, like the gangster in *Breathless*. Romantic revolutionaries could act out political plots instead of robberies. But he does not invest the political activists of *La Chinoise* with glamour or mystery, or even passion. His romantic heroes and heroines were old-fashioned enough to believe in people, and hence to be victimized; the members of Véronique's group believe love is impossible, and for them it is. Godard does just what will be hardest to take: he makes them infantile and funny—victims of Pop culture. And though he likes them because they are ready to convert their slogans into action, because they want to do something, he dares to suggest that they haven't thought through what they're doing. The whole movie asks, "And after you've closed the universities, what next?"

ANDREW SARRIS

Jean-Luc Godard's *La Chinoise* is as successful with its fragmented forms as *Made in USA* and *Two or Three Things I Know About Her* were unsuccessful. Almost everything works as it should in *La Chinoise*, and the result is the kind of charm and enchantment we had almost stopped associating with the increasingly joyless Jean-Luc. What bothered me most about *Made in USA* and *Two or Three Things* was Godard's confusing his fleeting impressions of reality with reality itself. The visual flair was still evident, but the ideas were banal. The poet was pontificating like a pundit, and his films were becoming bloated with redundant rhetoric. More and more, Godard was saying what he meant instead of showing what he felt. After the suicidal climax and confessional of *Pierrot le fou* it seemed that he was following the safe path of cerebral deviousness by exploiting the most provincial prejudices of the Idiot Left. Anna Karina in *USA* and Marina Vlady in *Two or Three Things* were less characters than puppets, less directed than manipulated by their master's voice.

Godard's apparent decline could not have come at a worse time for his American admirers. It was hard enough getting any of his films distributed without publicizing his clinkers. Godard's inane interviews did not help matters very much. His description of Hollywood movies as "the gangrene of world cinema" could be chalked up to the political passion inherent in a project called *Far from Vietnam*, but his cranky comments about other people's movies and motives sounded as if the thousand flowers of the *nouvelle vague* were withering away into the jealous, poisonous weeds of anti-Hollywood conformity. Long, long ago I had loved Godard's criticism for its open-mindedness. The movies were everything, Godard had insisted, from Hitchcock to Rossellini, from Eisenstein to Flaherty. Now suddenly the movies were only what Godard and his cronies permitted them to be. This moviegoer still prefers the original description of the cinema as everything from Jean-Luc Godard's *La Chinoise* to Donald Siegel's *Madigan*.

Critical orientation aside, *La Chinoise* is the most perceptive film about modern youth since *Masculine Feminine*, which is another way of saying that Godard is the only contemporary director with the ability to express through graceful cinema what young people are feeling at this time in world history. Not all young people, of course, only the heroic hotheads. Anne Wiazemsky out of Bresson's *Balthazar* has replaced Anna Karina as Godard's Galatea. At first it seems that Godard has sought to transform a severe ascetic into a Sorbonne soubrette, perhaps even Anne into a facsimile of Anna, eyes wide and lips slightly parted, but the impression fades. Anne Wiazemsky is all mandarin as Anna Karina was all marshmallow, and Godard has learned to keep his distance. Jean-Pierre Léaud is the actor of the troupe, and he too transcends himself by being himself as he walks the tightrope between Mao and Artaud, between the politics of terror and the theater of cruelty.

La Chinoise is filmed as if it were in the process of being filmed. We see the clap board banging together at the beginning of scenes that do not always come to a conclusion. Godard's voice can be heard in the background of *cinéma-vérité* scenes, but softly now, always softly, as if he were conversing with beings possessed of otherness rather than mere reflections and echoes. Perhaps Godard does not yet understand Anne Wiazemsky well enough to know her every move and calculate her every mood. Perhaps he was simply fascinated by the facility with which she expressed the inexorable intolerance of youth.

La Chinoise is beautifully photographed. Never have I seen posters and photographs so well integrated with characterization. This is what I missed in *The Edge*. Robert Kramer is too intellectual to let us see even the graffiti we encounter accidentally. No two people ever talk about a subject that could possibly be of interest to a third person. Kramer's directorial tact dooms him to inexpressiveness and boredom. I respect the dignity and intelligence of *The Edge*, and I might even be willing to grant that Robert Kramer is a better human being than Jean-Luc Godard, but *La Chinoise* remains a mountain of scenic splendor whereas *The Edge* remains an arid plain of unrelieved flatness except for the mechanism and symbolism of Kramer's Golden Bowl.

Such articulate defenders of *The Edge* as James Stoller, Roger Greenspun, and Stuart Byron have focused attention on the cups of coffee involved in the deliberations of the protagonists. By a strange coincidence, Godard has one of his characters dunk rolls into a bowl of café-au-lait while he is explaining his defection from a young Maoist cell in the New Left of Paris. Godard's character would rather eat than talk. Kramer's characters all would rather talk than eat: they handle their dingy utensils as if they were sacramental objects, they are never dominated by their décor or by the food they eat; but by thus being somewhat more than human they are much less than human. Godard's character succeeds in emphasizing what is most poignantly ephemeral about the proceedings because Godard's vision enables the director to see a meal and a message on the same level of history. Kramer's direction suffers from a visual paranoia that causes him to blame objects for human misery. Perhaps it is unfair to compare Godard and Kramer, but, unfortunately, *La Chinoise* makes *The Edge* and Clive Donner's *Here We Go Round the Mulberry Bush* seem somewhat superfluous as statements of the Sixties. It might be argued that *The Edge* is what happens to the people in *La Chinoise* ten years later, except that Godard will probably be on hand ten years from now with a superior version of *The Edge*.

Ultimately, Godard is superior to the New American humanists because he is cursed with a fantastic memory of the medium. There are bits of Lubitsch and Ophuls in the back-and-forth tracks within scenes across the obstacles of walls and the apertures of open shutters. These tracks, so effective here, were often irritating in *A Woman Is a Woman* and *Contempt*. (Godard even repeats a song from *A Woman Is a Woman* to link Anne to Anna.) However, the most extraordinary movements in the film come out of Murnau; a sliding gate reminiscent of the ship's sail entering the frame in Murnau's *Tabu,* and an extraordinary trip viewed through a train window situated between two speakers to remind us forcibly of the Janet Gaynor–George O'Brien trolley ride in Murnau's *Sunrise.* The fact that the two speakers—Anne Wiazemsky and Francis Jeanson—are debating the uses of terror in a smug society as the country to be terrorized passes serenely outside their window only enhances Godard's stylistic coup with thematic relevance. The world is so big, Godard implies, and time is so short (for youth as well as for revolution), and the bravest men of the past seem like cowards in the present. Jeanson himself was exiled for his stand on the Algerian War, but he can offer no encouragement to the Parisian Maoists. For his part, Godard now perceives fully the chasm between thought and action. He stays with the students for their summer and takes them on their own terms, but in the very heat of summer he can anticipate the winter of their discontent. *La Chinoise* is more than Godard's valentine to youth; it is also his valedictory.

Movies as Opera (CHINA IS NEAR)

Pauline Kael

Movies have been doing so much of the same thing—in slightly different ways—for so long that few of the possibilities of this great hybrid art have yet been explored. At the beginning, movies served many of the functions of primitive theater; they were Punch-and-Judy shows. But by bringing simple forms of theater and great actors and dancers and singers to the small towns of the world, they helped to create a taste for more complex theater, and by bringing the world to people who couldn't travel they helped to develop more advanced audiences. When Méliès photographed his magic shows, when D. W. Griffith re-created the Civil War or imagined the fall of Babylon, when Pabst made a movie with Chaliapin, when Flaherty went to photograph life in the Aran

Islands or the South Seas, they were just beginning to tap the infinite possibilities of movies to explore, to record, to dramatize. Shipped in tins, movies could go anywhere in the world, taking a synthesis of almost all the known art forms to rich and poor. In terms of the number of people they could reach, movies were so inexpensive that they could be hailed as the great democratic art form. Then, as businessmen gained control of the medium, it became almost impossibly difficult for the artists to try anything new. Movies became in one way or another remakes of earlier movies, and until inexpensive pictures from abroad began to attract large audiences the general public probably believed what the big studios advertised—that great movies meant big stars, best-seller stories, expensive production. The infinite variety of what was possible on film was almost forgotten, along with the pioneers, and many of those who loved movies lost some of their own vision. They began to ask what cinema "really" was, as if ideal cinema were some pre-existent entity that had to be discovered; like Platonists turned archaeologists, they tried to unearth the true essence of cinema. Instead of celebrating the multiplicity of things that movies can do better or more easily than the other arts, and in new ways and combinations, they looked for the true nature of cinema in what cinema can do that the other arts can't—in artistic apartheid. Some decided on "montage," others on "purely visual imagery." (There was even a period when true cinema was said to be "the chase," and for a while audiences were being chased right out of the theaters.) They wanted to prove that cinema was a real art, like the other arts, when the whole world instinctively preferred it because it was a bastard, cross-fertilized super-art.

"Cinema" in a pure state is not to be found, but movies in the sixties began to expand again, and so quickly it's hard to keep up with them. In France men like Jean Rouch and Chris Marker are extending movies into what were previously thought to be the domains of anthropologists, sociologists, and journalists, while in *Masculine Feminine* Jean-Luc Godard made a modern love lyric out of journalism and essays and interviews, demonstrating that there are no boundaries in the arts that talent can't cross. Not even the grave. In *China Is Near* the young Italian director Marco Bellocchio now brings back to startling life a form that had been laid to rest with modern ceremony—that is, with a few regrets, kicks, and jeers. The new, great talent—perhaps the genius—of Godard brought chance into the art of movies. Bellocchio's talent—so distinctive that already it resembles genius—flourishes within the confines of intricate plot. *China Is Near* has the boudoir complications of a classic comic opera.

Among the five principals in *China Is Near*, who use each other in every way they can, are a pair of working-class lovers—a secretary and an accountant—who scheme to marry into the rich landed gentry. Their targets are a professor, Vittorio (Glauco Mauri), who is running for municipal office on the Socialist ticket, and his sister, Elena, a great lady who lets every man in town climb on top of her but won't marry because socially they're all beneath her. Vittorio, the rich Socialist candidate, is that role so essential to comic opera —the ridiculous lover, the man whose mission in life is to be deceived—and Bellocchio, who wrote the film (with Elda Tattoli, who plays Elena) as well as directed it, has produced a classic modern specimen of the species: a man who's out of it, who doesn't get anything while it's going on. The fifth principal is their little brother, Camillo, who is a prissy, sneering despot, a seventeen-year-old seminary student turned Maoist who looks the way Edward Albee might look in a drawing by David Levine. Camillo provides the title when he scrawls "China Is Near" on the walls of the Socialist Party building—his brother's campaign headquarters.

Bellocchio uses the underside of family life—the inbred family atmosphere—for borderline horror and humor. His people are so awful they're funny. One might say that Bellocchio, though he is only twenty-eight, sees sex and family and politics as a dirty old man would, except that his movie is so peculiarly exuberant; perhaps only a very young (or a very old) director can focus on such graceless, mean-spirited people with so much enjoyment. As the pairs of lovers combine and recombine and the five become one big, ghastly family (with a yapping little house pet as an emblem of domesticity), Bellocchio makes it all rhyme. He provides the grace of formal design. The grand manner of the movie is hilarious. I found myself smiling at the wit of his technique; it was pleasurable just to see the quick way doors open and close, or how, when the scene shifts to a larger, more public area, there's always something unexpected going on—surprises that explode what has seemed serious. Bellocchio's visual style is almost incredibly smooth; the camera glides in and out and around the action. He uses it as if there were no obstructions, as if he could do anything he wanted with it; it moves as simply and with as much apparent ease as if it were attached to the director's forehead. In *China Is Near*, as in his first film (*I pugni in tasca*, or *Fist in His Pocket*, which was made in 1965 and is soon to open in this country), he probably exhibits the most fluid directorial technique since Max Ophuls, and I don't know where it came from—that is, how he developed it so fast.

Fist in His Pocket must surely be one of the most astonishing directorial debuts in the history of movies, yet it is hard to know how to react to the movie itself. The material is wild, the direction cool and assured. *Fist in His Pocket*, which Bellocchio made fresh from film schools in Italy and England, is also about a prosperous family, but a family of diseased monsters. And as epileptic fits multiply between bouts of matricide, fratricide, and incest, one is too busy gasping at the director's technique and the performances of a cast of unknown actors (Lou Castel, with his pug-dog manner, and Paola Pitagora, looking like a debauched gazelle, are the best strange brother-and-sister act since Édouard Dermithe and Nicole Stéphane in *Les Enfants Terribles*) to doubt his directorial genius. But the movie is a portrait of the genius as a very young man. It is so savage it often seems intended to be funny, but *why* it was so intended isn't clear. Though *Fist in His Pocket* is exhilarating because it reveals a new talent, not everybody cares about movies enough to want to see a movie—no matter how brilliant—about a family cage of beasts, and to a casual moviegoer *Fist in His Pocket* may seem as heavily charged with misguided energy as one of those epileptic seizures. But in a few years people will probably be going to see it as, after seeing Ingmar Bergman's later films, they went to see his early ones. After only two films, Bellocchio's characters already seem his, in the way that the characters of certain novelists seem theirs—a way uncommon in movies except in the movies of writer-directors of especially individual temperaments. Bellocchio's characters are as much a private zoo as Buñuel's.

It was not just coincidence when, a few years ago, first one young French director broke through, then another and another; it was obvious not only that they took encouragement from each other but that they literally inspired each other. Bellocchio was preceded in this way by another young Italian, Bernardo Bertolucci, who at twenty-one directed *La commare secca* and at twenty-two wrote and directed the sweepingly romantic *Before the Revolution*, which also dealt with a provincial family and sex and politics, and which suggested a new, operatic approach to movie-making. Both these young directors refer to opera the way the French refer to American movies; they not only use operatic structure and themes but actually introduce performances and recordings of operas—especially Verdi operas—into their work. (The bit of opera performed in *China Is Near* is the damnedest thing since *Salammbô* in *Citizen Kane*.) In the analogy they draw with opera, they seem to glory in the hybrid nature of movies, and to Italians movies may seem almost an outgrowth of the hybrid art of opera. If Verdi wrote a larger number of enduring operas than any other composer (perhaps a fifth of the total standard repertory), it's not only because he wrote great music but also because he filled the stage with action and passion and a variety of good roles for different kinds of voice, which is how these two directors make their movies. Maybe, too, these directors are saying that sex and family and politics in modern Italy are still out of Verdi. Both these young Italians are different from the older Italian directors—even those just a little older, like Pasolini—in the way that their movies move. Men like Fellini and Antonioni developed their techniques over the years, laboriously, and their early movies attest to how long it took them to become Fellini and Antonioni. This is not to put them down—most of us take a long time and never become anything—but to contrast them with Bertolucci and Bellocchio, who started their movie careers with masterly techniques, proving that it doesn't take decades of apprenticeship or millions of dollars to tell planned and acted stories, and that there is still joy in this kind of moviemaking. I think Godard is the most exciting director working in movies today, and it's easy to see how and why he is influencing movie-makers all over the world. But chance and spontaneity and improvisation and the documentary look are only one way to go—not, as some have begun to think, the only way. The clear triumph of *China Is Near* is that it demonstrates how good other ways can be.

ANDREW SARRIS

Marco Bellocchio's *China Is Near* may not be running much longer, and more's the pity for an art-house scene that is usually starved for genuinely artistic attractions. Bellocchio's direction is brilliant to the point of brilliantine. Not a hair or shot is out of place, nor a cut or camera movement. Everything counts and everything matters in this Stendhalian comedy of mores, but Bellocchio seems to have offended some of the reviewers by violating the sacred rules of exposition. The first shot of the film is a rigidly framed, discreetly distanced glance at two lovers dormant on an improvised bed in an unidentified room by the cold, gray light of dawn. Bellocchio cuts briefly to the stirring couple simply to identify their faces and then retreats quickly to the discreet distance that will keep the sensations of the plot from ever seeming sordid. We shall never completely escape the chilling grayness of this opening sequence. Indeed, *China Is Near* explores all those frayed feelings of conformity that awaken in the five o'clock of the morning of the soul when the ancient alarm goes off like the dreaded church bells of Italian Catholicism.

We are barely accustoming our eyes to the dimly lit and drably furnished scene before this first stage of exposition is supplanted by the next and then the next and then the next until three separate plots and five major characters merge into one comic canvas of Italian Leftism in complete disarray. Bellocchio's young lovers, Carlo (Paolo Graziosi) and Giovanna (Daniela Surina), are first introduced as the beleaguered victims of a class society, specifically the servants of a family of spoiled, self-indulgent aristocrats who dabble in the politics of the Old and New Left. Vittorio (Glauco Mauri) is a plump, pink plutocrat with acute guilt feelings about his enormous wealth. After a fling with the Communist Party, he settles down with the staid Socialists when they present him a place on the ticket as councilman. The candidate's younger brother, Camillo (Pierluigi Apra), leads a three-man Maoist cell in the municipality and refuses to countenance the brother's disgraceful desertion. The candidate's sister, Elena (Elda Tattoli), confounds her brothers with her political conservatism and sexual radicalism. Even when the world is going to pieces, Vittorio reminds her, an Italian expects his sister to retain her honor.

However, Bellocchio is no mere satirist like Pietro Germi, and his characters never degenerate into Germi caricatures at whom we can laugh so complacently. Bellocchio's five characters struggle vainly and grotesquely to escape their common destiny, but they are ultimately helpless against the fundamental lethargy of Italian

history. Bellocchio very cleverly keeps the audience off balance by
never allowing any moral situation to linger on the screen long
enough for facile audience identification. The fact that the impov-
erished Carlo is passed over for the Socialist nomination so that the
wealthy Vittorio can attract bourgeois votes is soon forgotten
when Carlo takes Vittorio's sister as his mistress. Discarded by
Carlo, Giovanna retaliates by allowing Vittorio to take her at long
last from his typewriter to his bed.

The plot takes an ugly turn when Elena becomes pregnant and
decides to escape her trap by obtaining an abortion. Carlo sets all
the machinery of family, church, and state into motion against her,
and the only truly admirable character in the film is broken by all
the bigotry arrayed against her. And yet she too is part of the system that entraps her. She is not as cowardly as her two brothers,
nor as calculating as the two proles who inveigle their way into her
household, but in the moment of truth she is not quite courageous
enough to sacrifice her reputation for her principles. The film ends
with Elena and Giovanna practicing their maternal exercises together in the splendor of a room seen for the first time in its awe-
somely ornate verticality. Elena will marry Carlo. Giovanna will
marry Vittorio. Unbeknownst to Vittorio, both women have been
impregnated by Carlo. It doesn't matter. The accommodations
have been made. Life must go on. China must wait a bit longer,
like any hope too long deferred.

On my first viewing of the film I somehow missed the posters
advertising Sean Connery in a James Bond film and Michael Caine
in *Alfie*. Also the reference to Bernardo Bertolucci's *Before the
Revolution* at a performance of Verdi's *Macbeth* through a lens
dimly. On a second viewing everything in the film fell into place
too neatly and concisely for comfort. Bellocchio's economy of expression is more impressive on first viewing than second, and yet it
takes two viewings to appreciate the initial brush strokes of characterization. Truffaut maintains in his introduction to his Hitchcock
interview that clarity is the supreme virtue of a director. Bellocchio's opening is anything but clear. Not only does he confuse the
audience with unexplained shifts of locale for the unheralded entrances and exits of unidentified characters on unmotivated mis-
sions, he also makes jokes about the characters before they have
been properly introduced to us, and hence throws away his punch
lines. For example, Glauco Mauri as Vittorio makes the most spec-

tacularly farcical entrance of a character since Alberto Sordi, bedecked in Arab garb, sang on a swing in Fellini's *The White Sheik*. Our first glimpse of Mauri's Vittorio is a medium (i.e., waist-high) shot of a man in the throes of masturbation or constipation begging God's forgiveness. Bellocchio then cuts discreetly but still devastatingly to a long shot of Vittorio virtually lurching out of the water closet to confront the guilt of a new day.

It all happens so fast that even the most discerning spectator lacks the buildup to give this gag the laugh its sheer audacity deserves. Indeed, there is barely time for a quiet chuckle; but it all turns out for the best, because Glauco Mauri's performance is one of the most beautiful characterizations in the history of the cinema. Mauri is the main reason I missed decorative trivia like the Connery-Caine posters. I couldn't take my eyes off his face, the face of a gloriously helpless bungler and bumbler, a frustrated lover and humanitarian, an inept traitor to his class who cannot persuade even his maiden aunts to vote for him, a born dupe and cuckold, in short a poor little fat rich boy who never outgrew his childhood dreams of romance and adventure and who, in a useless sort of way, is infinitely more precious than all the realists who make sport of his illusions.

The most beautiful moments in the film are derived at least in part from the richness of Mauri's characterization. The much admired off-key children's serenade to an ailing priest forms both background and counterpoint to Mauri's earnest plea for forgiveness from his unyieldingly fanatical younger brother. Later when the two brothers are confronted with the imminence of their sister's abortion rather than world revolution, a crisis more practical than theoretical, they are embarrassed to encounter each other in a movie theater, that modern refuge from reality. The older brother flees in panic, the younger averts his eyes with a shame-driven snap of his neck. Still later, Vittorio's sister drags him from bed for an impromptu night inventory of the library. Vittorio bounces a ball; Elena takes it away from him. He calls out the titles of first editions, then pauses over a bound comic book containing his childhood memories. He smilingly yawns, and Elena follows with a yawn of resignation to her own private five o'clock in the morning of the soul. Elda Tattoli as Elena (and co-scenarist with Bellocchio) gives a quite lovely performance, as do the other principals and supernumeraries, but Glauco Mauri is something special in making you smile when you really want to cry.

Bellocchio's direction may be too controlled for some tastes; his vision of the world too naïvely neurotic for others. I found myself liking and admiring *China Is Near* almost in spite of myself. There has always been a grotesque credibility gap between ethics and politics, between personal opportunism and social idealism, between the muddy trenches of man's sexuality and the marble pillars of his intellect. Perhaps never more so than in this very fateful moment in world history. The fact remains that a politician's truth can become an artist's truism. Fortunately, Bellocchio avoids the trap of schematization by implicating all his characters in his fluid frames even in those most dreadful moments when an honest civil servant is forced into corruption and a priest rolls his eyes skyward as he breaks in on an abortion. *China Is Near* is perhaps a prophetic film in its total despair.

UP TIGHT

STANLEY KAUFFMANN

Jules Dassin's *Up Tight*, financed by Paramount, is the first big-money film (as against several underground films) to tell uncompromised truth about black feelings in this country today. Not all the truth (what is all?); but, as far as I know, every aspect of black thought that this film treats is treated candidly. It's quite an experience to hear the political sentiments in *Up Tight* coming from a film that begins with that same old Paramount insignia, the lofty peak circled by calm stars.

The picture takes place in Cleveland and begins on the day of Dr. King's funeral in April, 1968. The camera pushes into the black community of the city—very few whites in the film—probing the varied reactions. (There is no mention that Cleveland has a black mayor, but for those who remember this fact, the implication is that, for militants, Mayor Stokes is irrelevant.) The militants feel that nonviolence has brought about its own demise in violence, and they are preparing an armed outburst. A veteran black "gradualist" tries to reason with them. A white radical who has marched in Alabama and been jailed in Mississippi is expelled simply because he is white. (Later on, we get a glimpse of the come-to-Jesus religious escape hatch as the script tries to touch every element of black feeling.) The film moves unequivocally toward a finale of revolutionary resolve, with the inevitability of race war as its conclusion. Radical social revision would obviate that conclusion, but the militants don't expect that from whites. *Up Tight* tells it as the militants feel it must go. There is no Stanley Kramer on hand—or, for that matter, no Bill Cosby or Sidney Poitier—to make it all come out merely ironic or possibly rosy. The heated irons are there.

But *Up Tight* is based on Liam O'Flaherty's novel *The Informer*, from which John Ford's famous 1935 film was made. I say "but" because I think that this is the new picture's undoing. Dassin and his collaborators on the script, Ruby Dee and Julian Mayfield, have felt bound to follow the O'Flaherty-Ford form; thus what starts as a dramatic conspectus of present tension shifts into a drama of one man that is intrinsically unrelated to those tensions. The three new writers have overlooked the fact that Ford's film was not about the rights and wrongs of the Irish Revolution or the conflicting ideological strands within it. It was concerned *entirely* with its protagonist, who, as far as his drama was concerned, could have been an Algerian under the French or a Palestinian Jew under the British. The O'Flaherty-Ford theme was the humanity of weakness and the futility of betrayal, not social-political issues. *Up Tight* begins with issues; then, in unfortunate obedience to the earlier structure, swerves right out of them, into another subject. Dassin's protagonist, Tank Williams, the renegade militant, does not have a race problem essentially: he has a drink-envy-weakness problem which could have landed him in an equivalent mess if he had been a white defense-plant worker with Soviet agents nibbling at him. Near the end, the hunted Tank says he wishes that someone in the world could tell him why he committed his treachery. This plea is made the crux of the film, but Tank's internal anguish is a long way from the wide-scale social drama with which the story began. The idea of a remake of *The Informer* is presumably what launched this project and made it possible—much more clever and exploitable than a new script on the race situation. But a new script would not—necessarily—have forced the film into a shape that works against it, as the remake does.

What is even worse is that this protagonist and his drama are feeble. We are not only switched out of what is valid and vivid; what we are switched *into* is poor. In the second half of the film, the screenplay becomes mostly a weak Americanized echo of Dudley Nichols' *Informer* script, and the performance of Tank is tedious. Julian Mayfield, who plays the role, is a big sweating man with no real power of agony. Victor McLaglen was no sterling actor, but he had a forceful personality and Ford knew how to use it.

Some of the cast are good. Frank Silvera, the gradualist, gives fire and contempt to his dissolving position. Raymond St. Jacques, the militant leader, is utterly convincing, never a trite film bravo. Although Roscoe Lee Browne, as a police informer, is blatant, his role is blatantly written—a blind man could see that he is a stool pigeon; at least Browne plays it with bitter style. The least flavorful performance is by Ruby Dee, pallid as Tank's prostitute girl friend.

The use of Technicolor seems wrong. (Perhaps this was Paramount's fault, looking ahead to future TV sales.) *Up Tight* cries out for black and white, to avoid any possibility of the very trap the production falls into. As designer, Dassin has used Alexandre Trauner, the Frenchman whose career of more than thirty years includes *Children of Paradise* and the recent *A Flea in Her Ear*. (His Art-Nouveau sets were the best feature of that last disaster.) When Trauner designed such grim French works as *Quai des brumes* and *Le Jour se lève*, he worked out of and toward something he knew. Here he designs like a fascinated tourist. He over-designs; his colors are lush and intrusive, many of the places look like settings (the room where Tank is "tried," for instance), and the over-all visual effect is of a musical.

Dassin's direction is his best since *He Who Must Die*, but that's a tiny compliment, because most of his work since then has been abominable (*Phaedra, Topkapi,* 10:30 P.M. *Summer*). At least *Up Tight* has allowed him to achieve a bit of the spaciousness of his Kazantzakis film. Some of the better moments—like a scene where tenement dwellers crowd onto balconies and toss bottles to protect a fugitive from the police—are reminiscent of early Fritz Lang: still, they have some size. But Dassin's grip is weak. He grabs suddenly and frantically for subjective effects: a hand-held camera when Tank goes into the police station to squeal, and a whirling camera when the fugitive plunges to his death, a device that's repeated when Tank dies. Dassin reaches his nadir in a penny arcade where Tank encounters some white people in evening dress. The white-backlash dialogue is sophomoric, and Dassin shoots his actors with equal subtlety—in funhouse distorting mirrors. It's enough to make you doubt that any honest statements *have* been made in the film.

The honesties are there, however. *Up Tight* is, in sum, a poor piece of work, but at least it allays our initial suspicion that it's going to crimp its explosive underlying ideas. Which leads to the next question: Why does a big studio, a subsidiary of a huge industrial combine (Gulf & Western), finance a frankly revolutionary film?

For two interlocking reasons, I think. First, there isn't a militant statement in *Up Tight* that will be news to readers of *Look* and *Life* or to viewers of CBS and NBC and NET. In the past, to tamper with matters like the militants' pronouncements would have made the film look phony only to readers of books and of small-circulation magazines. No longer so. The mass media now reach wide, and they can reach fast. They have biases and limitations, but they do have some sense of the dramatic; and nothing is more dramatic in America today than black militancy. TV coverage in particular—the visible actions, the audible statements, the resolute faces—have made Hollywood equivocation on this subject virtually impossible. If a picture is going to deal at all with a black group that is willing to kill a traitor, that group cannot be shown as working toward, say, the busing of schoolchildren.

Moreover, revolutionary ideas of all kinds have become a new spectator sport for the increasingly affluent, increasingly educated, therefore increasingly guilt-ridden (and guilt-enjoying) middle class. I was in Vancouver recently, and the first thing I saw on the morning I arrived was a hippie on a street corner selling the local "underground" newspaper, doing a brisk trade with white-collar types on their way to work. Not in San Francisco or L.A.—in Vancouver, British Columbia. Whatever Dassin's motives for wanting to make *Up Tight*, Paramount's motives were, I would guess, the knowledge that the trials had been well blazed by mass media, an awareness of the new sophistication in ideological thrill-seeking, and a professional sense of the narrowing gap between the front line of social fact and the threshold of film-audience acceptance. Plus the money of the growing black audience. In any event, the fact that Paramount backed this picture is more interesting than the picture itself.

FOR LOVE OF IVY and
DARK OF THE SUN

PHILIP T. HARTUNG

I suppose when the shouting about integration in movies and the film industry, and about black power and black culture, and about the new breakthrough of Negroes in films (although Sidney Poitier is still the only important star)—when all this clamor finally dies down, the proof of the pudding will be in the movies themselves. No doubt we are still in a transition period, but the pudding right now is pretty thin. And a couple of new pictures, although perhaps pointing in the right direction, are sad examples of the rise of Negro roles.

The only thing that differentiates *For Love of Ivy* from the comedies of the Thirties and Forties is that Negroes play the lead roles. Its cliché-ridden story is about a well-heeled white Long Island family who are thrown into a dither when their Negro maid announces she is going to leave. Distraught Mr. Austin (Carrol O'Connor), realizing they're losing the jewel who runs their house so well, offers Ivy vacations—even to Africa. Scatterbrained Mrs. Austin (Nan Martin), who can't even make toast, asks Ivy, "What *do* you want?" And very attractive, thoughtful Ivy, who's worked for this family for seven years and hopes to go to secretarial school, replies, "I'm not sure. I just know I haven't got it now." The Austins' giddy daughter (Lauri Peters) and hippie son (Beau Bridges) decide that what Ivy needs is some romancing; and for the job they tap a successful Negro businessman who operates a trucking company. When he's reluctant, the hippie practically blackmails the trucker into dating Ivy, because hippie knows trucker runs a gambling business in his trailer trucks at night.

From then on, *For Love of Ivy* belongs to Abbey Lincoln, who plays the maid role with endearing dignity, and to Sidney Poitier, who displays his usual boyish charm—first in mild anger for having to date Ivy, and then in ardent romanticizing when he falls in love with her. But the good performances of these two (and of Lloyd Bridges' son Beau, as the hippie) cannot disguise the old-fashioned vacuity of plot, the boy-meets-girl, boy-loses-girl, boy-gets-girl clichés, the silly bedroom scene designed to show how daring we are now, or the film's patronizing attitude toward the whites, who themselves are patronizing toward the blacks. Perhaps all this patronizing is meant to make up for all those false characterizations of Negroes in the past. In any case, two wrongs don't make a right. It's hard to know whom to blame ·for all the mediocrity in *For Love of Ivy*. Robert Alan Aurthur wrote the screenplay from an original story by Sidney Poitier, and Daniel Mann gave the film its colorless direction. Surely these talents could have come up with something more interesting.

It isn't Jim Brown's fault that *Dark of the Sun* is such a bloody mess. This picture, about mercenaries in the Congo who are sent to rescue some refugees and diamonds, makes Brown do the Noble Negro act, the kind of role Poitier plays so well. As a patriotic sergeant under a rough and cynical captain (Rod Taylor) and a still rougher ex-Nazi officer (Peter Carsten), Brown is almost saintly in his behavior. *Dark of the Sun* has as much violence, killing and miscellaneous carnage as any picture of the year. It also has the usual clichés in the dialogue that go with this kind of modern swashbuckling movie. What it doesn't have, alas, is much feeling or explanation about the suffering and birth of a new country. High-minded Brown does say to money-minded Taylor, "To you this is a job; to me this is our Bunker Hill." But *Dark of the Sun* is really not concerned with a fight for independence or with racism. It is an exercise in slaughter and mayhem.

3

MEN AT WAR

THE CHARGE OF THE LIGHT BRIGADE

STANLEY KAUFFMANN

The light on Vanessa Redgrave's cheeks, John Gielgud as Lord Raglan clucking over the British Army like a father hen, the sunny-misty air above smooth English lawns, Trevor Howard as Lord Cardigan turning pink at offense, Jill Bennett as Mrs. Duberly saying, "Oh, glad!" when she and her husband are invited to dine on milord's yacht—these are only some of the things I expect never to forget about *The Charge of the Light Brigade.* It's an extraordinary film, easily the best spectacle since *Lawrence of Arabia* and more ambitious than Lean's picture, since it wants to dramatize not one man's life but a civilization.

Cecil Woodham-Smith's celebrated book *The Reason Why* is given as the source of additional material, but it seems to me the source of virtually all the facts. Even some of the fictional material is adapted or arranged from facts that the book cites. The point of the film is to re-create mid-Victorian England in spirit and detail, to show how that spirit insisted on having a war, and how the most famous battle in that war, by its valor and stupidity, summed up the quality of the age. More than half the action takes place in England before the troops sail for the Crimea; Balaclava, says the film, is what England was heading for, the tea parties and balls as well as the drills and parades.

The picture's absolute triumph is the level of the acting. Gielgud is supreme: his Raglan goes far deeper than the caricature it might have been to become a genteel, gently shrewd, and finally failed man. Miss Redgrave, as a young officer's bride, continues to be magical; she can make us forget that she is acting *at the same time* that we admire her power to make us forget it. Trevor Howard's Cardigan is his best performance since *Sons and Lovers*, a perfect portrayal of a man with the power to exaggerate social conventions into dangerous lunacy. David Hemmings, despite his small size and unexceptional features, has fire and dash as Nolan, the officer who loves his friend's wife. Mark Burns has the right Victorian sweetness as his brother officer. Miss Bennett, as a gamesome officer's wife who follows her husband to war, spices the screen with elegant, nutty sexiness. In all the large cast there is not one false note, but I want particularly to mention Roy Pattison, a veteran sergeant-major who is wrecked by believing what the army taught him.

Onward the compliments must roll. The script by Charles Wood, in its scene-by-scene construction and its dialogue, is intelligent and literate. The sound track, handled by Simon Kaye, is so crisp we can almost taste it. The costumes by John Mollo and David Walker jump from the engraved page into daily use. The color camera of David Watkins is used superbly, particularly to capture the soft shine of Victorian photography (as on Miss Redgrave's face). And much praise must go to Tony Richardson, who directed.

I've taken a great many cracks at Richardson since he entered films and I have some more to take here, but a lot of his work in *Light Brigade* is fine. Apparently he has been to school to Lean and *Lawrence*, but that was a good school for this film, and Richardson has profited. He has learned especially how Lean plays off huge spectacle against huge intimacy to create a world. I don't mean the easy juxtaposition of vast panorama and tight close-up; I mean the delicacies and size of individuality poised against the immensity of history.

Richardson has succeeded better with the intimate than the panoramic. For instance, there is a lovely scene in the doorway of a country house where Miss Redgrave stops her lover, Hemmings, who is about to join her husband in the garden, to tell him that she is pregnant. We follow the pair as they step behind the open door, then they move to the front of the door and we see them through the gauze curtain, then we come around to join them, and we remain with her as he finally goes out into the garden. That little sequence of actor and camera movements, not quite parallel, curved in soft arcs, is a mute comment on the poignant helplessness of the pair. When Hemmings lay dead on the battlefield, I remembered his face through the curtained cottage door.

The direction of the Crimea sequences (actually shot in Turkey) is less secure. Richardson here seems more to know what he wants than to be able to get it. But some of this is because large-scale battle scenes are doomed to remoteness. Whether it's Borodino in *War and Peace* or Balaclava here, they always seem to reduce to the same shots in differing uniforms: the *Alexander Nevsky* shot, in which the camera rolls along looking down a line of advancing riders; the cannon exploding in our faces; the quick glimpses of men with lances through their guts; the riderless horses; the ground-level shots of the dead. The big film battle has become a ritual rather than an experience, often confusing and usually too long. (Having gone to all that expense, they're not going to use only a couple of minutes' footage out of it.) About all that ever really works is the long, wide horizon shot, which conveys only size, not heat. Richardson adds to the difficulty of making the battle *our* battle by including some shots from the Russian viewpoint. They only reminded me that Ensign Tolstoy was involved in this war, and so confused my sympathies.

And this brings me to other shortcomings. Richardson's social-significance touch has not become exactly light. His contrasts of London poverty and aristocratic *luxe* are plunked down more heavily than they were in *Tom Jones;* the difference between soldiers' squalor and officers' privilege is troweled on. He has also hit on the really abominable idea of using animated-cartoon sequences to convey facts and cover transitions. These cartoons blot the visual texture of the film; they distract us and jolt us back to a movie theater; and, worst of all, their blatant satire weakens the self-satire that the film otherwise achieves through realistic fidelity. Who needs cartoons about Victorian stuffiness when we have seen a scandal in an officers' mess because a captain allows wine to be put on the table without decanting? Further, the cartoons oversimplify the causes of the war. British jingoism and wealth and bumptiousness were largely responsible, but another important reason was liberal revulsion at Russia. It was vividly remembered in England that the Czar had helped to suppress the revolts of 1848 and had helped Austria to suppress Kossuth's revolt in Hungary in 1849. This liberal motive in the Crimean War is left out of the cartoons —out of the entire film.

And, finally, *Light Brigade* falters in the intent mentioned earlier—to show that Victorian society itself produced the tragedy at Balaclava. This idea just doesn't fit the facts. The costly blunder was not the result of class privilege or purchased commissions or inhuman treatment of troops. (Indeed, we see the survivors of the charge asking to "go again.") It was due, first, to a failure by the goodhearted and thoughtful Raglan to make himself clear and, second, to an ambiguous statement in the heat of battle by Captain Nolan—the most progressive and humane officer of the lot! The Crimean War, after Britain muddled through, did eventually bring about various reforms, but the fiasco of Balaclava was not directly caused by the ills that were later reformed. So, thematically, the picture is inconclusive and leaves us feeling slightly itchy, unsatisfied.

But if it's less than the sum of its parts, many of those parts are splendid. It's not to be missed and, I think, not to be forgotten.

The Bofors Gun is almost a postscript to *Light Brigade*. It's about the British Army exactly a hundred years later—1954, in occupied Germany. We spend a night with a squad doing guard duty over an obsolete antiaircraft gun in peacetime. It shows us the continuing inanities of army life and discipline, but, even without *Light Brigade*, that's an old idea for plays and films, to which the author, John McGrath, has nothing to add. He "tells it like it is," suffering from the common delusion of such tellers that "it" has not been told before. The focus is a confrontation between a sensitive, weak-willed noncom (David Warner) and a malicious, imaginative soldier (Nicol Williamson), but McGrath is as clumsy with the moral issues as he is banal with barracks naturalism. Williamson blazes, as those who saw *Inadmissible Evidence* would expect. Those who saw *Morgan!* may not be surprised that Warner is personally unappealing and a trite actor.

JOHN SIMON

As superproductions go, *The Charge of the Light Brigade* is preferable to things like *Romeo and Juliet*. Tony Richardson resembles Zeffirelli in more ways than I care to mention, except that he is more derivative. Nevertheless, he has conjured up here, with help from others, some remarkably faithful period atmosphere, so that even what has drawn most criticism, the cartoon sequences and the emphasis on glaring social contrasts, is truly Victorian, and worthy of corresponding passages in Dickens. For once, Richardson succeeds in eliciting fine performances that resist the pull toward caricature; John Gielgud as Raglan and Trevor Howard as Cardigan are particularly persuasive. David Watkin's color photography knows exactly how to coddle or jolt the eye, and the marvelous background music of John Addison often surpasses the foreground.

All the same, despite excellent bits, *The Charge of the Light Brigade* is not a satisfying film. For one thing, the story—or whatever one should call the haphazard incidents serving as pedestal to the Crimean episodes—is insignificant and uncompelling. For another, Charles Wood's dialogue verges on the unfortunate hyperboles of military stupidity he piled up in *How I Won the War*; here, moreover, the surreally imbecile dialogue uncomfortably clashes with the visual *verismo*. Most importantly, the final section of the film is impossible to follow; in fact, considering the lucid book on which it is largely based, it is almost as inexcusably muddled as the British commanders at Balaclava. Richardson was trying to say something about unduly heroic liberals being no less at fault than the finky old fogeys, but the intention gets lost in the battle scenes, whose turmoil is partly splendid and partly a mistake.

Two further complaints. It is regrettable to have both leading ladies in such a dashing film seemingly vie with each other for this year's Homeliness Award, just as it is misguided to entrust the gallantly swashbuckling lead to David Hemmings, who, besides being a mediocre actor, looks in long shots like something out of *Planet of the Apes*. A more serious grievance concerns the exhibiting of the film: I doubt that so vacillating a product should be turned into a road show; but for such prices the public is at least entitled to a larger screen than that of the Fine Arts Theatre, and a projectionist who will not add his own vacillations to those of the film.

LES CARABINIERS

PENELOPE GILLIATT

War is stupid, says everyone, fighting and buying armament stocks the while. No, says Jean-Luc Godard's blandly insult-
ing *Les Carabiniers*, it is soldiers who are stupid. War itself is very
clever. It gets the ill-placed to do the top brass's dirty work, it sanc-
tions acts of arson and genocide that lone criminals might jib at,
and it sells the recruitable on the idea that their lives are duller in
peacetime. Without great idiocy among the men who fight, says
the film—which has only just got a New York run, though Godard
made it in 1963—war could scarcely work so brilliantly. This startling, craggy picture is haggard with intellect, but the brains and
concern are disclaimed. *Les Carabiniers* wears an off-focus callousness that is peculiar to Godard. He proposes rock-faced paradoxes
upon which familiar sympathy can obtain no purchase. They are
illustrated with all the inhumanity he can muster, and he dares you
to presume pity in him at the peril of your own cool. But some
freezing alertness to people's suffering in the vise of modern arbi-
trariness seems to be there all the same, and his drive to deny that
he feels affection is part of the same racking contemporary trap.

The brothers who are the chief characters are Ulysses (Albert
Juross), a thin, resourceless man with a deceptive look of mastery,
and Michelangelo (Marino Mase), a cream-faced loon whose tiny
eyes are habitually screwed up in a hopeless mime of shrewdness.
Michelangelo's temperament finds silver linings all over the place.
When the king of the film's imaginary country tells him to fight,
he interprets the order as a chance to see the world. Nice of His
Majesty to write, he thinks. He swallows codswallop by the carload
and looks on the bright side with a fixity beyond Candide's. Neither he nor Ulysses has apparent forebears, or anything but the
most barren personal context. Godard always tends to abstract
characters a little from naturalism and to show them in outline
against lives that are like bare walls—much as Raoul Coutard, his
great cameraman, chooses to represent them physically.

The brothers have their civilian being in a shack and use an old cart as a couch for reading paperbacks. Their women are rock-bottom models of womanishness whose salient quality is a gift for staying numbingly cheerful through anything. While the girls hack public crisis down to the size of a mishap to the hair-dryer, the brothers feel manlier passions, and lust after a Maserati car. Soldiering presents itself to them as nothing but license. "Can I kill the innocent?" Michelangelo asks a policeman. "Yes." "Can I leave a restaurant without paying?" "Yes, yes"—impatiently. "It's *war.*" What a spree, the enlisted feel. There is carrousel music suddenly on the sound track. "Bring back a horse and a lot of ribbons," says one of the girls, blithely putting something lyric into rapacity. The women—called Cleopatra and Venus—are entranced by the idea of their men in khaki. They encourage them in their new careers with a long appreciation of the wonderful things that can accrue from battle. This sequence balances one at the very end of the film, when the soldiers are back from the fatuous massacre with a suitcase proudly stuffed with picture postcards. The postcards are thrown onto the screen in a mishmash symbolic of the fruits of war as the brothers' dimmed minds see them. The montage of photographs—ancient architecture, cars, famous beauties, cheesecake, a Persian cat in a soppy pose, a Modigliani nude—turns into a ghastly thank-you to systematized slaughter for the looting it allows, the sightseeing, the ecstatic dreaming forced on lonely, frightened men in pain. The jumble of empty mementos stands for all that the brothers can retain of anything that happens to them. Nothing is assimilated. Pictures of things are accepted in place of their meanings, and civilization is melted down into a souvenir. The girls look on indifferently. "I don't want the Parthenon," says Cleopatra. "It's ruined."

Cleopatra, Venus, Michelangelo, Ulysses. *Les Carabiniers* is about insensate people carrying legendary inscriptions of which they know no more than the postcard knows of the Parthenon. It is about minds that see history as garbage; about the way the world looks when insight and the sense of consequence have been lobotomized; about being a tool. Brecht often wrote of the same things. He was obsessed and saddened by our readiness to buy life as it comes and to believe the labels. The bemused clods in *Les Carabiniers* have been sold a fake, handed out the existence of curs, but they trust the tag and obediently act out the parts of fortunate men, just as the characters in *Mother Courage* truly suppose themselves to be doing well out of the war that exploits them. The intellectual substance of the picture is compressed into the device of attaching noble official pronouncements to scenes of harrowing military muddle that they don't match at all. Soothing slogans are intoned over images of wretchedness like benedictions uttered over a Catholic peasant woman at the end of her tether. Godard is really making a humane point of linguistics. Hang on like grim death, he says, to the difference between words and meanings. Language denies the visible truth all the time in this picture. There is a shout of *"La guerre est finie!"* but the explosions continue as usual. While a voice sonorously announces triumph, civilians in a town square scatter under a low bombing raid. The womenfolk at home trot out to the mailbox for lunatically stoic letters saying that the bloodshed proceeds magnificently and that their men kiss them. On the third Christmas Day of the war, beside a stingy tree in a corner of their shack, Cleopatra and Venus experiment happily with festive ways of doing their hair.

The film is full of the vilely familiar iconography of the news photographer—shots of women waiting, of scared people running for cover with children in their arms, of shopkeepers in doors looking up at a sky full of planes. It is a system of imagery that we recognize as fully as our forerunners recognized the emblems of the saints. By pushing the terrible very slightly toward the imbecilic, Godard makes it a little worse; in one of the rare close-ups in the film, for instance, Michelangelo stares at the camera wearing a gas mask. It is a mindless, ugly sight—some napalm-age cartoon of a knight with his visor down. "We captured Santa Cruz," the buffoon announces proudly in a hand-written title. "I went to the movies." He sits in the cinema, grinning, and then holds his arms over his eyes to protect himself from a head-on shot of a train in the film he is watching, although he has never twitched a muscle about butchering people in real life or even shown fear for himself. Then there is a bath scene from an old silent movie. Michelangelo goes up to the screen and tries to stroke the girl in her bath, yearning for the photograph of her as he never aches for the flesh of his wife. It is as if everything in life as he knows it were now ersatz, just as all history has become incoherent and all old endeavor been canceled.

But now and then, characteristically, Godard's black world will light up with an epiphanic flash of something better, so that the ground once won by the species seems not altogether lost. A Leninist girl condemned to be shot in a wood puts off the firing squad by reciting a poem of Mayakovsky's. The men usually love their work, but the ideas stored in her head make them stall. It is impossible to shoot her. She is so inconveniently in the middle of something—a recitation, or her life. The white handkerchief that they have hung over her face doesn't really help. It suddenly looks like a sculptor's cloth hung over a clay head to keep it damp for work next day. "*Frères!*" says the voice beneath the handkerchief, several times, wrecking resolve even further. To make murder routine again, the squad has to count "One, two, three" and fire in unison.

Les Carabiniers is a chilling fable about habit. It is also about the dizzying impulse to push the atrocious always a little farther. There are lines dealing with the same instinct in Godard's films about private life—moments when lovers wantonly say, "I do not love you," to test how much pain they can cause; and in *Pierrot le fou*, when Pierrot says to a badly off garage boy, "You'd like a car like that? Well, you'll never have one." The men in *Les Carabiniers* are inevitably less interesting than these characters, because their responses seem devised and not their own. They are the victims, never the agents, of the obscuring of their consciousness. The film is more of a thesis film than any other that Godard has made; it is deliberately even less particularized than usual, and sometimes even more contrary. I realize that the maddeningness is a device, but occasionally it can be—well, maddening. Perhaps it is a trick he uses to shield himself. (His ex-wife, Anna Karina, once touchingly said that his reason for wearing dark glasses all the time is not that his eyes are weak but that his universe is too strong.) The shrug that one catches in his work, the self-protective guise of cool, can sometimes look very like an updating of the hallowed and facile old French game of playing the unsurprisable cynic, but it can also strike you, when his films are most expressive, as the self-defense of a uniquely troubled, rancorous, and tender intellect. Godard regularly uses affront as a style for statement, maybe to stop our gum-chewing or maybe to give himself something to hide behind. In *Les Carabiniers* his weapon is stupidity—woodenheadedness in the soldiers, and even a surface of simple-mindedness to the thesis of the picture. But after you have thought about the film for a while you haven't much doubt that what drives it is not willful flippancy but distress. In his own way, Godard belongs historically to the line of great intellectual cartoonists—the witnesses who goad by deforming the familiar and by pretending callousness, the provokers who deliberately seek to be drastic because they see themselves as the reporters of last chances.

A FACE OF WAR

RICHARD SCHICKEL

Even the title is unassuming—A *Face of War*, not *The*, modestly implying that the experience of war has as many interpretations as it has participants and observers. Its technique is in keeping with this spirit, low-keyed and straightforward. Producer-director Eugene S. Jones and a crew of three simply moved in with the point squad of the lead platoon of Mike Company, Third Battalion, Seventh Marine Regiment, for ninety-seven days in the summer of 1966 to record on film and sound tape the quality of their lives in Vietnam. This is presented, without narration or musical score, in a seventy-seven-minute film of almost unbearable poignancy, one which must rank with *The Anderson Platoon*—and perhaps ahead of it—as one of the great documents of our Asian agony.

The stuff of this film is the ordinary stuff of war—a patrol through a rice paddy, a search for a sniper in a hamlet, the destruction by land mines of a couple of troop carriers. A great deal of footage is devoted to the activities of the men when they are not actually in combat—an impromptu rodeo as they try to ride a peasant's panicky bullock, a football game in ankle-deep mud, the treatment of villagers' minor illnesses and accidents by medical-corpsmen.

The peculiarity of the war is, of course, the shocking juxtaposition of its demands with the works of peace. Both the little rodeo and the sick call are interrupted by the explosion of mines and the necessity of attending to the ghastly consequences ("It hurts," a

wounded Marine says in shock, "it hurts"). The hunt for the
sniper ends not only with his death but with the death of a little
girl accidentally caught in the crossfire. Her last moments are spent
in a circle of Marines, and the anguish of their expressions, the
sheer damned helplessness etched in the faces, is almost as terrible
to behold as the child's senseless death. One cannot help but reflect in this moment that an age that has produced the philosophy
of the absurd has also produced, without really meaning to, a kind
of warfare to match, and that all of us—the child, her mother, the
Marines, even those of us who are merely distant witnesses—are
equally helpless victims.

The point is driven home in another, longer sequence. A village
that has harbored Vietcong is burned, its people weep, and up
lumbers an armored vehicle of some kind. Its great metal jaws,
cruelly pronged, open wide and the people are herded in. The jaws
grind shut, swallowing the entire population of a place, and off it
clanks, uncomprehending. Technology has granted these people a
kind of peace, but at the price of destroying the community they
shared, the fabric of the only life they have known. It is as if this
machine, only part of a much larger machine, runs mindlessly by
itself. That, of course, is the meaning of this war and one of the
reasons it so fills us with dread and impotent rage.

But it is in a less frequently observed side of the conflict that *A
Face of War* earns its greatest distinction. We have heard a great
deal about how this war is corrupting us, destroying our tradition
and our morality. That may be so, especially in our political command posts, but the rot has not yet reached the men of M Company. Surrounded by, dependent on, ruled by the engines of destruction, they remain triumphantly human, roughly tender with
one another and with the civilians they encounter.

One sequence is particularly telling in this respect. A peasant
woman, attended by a midwife and a Marine medic, is giving birth,
and a small group from the company stands around, unable to resist the ironic wonder of life beginning in the midst of death.
Gently, awkwardly, with beautiful shyness, they welcome the child
to a world that they, no more than anyone else, wanted to make.
"Hey, tiger," they whisper as they reach out with tentative hands
to touch the baby boy, exercising for the first time his right to
protest. "Hey, little tiger."

One may be ashamed by the thing they have been asked to do,

but one is not ashamed of them. Quite the opposite. That irreducible measure of goodness that is present in our national character, and which is too often ignored, is artlessly, uninsistently revealed by the brave men who appeared in—and made—this film. In this time when we search anew, as each generation must, for the meaning of who we are and what we are, the men of Mike Company remind us of our capacity for grace, even in torment, that we are in danger of forgetting.

TELL ME LIES, THE ANDERSON PLATOON, and INSIDE NORTH VIETNAM

STANLEY KAUFFMANN

Peter Brook's film against the Vietnam War is the wrong film at the right time. The filth of outrageous government falsehood, of responsibility for pointless death and destruction, is piling up in America in a way that makes this country seem a very great deal worse than New York during the garbagemen's strike. If we are to have a big Eastmancolor picture on this subject now, it ought, in heaven's sweet name, to be one that heightens and thrusts forward all possible American opposition to the war. Which means, for the most pragmatic reasons, not for dainty aesthetic ones, that it ought to be a good film. *Tell Me Lies* is not.

A couple of years ago Brook produced an antiwar theatrical work called *US* with the Royal Shakespeare Company of London, parts of which were included in a short film called *The Benefit of the Doubt*, directed by Peter Whitehead, that was shown at the last New York Film Festival. Now Brook has used *US* as the starting point for a long cinema fantasia on the same theme and has used most of the same actors. (Note, to our additional shame, that both of these films were made in Britain. The only major American picture I know of on this subject is John Wayne's *Green Berets*, whose aim is presumably somewhat different.) *Tell Me Lies* begins with Mark, a young Londoner, becoming upset by the magazine photo of a bandage-swathed Vietnamese baby. He sets out on a kind of pilgrimage around London, asking questions, attending rallies, having conversations with known and unknown figures. There are also reenactments of some actual events, like the self-immolation of Norman Morrison, the American Quaker, before the Pentagon. There is a portion of the (New York) Open Theatre's ribald playlet on how to beat the draft. There are songs and sketches. There is a general air of tension.

But it is an air of theatrical tension, of self-dramatization. After Mark and his girl leave a cinema where they have seen a Buddhist monk burning himself in Saigon, she asks him, "What is there that we would be prepared to burn ourselves to death for?" The question seems to me typical of what is wrong with this film—thin dramatics over a void of thought. The answer to her question, I should think, is: "Nothing, I hope. And I really don't feel remiss about it, either. But I also hope there are some things I would want to stay alive as long as possible for—and to fight about. There are far too many burners in the world already. Why do their work *for* them?"

The attitudinizing songs, the soul-baring professions, the "daring" sketches, are all in a mélange of Brecht-Artaud modes that is supposed to assault our minds and our nerve ends, but it only distracts us to the *surface*, to the actors themselves being personal and rather designedly uninhibited; so we lose sight of Vietnam in a welter of uninteresting candor, as well as of theatrical theory. I am not much interested in sophomoric political discussions in Chelsea basements simply because familiar juvenilities are couched this time in British locutions. I am not the least bit interested in the actress, Glenda Jackson, being vibrant at me with banal discoveries she has made in the recesses of her soul. (I would be *very* interested in seeing this fine actress—who was Charlotte Corday in *Marat/Sade*—in a good script that dramatized the putrescence of this war.)

Earlier, at an outdoor rally, Miss Jackson reads a ringing statement, and when Mark asks her who wrote it, she says quietly, "Che Guevara," and passes on. We are meant to reel, some way or other, without any questions at all, silenced by that charismatic name. This is totemism, not politics.

And this leads to a terrible irony. I think that Brook's film works just against the crusading effect he meant it to have—precisely because of his cavalier treatment, or dismissal, of politics. This was crystallized for me in one incident. At a party Mark converses with Kingsley Amis and Peregrine Worsthorne, two of Britain's staunchest supporters of Johnson's Vietnam policy, who are clever polemicists. Their arguments about stopping Communism and drawing the line in Vietnam were for me the points that were made most strongly in the whole film! I emphasize as loudly as I can: they are points with which I disagree. But the rest of the film is so woozy or quivering-souled or East Village Other bawdy about matters I agree with, that the Amis-Worsthorne views stand out as a (deceptive) moment of clarity. I would have given all the songs, all the blue jokes, all the squiggles of soul-searching, for one minute of cogent reply to their views. The Amis-Worsthornes need to be answered, especially to convince the unconvinced; and pictures of charred babies will not move their supporters. No one displayed pictures of the charred babies of Hamburg in 1943 or of grievously wounded Egyptians in June 1967—at least not as arguments against the Allies or Israel. Why? Because the horrors of war were taken as necessary for political ends. Well, that is exactly what the Amis-Worsthornes of the world are saying now, and all the pictures of blasted villages and burning Buddhists are only clucked over as part of the price for necessary ends.

Two other recent films about Vietnam also fell far short of the point for which they were presumably made. The Anderson Platoon, by the Frenchman Pierre Schoendoerffer, was a documentary about some U.S. soldiers, their courage and their hardships. Some of the footage was fine, but it said nothing about this war; with a change of helmets and rifles, it could have been made on Guadalcanal. Felix Green's Inside North Vietnam showed us in color how lovely the Vietnamese countryside is and how graceful and winning the people are, even if the cheerful workers were possibly under the eye of an off-camera commissar. But all it accomplished that was really relevant was to refute the American contention that we have never bombed North Vietnamese civilian centers. And Greene completely avoided the political issue that is the reason for the war; his sound track never once mentioned the word "Communist."

It can be argued that any film that pushes the daily ghastliness of this war into people's faces is worthwhile. But many of those who support the war know about the ghastliness quite as well as the war's opponents. I cannot imagine that *Tell Me Lies* would change a war supporter's mind; and unless more and more minds are changed, the war will not quickly end.

In my view, what we need most are not productions like *Tell Me Lies* or *US* or *Viet Rock*, which are, finally, coterie works; and we certainly do not need works as blithe about hard political issues as *Far from Vietnam*, a French film that was also shown at the last New York Film Festival, some of which assumed that the problem of Communism bothers only squares. We need some first-class film documentaries on the political answers to the Amis-Worsthornes: documentaries that, among other things, tell the truth about the belated veneer of purpose applied to an initial misadventure; about the escalation of military mistakes and political falsehood; about the impossibility of achieving the very aims our government professes (because we have to either occupy Vietnam permanently or else submit *after* a treaty, rather than before, to its Communist domination); documentaries that show that the "line" has been drawn in the wrong place. Such documentaries would change those of the opposition who *could* change much sooner than pictures of charred babies. If enough people changed, then politicians—most of whom are essentially amoral—would respond; and it is only through the response of those with power in Congress and elsewhere that matters can improve. Take an example from the lower end of the integrity scale in politics—Richard Nixon. If a sufficient number of people expressed opposition to the Vietnam War tomorrow, it is a safe bet that Nixon would make his next campaign speech under a huge photograph of Dr. Spock.

THE GREEN BERETS

PENELOPE GILLIATT

Leaving aside the effect of close contact with John Wayne's *The Green Berets*, a film best handled from a distance and with a pair of tongs, I would never have guessed that any statement of the right-wing argument for the war in Vietnam could remind me so forcefully of the voice of the traditional English nanny. It took me back to the days of Britain's Suez adventure in 1956. Nanny's brain was there too. The old guard of nannies is dying out but not yet extinct—not by a long chalk. Members still patrol Kensington Gardens, swapping snobberies over expensive baby carriages. The concept of Nanny looms large in upper-middle-class life, and it is responsible for a lot. One day somebody should do a study of the ethical effect of Nanny on British foreign affairs for the last hundred and fifty years, for most British prime ministers and foreign secretaries of the past have emerged from nurseries where she ruled unchallenged. Mummy ranked nowhere.

The archetypal nanny figure is authoritarian, proselytizing, both Spartan and greedy, and conservative through to her bootheels. She is also often kindly, faithful, and impossible to budge, with the compound of benignity and insensibility that has distinguished much imperialist policy. She may be what is called a "paragon" (meaning that Mummy won't ever have to look for another one), or she may be a "gorgon" (meaning that Mummy can't face her, and the children will have to get on with it), but her morality doesn't vary much, and it has been in force since the early days of the British raj. Even now, in swinging London, considerable numbers of infant toffs are inculcated with Nanny's awful saws: "Good, better, best,/Never let it rest/Till the good is better/And the better best"; "Satan finds a mischief for idle hands to do"; "Don't give me no buts. Nanny knows best"; "Eat up your carrots, Lord Rupert. Little children less well off than yourself in Africa could live for a week on the lovely things you leave on your plate"; "Come along, Simon. Plenty of poor children in Asia would be *grateful* to go to Sunday school." When little Lord Rupert and little Simon grow up into the Tory Minister of State for Commonwealth Affairs and the Tory Prime Minister, no wonder they behave toward Africa and Asia like nannies in their turn.

The nanny-bred Tory's objection to Eden's Suez adventure was not that it was internationally immoral or the act of a flouted former power in a fit of pique, but that it wasn't militarily efficient. ("Lord Rupert, you're not trying.") Much the same attitude animates the fury of the American extreme right about the management of the war in Vietnam: if the President only put his mind to it, we could be finished in no time and then we could all go out and play instead of being punished on this lovely day. Nanny's sentiments underlie every scene of *The Green Berets*. "If we're born fortunate, we can't expect life to be all fun. Queen Victoria didn't *enjoy* ruling India. Do you think putting down the Indian Mutiny was nice for her? She did it for the Indians' own good." I don't know who was responsible for the upbringing of the people who created *The Green Berets*, but the film has the real touch of Nanny's fist. Vietnam is treated as if it were a little savage in dire need of moral upbringing and probably infected with lice. As the picture sees things, all the appalling butchery carried out by the Americans in it is for Vietnam's own good. The Vietnamese haven't had our advantages; they don't know what's best for them yet. The green-bereted soldiers speak to the Vietnamese in a dismaying version of baby talk, and the Vietnamese answer like Nanny's idea of rude-tongued village idiots, using naughty words like "stinking." ("My home is in Hanoi," says a Vietnamese who is on the Right Side. "I go home someday. First kill those stinking Cong. Then go home.") The Green Berets in John Wayne's charge are the nicely brought-up children, brought up to say "please." ("Sir, could I have a choice, just for the hell of it?" "Yes, you can have a choice," says Wayne. "I'll take a point," says the soldier, bravely choosing to kill off a few more stinkers, or villagers, and getting further into Nanny Wayne's good books.) Wayne knows that everything is for the sake of the Vietnamese in the end. A sickening child who stands for the Vietnam that needs "protection" says to him in the closing shot (which is a back view of the two of them against—I swear—a rosy sunset), "What will happen to me now?" "You let me worry about this, son," says Wayne. "You're what this is all about."

The Green Berets must be the first film to put the unadulterated right-wing case for the war. With a clumsiness that would be funnier if it were less terrifying, it includes a primitive lesson in dogma, set at the John F. Kennedy School for special instruction in guerrilla warfare and inane derring-do. A planted liberal journalist is allowed to put some tricky questions, which the soldiers begin to answer for themselves. One of them triumphantly explains away the delay in a settlement with Hanoi by equating it with the eleven years that it took the original American states "to come up with a paper that everyone would sign—the Constitution." Another, justifying everything, shows a crateful of Czech arms and says,

"What is involved here is Communist domination of the world." The liberal journalist retains his doubts for a minimal amount of time. The only sure way I had of knowing that he was supposed to be liberal was that he waggled his pencil. Later on, in combat, where he does no visible research of any kind, he is a quick convert to Wayne's opinions. One is supposed to believe that he has an intellect. It gets hard.

The film's serious moments are tough to bear, but its sense of humor is worse. Sudden death is often a practical joke, and a Vietcong face blown apart in mid-grin is a sight gag. I deliberately went to the film when there was an audience, and the response to it was enough to make your bones shake. On a weekday afternoon, the cinema was crammed. Many, many times, when a character of *any* nationality was startlingly blown up or thrown off a toppling structure or impaled by a booby trap, there were cheers and gales of laughter. Purely patriotic moments left the audience relatively cold. When John Wayne ran down the Vietcong flag after a long battle to "liberate" a village, there wasn't a sound. Not even a simple rah-rah chauvinism dignified the glee. Preserve us.

4

MEN AND WOMEN

PETULIA

RICHARD SCHICKEL

Let me put the matter very simply: *Petulia* is a terrific movie, at once a sad and a savage comment on the ways we waste our time, our money and ourselves in upper-middle-class America. It is a subject much trifled with in movies these days, but rarely—if ever—has it been tackled with the ferocious and ultimately purifying energy displayed in this highly moral, yet unmoralistic, film.

Its strength stems from two sources: the passionate intensity with which Richard Lester fastens his camera's eye on the inanimate artifacts of our consumer culture, and the complex, highly charged style—rather like a mosaic set in very rapid motion—with which he presents his vision of a world where the Thing is King. D. W. Griffith, the first master of the American movie, thought film was uniquely qualified among the arts to examine the psychological meaning of the objects from which we fashion the modern landscape—"the visible hieroglyphs of the dynamics of human relations," as a critic once put it. They are, I think, the true subject of *Petulia*. A fully mechanized motel, a parody of a *Playboy* bachelor's pad, an inhumanly efficient hospital (a sort of medical factory)—what these hieroglyphs tell us about our doomed hopes for ease and grace! From the place his characters choose to eat lunch, from the show flickering on an unwatched TV set, from the stuff they give their kids, we learn who his standardized people are in a way that almost makes dialogue superfluous. The basic technique is not untried—not in the age of Mike Nichols—but Lester never

107

presses his points, repeatedly passing up big gadget laughs to stick to his small truths.

As for the style, it is the now conventionalized and commercialized one based on the quick cut and the deliberate jumbling of time sequence, no longer worth discussing, let alone deploring, since it is *the* style of the Sixties. The point is that Lester uses it with superb natural ease. Too often in American films it is regarded as no more than an opportunity to show off. Here the technique, which emphasizes the fact that movies are themselves a mechanical art, works brilliantly; style and substance are organically related, working like a reciprocating engine to drive home Lester's point.

I do not wish to suggest that there is no story in *Petulia*. It is a perfectly adequate little thing—a romance between the girl of the title (Julie Christie) and a doctor (George C. Scott) whom she sort of wins at a raffle. She is on the verge of a mental breakdown, driven there by a faggoty husband (Richard Chamberlain, who is for the first time not nice and therefore memorable) and his rich, devouring family, who give the kids every*thing* except understanding. Scott is on the verge of a social breakout, sick to death of material preoccupations which seem to him a travesty of his profession's ideals. For the length of the movie they twist and turn, attempting to elude the destinies imposed on them by the distorted values of their time, place and class. But, for all their venturings, both comic and grisly, they remain pretty much as we find them, screwed-up prisoners of a screwed-up world.

This is a measure of the film's honesty, but there are others. Petulia and friend are nice enough to identify with, but they are not so delightful that you feel like indulging them to excess. Each has a hard core of selfishness and foolishness that cannot be washed out; since they too are creatures of their era, they contain within themselves the very qualities against which they are in rebellion. Their tragedy is that, unlike their fellow sufferers, they are aware of what's happening to them. They are not the blind bourgeoisie of *The Graduate*; they do not need an insufferably superior adolescent to show them what's wrong with them. They know, they know—and still they can't quite make it to decency and repose.

After the idle pleasantries of his Beatles movies, the disappointing heaviness of *A Funny Thing Happened on the Way to the Forum*, the desperate preachments of *How I Won the War*, Lester has at last controlled his enormous gift for movie-making with a brilliantly conceived, carefully aimed, splendidly detailed satire. He demands much of the audience, a stern ability to put down that inevitable wish for the happy-ending cop-out. In return, he gives a rich, terrible examination of the contemporary social and psychological malaise. It will be interesting to see if we are up to it, if this film will attract the audiences that movies working the sunnier side of this same street have gained.

WILFRID SHEED

The real Richard Lester has made a movie called *Petulia*, applying his flighty methods, for once, to a solemn subject: how we live today, if I'm not mistaken. A jet-set specimen (Julie Christie), shiftless and kooky (her word, not mine), tries to recharge her batteries with a doctor (George C. Scott), soiled and bourgeois. His marriage has been eroded by banality, hers by the pointlessness of wealth. Can they get together and form a third force—a class that cares, without being boring about it? Their story is told in flashes fore and aft, timeshifts which a novelist might use to backlight his subject, but which here serve less to illumine than to confuse. Telling a story backward and sideways does not *necessarily* add anything to it.

Beyond that, Lester tries to portray Our Society by stockpiling quick takes: social vignettes, style hints. Watch the rich at play, compare them with these fine sad people in the hospital; see the yachts, see the nightclubs; now see the poor Mexican boy under the surgeon's knife. The trouble is Lester's old one, a slickness and shallowness that is built right into his method. His hospital shots have the slick instant-pity effect of charity ads. His high life and his low life have an identical shine on them. His social observation sometimes looks and sounds fresh, but it rests on a bed of stereotypes—has to, at that pace. And he undermines his own scenes again and again with cutie-pie photography and smart-ass irony.

However, superficiality can have its charms. Lester forms some elegant patterns with his paperweights, almost like real. He knows how to make the most of his actors' exteriors: Richard Chamberlain and Joseph Cotten have never seemed more interesting, yet their parts as written do not amount to much. If Lester's brain ever catches up with his eyes, and if he quits tap dancing for a minute, he will be quite some director.

THE THOMAS CROWN AFFAIR

WILFRID SHEED

Just a quick word about movie violence, before you have time to turn down your hearing aid. The talk is that movie violence makes people immune to, therefore callous about, the real stuff (well, that's *some* of the talk—I wouldn't attempt to give you all of the talk), but I think for most of us cold-blooded mammals, m.v. only makes us immune to more m.v. I believe a real-life killing or beating would shock and sicken about as much as before, and possibly more, because we think we know about it and we don't. A real kick in the groin is quite a piece different from a pretty picture of one.

These thoughts occurred after watching the hysterical scenes that followed the Robert Kennedy murder, on color TV. The people in the Ambassador ballroom were, presumably, average citizens who sup their fill on war every night and supplement their blood-rich diets at the local flick. Yet, faced with an actual shooting, they went berserk, screaming and threshing in fear and outrage and forming a tableau of torment out of Goya.

This panic-in-a-stockyard aspect of violence is either faked or omitted in most movies. Most of the popular violence pictures approximate, as nearly as possible, ballet. We are not, on the whole, a body-contact people. That the hippies have made such a business of touching shows what a rarity it is on American soil; an Italian, tapped out from embracing relatives, friends, Fuller Brush men, wouldn't know what the hippies were talking about.

Thus, we celebrate the punch, crisp and distasteful, over wrestling, which tends to be warm and sweaty, and over Frenchman's bite; and above the punch we place the gun, where nobody touches anybody at all. Clean as a bullet, we say, approvingly. And above the gun the clean bomb, the long-range missile: the ultimate puritan weapons.

But violence isn't the only thing that's ethereal about our movies these days. The new thing in films, typified by Richard Lester or by such a recent sub-Lester film as *The Thomas Crown Affair*, is to etherealize, decarnalize everything in sight. Even the lovers only appear to make love—you wouldn't be surprised to learn that the principals were in different cities when those scenes were shot. Steve McQueen and Faye Dunaway have a love affair in *Crown* that can only be compared to a protracted Salem cigarette commercial. When they kiss, in a floating dance of the mouths, lip over lip over lip, it has no more connection with actual kissing than a mountain stream has with the taste of tobacco. But this dissociation of image from substance is the very stuff of the new thing in middle-class films.

Thomas Crown is itself a prize-winning commercial for the anti-hip, anti-touch American alternative. The hero is a millionaire sportsman who conducts glossy burglaries for kicks. These are beautiful affairs, as smooth as the Dodge Rebellion, as whimsical as a plea for Alka-Seltzer. There is no scene in McQueen's career that you would be ashamed to run in a quality ad. His days are an Abercrombie and Fitch catalogue of natty outdoor fantasies—sports planes, beach romps, the very best cashmere sweaters. At night, his sex life contains only the finest merchandise. That his inamorata works for a rival company (she is an insurance shamus) adds that spice of product competition that gets your campaign off the ground.

The movie's grim efficiency breaks down in a place or two. The smart chat is not up to snuff. McQueen's slow smile is down to a crawl. And I doubt if a man like this would blow his wad on an impossible golf bet. A man who enjoys gambling does not take even money on thirty-foot putts, even when Jack Nicklaus is conducting them.

Stefan Kanfer

"Fashion can be bought," said one-time *Vogue* editor Edna Woolman Chase. "Style one must possess." *The Thomas*

Crown Affair has spent millions on fashion; Faye Dunaway makes thirty-one smashing costume changes, while Steve McQueen appears in $350 suits and consults a $2,250 Patek Philippe watch. The screen that exhibits them is a flashy replay of Expo-67 techniques, fragmenting into scores of tiny separate images like a mint sheet of stamps, or simultaneously showing five characters in five different places. If style could be purchased, Norman Jewison, normally a versatile, canny director (*The Russians Are Coming, In the Heat of the Night*), would surely have included it. Unable to do so, he has turned out a glimmering, empty film reminiscent of an *haute-couture* model: stunning on the surface, concave and undernourished beneath.

Thomas Crown (Steve McQueen) is a Boston tycoon with a brilliant criminal mind. Uneasy lies the Crown that wears a head. To pique the Establishment that he is part of, he hires some crooks and stages a flawless $2,660,527.62 robbery that leaves the police without a clue. Enter Faye Dunaway, girl insurance investigator who has slept her way to the top of the business.

All pro, Faye swiftly identifies McQueen as Mr. Wrong, bird-dogs him around town, and eventually gains entrée to his mansion. There ensues a ludicrously erotic chess game, out of Mae West by Tom Jones, which Faye wins. After the check comes the mating, visualized in some lurid camera work that focuses so long on the stars' lips that they come to resemble two kissing gouramis in a tank.

Cop and robber soon fall in love; but McQueen trusts no one, and to put Faye to the test he bitterly stages another heist. She counters with an ambush that leads to a surprise ending slightly less suspenseful than the one in the Hansel and Gretel affair.

Impeded by a script that has lines like "It's my funeral; you're just along for the ride," McQueen stops acting and settles for a series of long poses. Dunaway, hired before *Bonnie and Clyde* was released, is used solely as a clotheshorse out for a long gambol. Giving his film a "now" look and his characters an ironic, detached air, director Jewison obviously hoped to play his movie cool. But there are several degrees between cool and frigid: a degree of wit, a degree of plot and a degree of that old unbuyable, style. Their absence stops the movie cold.

JOANNA

Hollis Alpert

Every now and then a movie comes along that gives one the feeling that things are going to change. They don't really, or at least very slowly and haltingly, for habits of mind and operation in so expensive a medium as that of feature film are relatively fixed, and the tendency is to do it the old way. But then *The Graduate* suddenly breaks through, or *Bonnie and Clyde*, and a few more people get the chance to do it their own way. This year it may well be *Joanna*, which Twentieth Century–Fox is releasing, that will signal another change of direction. In technique it is fresh; its spirit is contemporary; its attitudes are youthfully free of cant or moralizing.

The movie was made in London, and it tells a relatively simple story. It's all about a pretty, leggy teen-age girl called Joanna who comes to London to study art and who, let us say, is inclined to diversify her affections. It would be wrong to call her promiscuous, because the word has a moralistic ring. There's nothing bad or wrong about Joanna. She enjoys sleeping with whoever happens to strike her fancy at the right moment. Her view of reality is slightly askew, mainly because she's almost childishly caught up in a fantasy of who she is.

Michael Sarne, a twenty-eight-year-old former pop singer and composer, photographer, journalist, and book and film critic, wrote the story and directed it; Michael Laughlin, a twenty-eight-year-old American from Illinois, produced it; and, very importantly, Walter Lassally, the brilliant young cameraman of *Tom Jones*, photographed it. They all somehow provide the conviction that they knew exactly what they were doing and how to do it. It's as though they said to each other, "Let's make a story about a crazy, cheeky, beautiful girl, the kind who comes to London and wanders into someone's bed, who shows up at parties in Chelsea, who seems built by nature to wear mini-skirts, who doesn't understand a thing, and who yet is somehow lovable. And let's tell about the

people she runs into, and what happens to them and to her because of them."

That's about all that the movie does for its two-hour length, but
it does it so winningly, with such tender, tolerant understanding of
the girl, that it is a joy to watch. For a while, one is not even much
aware of the fact that a story is being told. We meet Joanna casually; catch glimpses of her here and there; suddenly are catapulted
into one of her girlish fantasies; see her yawning, running, talking
to someone at a party, learning about life from a serious young
artist, being rejected by a boy who is as diversified in his affections
as she is inclined to be, visiting a girl friend about to have an abortion. In Joanna's little world, black and white are equally beautiful.
Her best girl friend is a beautiful black girl, whose brother, handsome and arrogant, Joanna falls most in love with. The black girl
has a boy friend, Lord Peter Sanderson, a young man dying of leu-
kemia, who doesn't want his friends to know about it or to grieve
over him when he goes. What helps make the movie so pleasing
(rather than pleasant) is that it doesn't make a "thing" out of its
racial mixing.

The film is helped immeasurably by Genevieve Waite, who plays
Joanna as though playing herself. Maybe Miss Waite *is* Joanna, for
I can't separate her from the role, and I don't ever want to meet
her, because it might spoil the spell she has cast over me. Miss
Waite makes you understand why all those intelligent, talented
young people wanted to tell Joanna's story. And she is wonderfully
abetted by those who play the people who flow in and out of her
life, such as Donald Sutherland as Lord Peter. Because we are
made to see everyone through Joanna's hazy view, Lord Peter is a
modern-day saint, even though he is rich, idle, and hedonistic. He
just wants people to enjoy life while they have it, and he contributes what he can to that enjoyment. Then there is Calvin Lockhart, as the black nightclub owner with a streak of innate violence,
who has his pick of girls but likes best the complaisant Joanna; and
Christian Doermer, who won't let his birds interfere with his pursuit of art. In a fantasy ending, these and others (and here, I think,
Mr. Sarne was perhaps influenced by the ending of Fellini's 8½)
perform a show-business salute to the happy-sad-go-lucky spirit of
Joanna. A little too cheeky, maybe.

But providing the ambience, the beauty, the nostalgia, the
charm, is that limpid photography of Mr. Lassally. And for mood

there is Rod McKuen's score, which has a "sound" and some simple, evocative songs. *Joanna* doesn't say anything "important," but it's right out of today, or perhaps what young people think is today. In its way it is brave and bold, and I hope it does well.

JOSEPH MORGENSTERN

As a virtuoso display of vacuousness, *Joanna* beats the competition all hollow. Hollow people living hollow lives in hollow London. You know, putting *Blow-up* through some changes, except that you can't possibly know unless you can imagine the worst of Antonioni, Tony Richardson, Richard Lester, and Godard combined with meretricious compassion—*Marty* in mini-skirts and mini-souls—and then further compounded by the sort of self-satisfied lyricism that finds its finest flower at Forest Lawn or in Kahlil Gibran's poetry.

The heroine of the title is a young art student who sleeps around a lot because she's uncommitted. The film, written and directed by a twenty-eight-year-old named Michael Sarne, purports to know and care a lot about its heroine and other creepy-sleepies trying to find love and purpose in the desolation of modern society. "People are such—lovely things!" Joanna says ardently. Joanna is such a lovely thing, the sound track says with a single-note piano melody intended to signal the presence of a soft, simple human being. (Rod McKuen did the music and lyrics, most of them insipid.)

Well, Joanna *is* a lovely thing, every brief once in a while. Genevieve Waite, the newcomer who plays her, may have the makings of a first-rate comedienne. But all that caring about her by the writer-director is, like everything else in his movie, for effect only. It is a caring for the idea of people being nice rather than for any specific people themselves, and the ignorance underlying it leads to wild oscillations of style and attitude in which people are contemptible grotesques or saints in mufti.

Take the character of Lord Peter Sanderson, a wealthy patron of the arts who's dying of some kind of crud in his blood. Early on he's played quite wittily, by Donald Sutherland, as a parody of your typically stuffy, stuttering young aristocrat. Later you realize to your horror that it wasn't parody at all, it was a characterization intended to engender pity, compassion, admiration, even love. For Lord Peter turns out to be the poet of the film—the guy who gets to say lines like "It makes sense to die! Only then does it make sense to live!"

Conversely, the same film which has taken itself so seriously for most of its great length suddenly puts itself down when the whole cast trots on for a good old music-hall finale and sings, in measures strongly redolent of *Mame*, the praises of its heroine. "You fill my heart with hope/Your smile's like CinemaScope," go the lyrics. The ending is perfectly charming and in no way to be faulted. It's only what comes before that confuses and cloys.

RACHEL, RACHEL

ARTHUR KNIGHT

The role of Rachel Cameron in *Rachel, Rachel*, a tender and moving film based on Margaret Laurence's novel *A Jest of God*, is the sort that every young actress dreams about. Rachel is a small-town schoolteacher well aware that she is sacrificing her life to her demanding, domineering mother, aware that her best years are all but behind her, but terrified at the thought of breaking out and changing the even tenor of her ways. The film covers the crucial summer of what may well be Rachel's last fling—a reluctant sampling of some old-time religion at the instance of a fellow schoolmarm with barely suppressed lesbian tendencies, followed by an outburst of unrequited passion aroused by a neighboring farmer turned teacher.

Obviously, Rachel is a role that runs the gamut, and actress Joanne Woodward did more than just dream about it. She purchased the book while it was still in galleys, then convinced her husband, Paul Newman, first to produce the film and ultimately to direct it. To complete this family affair, the Newmans' charming daughter (masquerading under the name of Nell Potts) plays Rachel as a child in the numerous flashbacks.

It proved a wise decision all around. Newman, who has long wanted to direct, had the good sense as producer to surround himself with first-rate talent—New York editor Dede Allen, who cut last year's *Bonnie and Clyde*; cameraman Gayne Rescher, a resourceful recruit from the TV commercials with a knack for making New England's red barns and brick schoolhouses look like Charles Sheeler's clean, needle-sharp version of Americana; and composer Jerome Moross, who probably remembered from his ballet days that a simple phrase on a piano can often convey more to an audience than an entire symphony orchestra in full cry. The cast, also largely New York based, he apparently chose less for name value than for character verisimilitude and ability to act. (Estelle Parsons and Geraldine Fitzgerald may be the familiar names going in, but James Olson, Kate Harrington, and Frank Corsaro linger in the memory as belated discoveries.)

But, quite properly, it is Miss Woodward who carries the picture and makes it the affecting thing it is—and reminds us, incidentally, how long it has been since she had a picture worthy of her talents. No ravishing beauty, she projects instead an inner radiance, a winning wholesomeness and integrity that is the essence of Rachel Cameron. Unlike the star who is intent on maintaining an image, however, Joanne Woodward is willing (and superbly able) to distort her features in response to the surges of emotion that her role demands. Docile or desperate, hysterical with fear or with laughter, whether loving or brooding over the rejection of her love, she brings to the mobile surface of her face, without self-consciousness or any sense of "acting," the full force of what is felt inside. One recalls Helen Hayes and Barbara Stanwyck in films of the Thirties —actresses with a similar intensity and range—and suddenly we realize how much has been lost in the name of underplaying or "cool." Certainly, without Joanne Woodward (and, be it mentioned, the sympathetic support of Stewart Stern's script), *Rachel, Rachel* might easily have degenerated into a fairly ordinary, tear-jerking soap opera. Instead, Miss Woodward goes for the heart— and it makes all the difference.

RICHARD SCHICKEL

Rachel, Rachel turned out to be a discomfiting movie for me, one that calls into question a widely held assumption about the movies. The film was clearly undertaken in a spirit entirely too rare in the American film industry. That is to say a star, Joanne Woodward, and a screenwriter, Stewart Stern, discovered a novel, Margaret Laurence's *A Jest of God*, that was, to them, something more than a mere "property." Instead, it was a difficult and delicate thing that challenged them as artists, something they felt they simply had to make. They apparently encountered enormous difficulties in obtaining the relatively modest backing they required, and it was not until Miss Woodward's husband, Paul Newman, put his plentiful clout behind the project by agreeing to direct it that they could go ahead.

Everyone involved thereupon did his work with taste, conviction and solid, sometimes brilliant, craftsmanship. Stern's script, despite a tendency to tell rather than show, rings with gentle irony and rueful truth. Miss Woodward demonstrates again that she is perhaps the only major female star of our day capable of genuine naturalism, submerging self and image in a subtle, disciplined performance that avoids showiness, excessive sentiment, self-consciousness. As a director, Newman is anything but the bouncing boy-o we are accustomed to seeing on our screens. He has a sensitive, slightly melancholic eye for something most American movies miss—the texture of ordinary life. He displays, moreover, a feel for emotional nuance and a technical sureness; he is neither too radical nor too conservative. That is remarkable in a first film.

In short, all the elements of an excellent movie are here and yet, somehow, I emerged from *Rachel, Rachel* strangely unmoved by it, despite my appreciation of it and respect for it. Why, I must ask myself, does a rightly motivated movie go wrong?

The trouble is that the story itself is simply too slight, too familiar to engage us fully. It is merely a slice of the thirty-fifth summer of a spinster schoolteacher acutely aware that life is about to leave her permanently behind. She is nagged by familiar problems: persistent virginity, a sickly, aging mother to whom she is nurse-companion, memories and missed opportunities—problems that do not support for us dramatically the psychological weight they must carry for her.

The movie records her ambiguous triumphs over these afflictions: a loss of virtue that simply substitutes new problems for old; the neutralization of Mom, which is only partial and probably temporary; a breakout from her small-town existence that is no more than vaguely hopeful. It is all very right, very believable, very honest. But one merely sympathizes; sympathy is a mild emotion that implies a basic, irreducible alienation from its object.

Could the movie-makers have forced us across this gap? I don't know. Perhaps their basic material is just too true to be good dramatically, too much like unexciting, unclimactic, unresolved life to be an exhilarating or emotionally purging experience. Perhaps everyone was just a trifle too careful, too craftsmanlike, to take the kind of risks that stimulate us even when they fail.

But, as I said at the outset, I believe in the spirit in which this project was undertaken. Like all such attempts at artistic integrity, it is a test case, the performance of which will be carefully watched by the moneymen. I think, therefore, that you should test it on your own sensibility. It contains many rewards, not least of which is an almost perfect supporting cast. Estelle Parsons, touching and funny, achieves a marvelous individuality in her characterization of another old maid, trying to dissolve her loneliness in revivalistic religion while suppressing a leaning to lesbianism. Equally good are James Olson as the tricky fellow who liberates Rachel sexually—decency and maleness warring quietly beneath his fast talk—and Kate Harrington as Mom, somehow achieving depth in what could have been nothing but a stock role.

Rachel, Rachel is less than the sum of its parts, but in its intent and in much of its execution it is a good deal more than one is accustomed to getting at the movies.

ZITA

JOHN SIMON

A small, intimate film about ordinary people, yet with subtle implications, Robert Enrico's *Zita* is a gem of purest ray serene; well, let's except one or two impure rays. Enrico, who made the extraordinary *In the Midst of Life* (seen here, unfortunately, only piecemeal, episode by episode) and some excellent shorts, subsequently turned to commercial adventure films. With *Zita*, based on a story by his wife, he returns to delicately personal themes resonant with understated universality.

Annie, a young student living with her mother, is unable to bear the fact that her beloved Aunt Zita is dying in the next room; she escapes into a big night on the town. Her father (Zita's brother) was Spanish and died in the civil war; now the whole Spanish, paternal side of her family is becoming extinct. During her nocturnal adventures, encouraged by the sage family doctor and friend (a charmingly and unsentimentally drawn figure acted to perfection by Paul Crauchet—antiseptic, acerbic, yet ruefully human), Annie meets up with all kinds of men. Each of these gives her a lift, contributes more than a vignette. They are all individuals with some special forte they hold out to Annie, who learns from them whether she accepts or refuses.

One man is a sardonic young Negro activist who nevertheless keeps his cool; another is a handsome farmer from the south of France whose beribboned prize ram escapes and leads them all a merry chase through nocturnal Paris; still another is a young double-bass player and sports-car enthusiast who finally becomes her first lover. There are other people and incidents, such as a near-rape by a bunch of hippified hoodlums, and much riding about in various vehicles, which, however, is never boring as in Godard and Lelouch.

In one exquisite scene, Annie sits in the police station with a Spanish refugee who has been brought in for killing a cat he meant to eat to keep from starving. Annie first tried to protect the cat, then she tried to defend the Spaniard against the cops; now he sits in that cage where the Paris police put their pickups, and she sits just outside it. He speaks no French and she very little Spanish, yet she attempts to tell him about her father, who could blow up bridges; finally she is talking in French just to herself to keep her courage up. When Annie alone is released, she has a splendid outburst against the police. The dialogue, as always, is free of platitudes and literate.

The climactic scene is both brilliant and on the verge of soupiness. Annie takes her bass player to the suburban house in which she grew up under Aunt Zita's care. We know that Zita lies in another house, dying. But here she is, alive and bustling about, and Annie (without changing appearances) is both the child she was and Simon's girl friend showing him around the house. They rub shoulders with Aunt Zita, and the past and the present merge. Such is Enrico's artistry that the scene functions joyously as reality even though we know that it is fantasy.

The editing here is masterly. There is a sequence in which Annie goes up the stairs to what used to be her room, and the simple ascent of a stairway becomes, through brilliance of photography and montage, an adventure to make you hold your breath and heartbeat. The imagined seduction scene is a mite gooey; but the real sexual initiation, later on in Simon's apartment, has thus been provided with an effective counterpart. The latter scene is fresh, tactful, and savory.

When Annie gets home, she finds that Zita has died, but mother and doctor are there to offer quiet support. She insists on going in to see her aunt, whose agony was so unwatchable. Now that Zita is dead, Annie has a vision of herself as a child once again playing in Zita's garden as the camera fairly rapidly pulls away. Zita suddenly turns a corner around a hedge, and the skipping little girl's figure continues its dwindling alone—right into the final fadeout. This, again, might be sticky, but it is handled with a winning lightness and purity.

Zita is greatly helped by François de Roubeix's discreetly penetrating music, often just a Spanish guitar solo. Even more outstanding is the color camera work of Jean Boffety, who, by a slight change in lighting, can make the same room exude vastly different hues and emotions. Boffety's colors may not quite match the sheer loveliness of a *Red Desert* or *Elvira Madigan,* but they have a flexibility and variety that would be hard to equal.

The performances are all good, crowned by Joanna Shimkus' Annie. Miss Shimkus, besides improving from film to film, has an incomparable basic warmth and simple naturalness. Her Annie is child and girl by turns or both at once, and zigzags into ripeness before our eyes. Her infinitely various face—tomboyish from some angles, flawlessly beautiful from others—helps; but, ultimately, it is her unselfconscious, unhistrionic acting that lends Enrico's fine film its final glory.

FACES

ANDREW SARRIS

I would like to recommend *Faces* without restructuring the reader's aesthetic expectations, but I know by now that I can't escape the consequences of my criticism. *Faces,* if seen at all, should be seen with a degree of tolerance for its rough edges and raw nerve endings. Indeed, the first half hour strains so hard for its strained conviviality that the movie becomes a bad bet to last two hours without bursting a blood vessel.

Writer-director (but here not actor) John Cassavetes begins the proceedings with a framing scene that is recalled in retrospect as a half-baked Brechtian distancing device. It doesn't really belong to the picture, but curiously it works on its own terms. A comically hard-boiled TV producer (John Marley) grumpily sips his early-morning-dawn's-ugly-light coffee in a screening room consecrated by his staff to the exhibition of a slice of real life in which Mr. Marley himself is to be reincarnated as one of the pathetic protagonists. Already we are being treated to the ear-shorn, nose-heavy facial distortions of *caméra-vérité,* not to mention the serpentine person-to-person and room-to-room camera movements with which we have become so familiar on television's more realistic spectacles, such as the when-is-Mr.-Nixon-coming-down-Herb show on election night. Look at me! the camera screams too stridently. Look how honest and real and true I am! This viewer, I must confess, braced himself at this point for a strenuous session of formlessness masquerading as fearlessness.

And who are all these strangely worn unknowns? The only familiar face among the players is Gena Rowlands (Mrs. John Cassavetes), and even she has hardly been victimized by overexposure these past few years. The whole project smells so strongly of Poverty Row that the more cautious critic may beware the thin line between inspired naturalism and nagging indigence. Exterior shots, for example, are rarer in *Faces* than in the raunchiest sexploitation films. Scenes go on and on with Warholian exhaustiveness (though not exhaustion). And Cassavetes lets all the players laugh their heads off to the point where nervousness is transformed into purgation. Strange, different, but is it good? The notion of art as selection and compression gets short shrift in *Faces*. All in all, there are only seven master scenes, with three very brief transitions and virtually no parallel editing for contrast or irony. No one seems to be cut off, and nothing seems to be cut. Even at its best, *Faces* cannot be considered a triumph of cinematic form, and the formalist in me has been resisting the sloppy eccentricities of Cassavetes ever since *Shadows* a decade or so ago.

Ultimately, however, *Faces* emerges for me as the revelation of 1968; not the best movie, to be sure, but certainly the most surprising. (Buñuel's *Belle de Jour* merely caps a career that has crested many times before.) After its somewhat strained beginning, *Faces* not only works, it soars. The turning point is the first desperately domestic conversation between John Marley and Lynn Carlin, a conversation swept along on its banal course by gales of nervous laughter, a conversation accompanied by physical withdrawal behind the luxurious barriers of space, walls, doors, and furniture, a conversation that in its lacking topical details and symbolic overtones is perhaps closer to aimless soap opera than to deliberate drama. But it works in ways that are mysterious to behold, as if for once a soap opera were allowed to unfold out of its own limited logic for two hours without interruptions for commercials or station identification. What we have in *Faces* therefore is not only a failure to communicate but also a reluctance to terminate, and this reluctance is one of the reasons *Faces* achieves an otherwise inexplicable intensity of feeling that transcends the too easily satirized milieu of affluently superficial southern California. Although it is concerned almost exclusively with the lecherous delusions of pickups and pick-me-ups, *Faces* is never sordid or squalid. Cassavetes stays with his tormented, alienated characters until they break through the other side of slice-of-life naturalism into emotional and artistic truth.

Faces works even if we question its creator's original intentions. Who can ever say for sure that *Faces* is not a kind of serendipity cinema—that is, a movie that started out as a dull diatribe against American life and ended up as a heroic saga of emotional survival through an endless night of loneliness and shattered defenses? *Faces* is certainly more interesting in itself than for all the things that can be said about it, a mark of merit more intrinsic than extrinsic. Still, Cassavetes deserves full credit for the inspired idea (possibly intuitive) of developing characters objectively in odd-numbered relationships before exploring them intimately in even-numbered couplings. Hence, the first scene features two men competing in the apartment of the girl they've picked up in a bar. The infernal triangle brings out all the self-hatred of the errant husbands and takes us quite logically into a scene of domestic coupling through which self-hatred takes on new dimensions. The husband tells the wife he wants a divorce, and thus two become one and one; but when he calls the girl he picked up earlier in the evening, it turns out that she is occupied with a double date. No matter. The tormented husband bursts in on the party of four, to make·an unwelcome fifth, and scuffles grotesquely with an equally aging, equally affluent philanderer, but then everyone makes up as a sixth girl is recruited to restore the original double coupling of the evening and leave the husband alone with his original date. The arithmetical progression proceeds four to five by intrusion, five to six by augmentation, and finally two and four by division. Meanwhile the deserted wife and three of her more domestically disaffected girl friends visit a go-go dance joint, where they allow themselves to be picked up by a swaggering but thirtyish hippie. (The movie was shot at least two years ago, and thus the skirts look curiously long and the dances relatively coherent, a good sic-transit-go-go-gloria argument against ever trying to be too timely.) The circle of five disintegrates into a series of jealous explosions until wife and hippie are left alone in illusory togetherness, a dubious coupling that leads the wife to the medicine cabinet in search of the ultimate number—zero.

All through the movie, people are intimating that they want to be alone with each other even though they have been conditioned to function only in a crowd. They are driven to sex not by desire but by an adolescent bravado that they know instinctively is spiritually futile, but still they pay lip service to the ideal of intimacy, the very ideal their society has degraded with its dirty jokes and infantile inhibitions. The characters in *Faces* start off as a lineup of emotional cripples, but somehow they all make it to the finish line with their souls intact. Among the players, I would single out Lynn Carlin, John Marley, Seymour Cassel, and Gena Rowlands for special praise out of a virtually flawless ensemble, and if this be actor's cinema, long may it flourish. At the very least, Cassavetes deserves full credit for staging the spectacle with both conviction and compassion.

ARTHUR SCHLESINGER, JR.

One's main memory of *Faces* is the echo of laughter—nervous laughter, false laughter, compulsive laughter, hysterical laughter. It is the laughter of men and women who smoke too many cigarettes, drink too much coffee and alcohol, tell too many bad jokes, and hate their lives. It is Los Angeles laughter, businessmen's laughter, suburban laughter, middle-aged laughter.

Like *The Graduate*, *Faces* detests middle age and will doubtless win a grateful audience among the young. The only likable character is a benign hippie who serves as the mouthpiece for the deep thoughts of John Cassavetes, its writer and director. Italian and Czech films invest the old at least with pathos; the American film these days takes a savage delight in stripping the old of all trace of dignity.

Faces catches a marriage in a state of decay. The husband leaves his wife and visits a call girl; the wife goes to a discothèque with other wives, returns with the hippie, sleeps with him, and attempts suicide. The hippie saves her life. The husband comes back in the morning and surprises the hippie. Husband and wife end locked in reciprocal sterility.

"The mass of men," wrote Thoreau, "lead lives of quiet desperation." In California they lead lives of noisy desperation. Cassavetes' camera, fluid and inquisitive, records this desperation in harsh close-ups given a specious authenticity by the anonymous excellence of the cast and by the grainy quality of the film. His dialogue exploits the sounds of despair underneath banality; his pace is hectic and pitiless.

5

THE ARTIST AS ANTI-HERO

HUNGER

Penelope Gilliatt

Christiania—now Oslo—in 1890. Back view of a thin man, dressed in black, legs crossed. Leaning over a bridge, writing on a piece of paper, "Crimes of the future." A pencil putting a box of lines around the words. Now the man can be seen from the front. He seems to be chewing something. He looks like Dostoevski. Triangular face, pointed chin, wide forehead with the skin stretched tight over the bone, tunneling dark eyes like the firing ends of rifle barrels. He is seized by a cough, and spits into the water.

The man wears a high white collar, no tie, a striped shirt, a worn but genteel suit, and muddy boots, which he sometimes talks to and sometimes rebuffs on the basis that he has no time for them. ("Talk to each other instead," he says.) The man is the central character of Henning Carlsen's *Hunger*, a nobly comic account of what it is to be a potentially remarkable writer starving for food and famished for work. The film comes from Knut Hamsun's classic Norwegian novel, but it bears no sign of a bookish source. It seems—is—a true invention of subjective cinema. It stays inside one man's skull, and everything in it expresses that man. We see the world through a singular mind housed in the body of an indigent. His moods sweep the film: bile, pride, phantom hope, fury, fantasies of due grandeur that are outwardly unapt in a bum. Stomach sticking to back of spine, he concocts encouraging projects: enemies in bowler hats to be patronized; tail-twisting of the safely off to be done; the park to enjoy; a certain calm and ache to be savored, left by the sight of the beautiful women who walk

127

there, wearing muffs and high fur collars and hats freighted with feathers. The character conveys a sense of having no time, because of his throttled impatience to write, but also of having far too much time, because he isn't writing. No chance. God help us. No, ignore Him. Instead, answer an advertisement for a job as a grocers' accountant, in a copperplate hand too good for them. It will be better by three o'clock, or tomorrow. Tomorrow will be quite a day—no doubt of it.

The writer, on his knees, has no proof of talent apart from his own instinct, or his own paranoia, which he actually calls madness as the hunger gets worse and he begins to see a *Doppelgänger* of himself in his lodgings. We can tell more for ourselves. He is no born down-and-out. He has fugitive impulses that look much like genius, visible in the farcical energy he musters when others would be beaten. Encounters with the sentries of the bourgeoisie are converted into brilliant victories. He contradicts a startled policeman about the time of day, their breath spurting at each other in the freezing weather like the exhausts of early motorcars. And he shouts, "Do you have to sit on this bench?" at a well-dressed citizen who has the nerve to share his seat in the park. Fumes of resolve fill him. No melancholy. He exists on banked-down ambition, fire in his guts, and a sure knowledge of the possibility of better things. In the meantime, improvise variations on the minimum. Make another courtly application for a menial job. Speak to another policeman, to keep the spirits up. Ask for the time again. "Half past three," says the cop. "I see you know your job," says the writer ferociously, who is shortly to be crawling on all fours in combat for a bone with a ravenous dog. Manhood returns, after an interval. He raises his sights and keeps a speechless love vigil under the window of a sumptuous tart he has seen in the park. A princess, he insists to himself. He has an argument about her with some innocent who strikes him as supposing that he's exaggerating. A diatribe on her behalf, delivered with high dignity: "Do you think she's someone in the fire brigade, or a female debt collector? . . . Kindly remember her father's name. You should see his wife. She's the fattest woman in the world. Do you think she isn't the fattest woman in the world?" Flailing in a null interlude of his life. Twisting and turning for an enemy, when the real enemy is the fact of not writing. Fabricating names for himself so that he can speak invisibly to someone—anyone—and knock on the doors of the better placed. Inventing pretexts to meet fit company on his own terms. "I've come to fetch a parcel from a young musician called Grieg," says the rock-bottom man with fine ease, raising his hat at one doorway. At another: "An invalid gentleman advertised for someone to push his chair. I want to recommend a man with a philanthropic outlook." He would never recommend himself. He hasn't the taste for cringing. He asks a butcher for a bone, but his temperament makes him pretend that it is for a dog and that there doesn't have to be any meat on it. End of bungled encounter, leaving him haughty but foodless. Shot of him later gnawing on some other bone, hiding against a street wall. On an empty stomach, the scraps of meat make him sick. Damnation. *Is there nothing one may keep for oneself?* A sob against the stone. To recover, more grandee contempt for a cop: "Do you thank God for your blessings? Then thank him warmly for me, too." (In five minutes, I shall be happy.) The pawnbroker—detestable good-heart—whom he has been seeing too often, says, "I've told you, I can't accept your buttons. But God help you." Rage at mercy blows the writer's head open like a burst boiler. Nothing to be done; on the other hand, something must be. So he yells back, "I've told you, God doesn't want to help me! Even if He did, He could go to hell! I'll tell you what you are—you're His pack mule!" Dear Lord, he thinks, to his boots, I can't manage. No—I'm a little indisposed, but later I shall be the happiest man in the world. Again he addresses his boots. His dependents. Courage, he tells them loftily. Today is the big day. Stick it till three o'clock.

He feels no fraternity with other underdogs. He treats beggars in the style of some stately gentleman who happens to have left his purse at home. Manners, play-acting—devices to keep his mind off his place at the bottom of the heap. Obsession with the princess, who strikes him as plainly his rightful love, and with writing, which is his calling, and one day the world will know it. An editor accepts a piece on condition that the tone is cooled down a bit. By tomorrow. The editor looks carefully at him and thinks that he may need money, but the writer refuses an advance. Self-respect, huffiness, persecution mania, possibly art and starvation give him the deluded imperiousness of a descendant of some inbred old line of kings. Mournfulness is a response that he rejects. It is the mood of crawlers. When his princess starts to let him make love to her and then kicks him out, his form of grief is fiercer. His contempt for the shabby voyeurs and numb victims around him is absolute. His landlady robs him of his room after his girl has tricked him, but no matter. Perfidy everywhere, punishments idly dealt. He beats his feet on the ground. "Ladies and gentlemen, all is lost!" A boat is leaving its dock. Another possibility. Glee fills his face again, like the great sweetness that lit it when his princess miraculously smiled at him. He was once a big laugher—she told him she remembered it, from some sight of him at a concert a year or two ago. Yes, he laughed and laughed, quite lately.

I've now see *Hunger* three times since it was shown at Cannes in 1966. Fragments of this account are quoted from the dialogue, most of it is not. It is as near as I can get to a prose that might reflect something of the way the film is shot and edited, and of the hero's way of addressing his life. He spits in the eye of his stalemated situation, and sometimes he is swept by winds of resolve and fun that are mysteriously brave. Per Oscarsson's performance is phenomenal. It rules out any trace of despondency. The experience of the film is the experience of being this character, and there is no flagging anywhere in that—only fury, antic courage, a rather Beckettlike stoic humor, and a suppressed wild exhilaration that is equal to the grip of writing, or love. It is quite a film. It applies a desperate funniness, delicacy, and control to its tale of barbaric fret in a pent-up great man whose fiber is so far known only to him—unnourished by the right work or the right company but heroically jealous of any spirit spent on the mediocre.

HOUR OF THE WOLF

JOHN SIMON

A film by Ingmar Bergman that does not work is saddening in itself, and when the failure comes as a sequel to the magnificent *Persona* it is that much more disheartening. *Hour of the Wolf* returns to the problem of two people's interaction and interdependence to the point where two destinies become, or threaten to become, a single fused one. This time the question is to what extent the lover can help the beloved who is torn between sanity and a world of visionary horrors, the madness that (Bergman seems to feel) imperils the artist with its cruel yet cajoling lure.

A painter, Johan Borg, disappears from a small Frisian island where he spends the summers with his wife, Alma. The film reconstructs, from Johan's diaries and Alma's confessions, the events that lead up to the disappearance. First Johan begins to see demons and to sketch them; then they appear to his pregnant wife as well. They are a rich, eccentric group inhabiting a dilapidated château, and among them seems to be Johan's former mistress, Veronica. In a climactic scene, Johan and Alma have dinner with this company and are humiliated and divided against each other.

Johan's madness—if that is what it is—gains; he is particularly afraid of that hour before dawn when nightmares and hauntings preponderate, when most deaths but also, parodoxically, most childbirths occur: the hour of the wolf, as Swedish country folk call it. Finally, one of the ghostly crowd—if such they be—leaves a gun with Johan, who shoots his wife and thinks he has killed her. The painter runs off to the château, where he is subjected to all kinds of horrors; his host, the Baron, announces that he is now Veronica's lover, then scurries off across walls and ceilings.

After watching an old lady (the superb Naima Wifstrand) remove her face—an especially brilliant bit of film-making—Johan is made up *en travesti* by the sinister Archivist Lindhorst and invited to make love to the nude, seemingly dead Veronica on a stone catafalque, while the Baron and the Baroness and their ghoulish crew leeringly watch. Under the triple assault of homosexuality, necrophilia and exhibitionism, there cracks a noble mind. Alma runs after Johan into the woods, where he is attacked by the entire company, led by Curator Heerbrand. Lindhorst changes into a bird of prey to deliver the *coup de grâce*. Alma is left to bear the child, presumably in the wolf hour, and to wonder whether by falling in with her husband's demonology and visions she loved him too much or not enough.

Thus, roughly, the plot. What this is, though Bergman does not tell us so, is an improvisation on themes from E. T. A. Hoffmann, the great German romantic storyteller. In *The Magician*, Bergman had already borrowed a thing or two from Hoffmann's weird fantasies. In *Hour of the Wolf* the borrowing is chiefly from "The

Golden Pot," but there is also a faint parallel to the story "Don Juan," in which a performance of the opera *Don Giovanni* figures rather as *The Magic Flute* does in the film. There is, moreover, a sudden and unintegrated appearance in the film of Maestro (Kapellmeister) Kreisler, the hounded musician, who is Hoffmann's alter ego in two of his major works. In Hoffmann (who was a composer and conductor as well as a writer), Kreisler is called Johann, just like Bergman's hero; thinking this to be a dig at poor old Fritz Kreisler, American audiences giggle inanely.

In "The Golden Pot" (1814), which no less a man than Thomas Carlyle first translated into English, the student Anselm is torn between two realms. There is the supernatural one of Archivist Lindhorst, who is a demon prince and sometimes changes into a salamander or vulture, and his lovely and loving daughter Serpentina, who can turn into a little green snake. And there is the philistine, bourgeois world, typified by Rector Paulmann and his merry, calculating daughter Veronica, who loves Anselm but settles for the prosaic Registrar Heerbrand when he is appointed counselor. Earlier, Veronica enlists a hideous witch to help her win Anselm; yet the student ends up happily married to Serpentina, and is translated by Lindhorst to their magic castle in Atlantis. Lindhorst's world is that of art and the spirit, of white magic; Veronica's is that of middle-class stolidity, which, once the black magic of its youthful seductiveness has worn off, must lose out to the creative imagination.

In *Hour of the Wolf*, we find a Lindhorst, a Heerbrand, and a Veronica not unlike those in Hoffmann, although the symbology has been inverted. The world of the spirits, for Bergman, becomes the seigniory of evil: the supernatural corrupts the artist who is exposed, precariously balanced, corruptible. (To be sure, in other stories, such as "The Mine at Falun," Hoffmann too saw things in this way.) Along with these reverse-Hoffmannian figures we get typical Bergman characters: the patient wife, Alma, bears the same name as the sympathetic nurse in *Persona*; Veronica's last name is Vogler, the same as the disturbed actress's in the earlier film.

Unfortunately, the real and the unreal in *Hour* do not mesh. Hoffmann's supernatural is acceptable to us because even his natural world is remote, romantic, fabulous. In Bergman, however, the real is too near to us with toothbrushes, radios, revolvers. And a demon that drives a jeep is simply not a demon or even the raw material out of which the overexcited mind can make a proper demon. Consequently, instead of the real perfectly suffused with the superreal, we get the mundane and the hallucinatory each in its corner—except for one or two marvelous scenes where the two indeed coalesce.

There is a contradiction in Bergman's mind. In a recent filmed interview, Bergman spoke both of not believing in God and of actual demons that chased him out of habitations. Regrettably, the interviewer was not astute enough to ask how a cosmos can be at the same time godless and demon-filled; in any case, it is this kind of discrepancy that damages the film. There is even a sequence, deliberately overexposed, in which Johan kills a little boy (again, shades of *Persona*), about whose meaning Bergman himself, I suspect, remains unclear.

There are scenes, or at least shots, of great beauty, such as the grisly dinner party that aptly absorbs elements from Fellini and Buñuel; or the slow, choreographed entrances of the Baron and Veronica; or, contrariwise, the sudden and chilling appearances of the old lady with the hat and of Heerbrand at the hour of the wolf. Sven Nykvist's dependably inspired camera is there to catch the most haunting compositions, trajectories, varieties of shade and texture, capturing as many nuances in black and white as the richest palette could with color. A rowboat at dawn gliding past rocks; a penumbral lamp between darkling faces; Johan's sharp, shadowed profile bisecting Alma's tear-lit face against the gloaming of the Scandinavian night; Johan striking match after match in front of his slitted eyes in a vain attempt to domesticate the horror of the wolf's hour: so many master images!

My own two favorites are, first, Alma's anxious face in the dark room comforted suddenly by one and then two disembodied hands —the rest of Johan is submerged in night; and, secondly, Johan and Alma embracing in the late-afternoon light on the threshold of their cottage. In the brisk wind, the laundry on the clothesline flaps hostilely around their faces. It reminds me of my favorite lines from Hölderlin: "*Sprachlos und kalt, im Winde/ Klirren die Fahnen.*" (Speechless and cold, in the wind/ The weathervanes are clanging.)

The cast, headed by Max von Sydow and Liv Ullmann, is splendid from top to bottom, and the sound track, often using electronic music, is one of the spookiest within memory. Yet the film tells us remarkably little about the crises of the Mad Artist, or of those of the loving woman who tries to save him.

RICHARD SCHICKEL

Ingmar Bergman likes to speak of himself as a magician. The filmmaker, he notes, bases his art on the use of a machine that exploits a weakness in human vision in order to impart the illusion, not the reality, of motion and therefore of life. In other words, a highly complex art—and an industry hardly less complex—is based on a gadget that is fundamentally a toy to amuse and mystify children (or at least the child who resides in all of us). "Thus," says Bergman, "I am either an impostor or, when the audience is willing to be taken in, a conjurer."

There is both disarming modesty and admirable self-awareness in this statement, for I must confess that I have never been able to definitely decide whether Bergman is, indeed, a consummate magician or merely a mountebank. I change my mind from film to film and even from sequence to sequence in the same film. He is a journalist, not quite a philosopher, of the guilty soul, and the necessity to probe the unconscious states of his characters leads him to a highly symbolic style, in which he has created (a) some of the most memorable screen images and (b) some of the most annoyingly obscure and/or pretentious images of our time. In short, he fascinates as he irritates. All I know for certain is that the hold he has on me—and, I suspect, on almost everyone else—is his attempt to resolve the basic tension between the artist and the trickster.

It is no wonder that Bergman, so aware that his art (perhaps all art) is based at least partly on trumpery, should be obsessed with the tragedy of the artist who suddenly, mysteriously, loses the power to cast his magic spells. *Persona*, released a year ago, and his latest film, *Hour of the Wolf*, both deal with this theme and are, in fact, twins more understandable and rewarding when considered together instead of separately.

You will recall that in the former an actress loses her ability to speak and, as therapy, goes to live in an isolated seacoast cottage with a nurse-companion of resounding normalcy. There the source of the artist's malaise is revealed. She is haunted by guilt over past failures to love and to respond to love, and she has come to believe she has lost the *right* to speak to the world. She also discovers a frightful cure for her condition. Her silence encourages her simple, healthy friend to blather on about herself, and the more she talks the more the nurse realizes that she is as guilt-ridden as the actress. By the end of the film illness has been transferred from patient to nurse and we have learned a terrible lesson: the artist *must* discharge his neuroses somehow; if he cannot do so constructively in imaginative works, he will do so destructively by imposing them on other people.

Hour of the Wolf carries this logic one step further. Again the artist blocked by guilts (this time he is a man and a painter), again the placidly normal companion (this time his pregnant wife), again the isolated cottage (this time on an island). There is, however, one important difference. The companion will not allow herself to be drawn into the artist's insanity, perhaps because she is defending her unborn child, perhaps because she knows the wiles and dangers of her "case" more intimately than the nurse in *Persona* knew hers.

Anyway, the painter (played with his usual fine craftsmanship by Max von Sydow) cannot fight off his demons. They rise up to fill his mind—and the screen—blotting out every shred of reality until, at last, he attempts to kill his wife and thereby states openly what was only implicit in the earlier film: madness will out. If it remains undischarged in art or in human relations it must be exorcised through destruction.

As a journalist Bergman is an objective observer of such phenomena, and he betrays little overt emotion over this denouement. He accepts destruction as coolly (one is tempted to say coldly) as he accepted, in *Persona*, the destruction of an innocent bystander. He is, as all his films testify, the sort of completely committed, perhaps self-absorbed, artist who has long lived with full awareness that the creative spirit can turn rogue, can destroy with the same passionate intensity that it builds. Indeed, such terror as one feels for the characters of these films is a direct product of Bergman's easy acceptance of this possibility. One imagines that the idea once frightened him; now it is merely another psychological phenomenon for him to examine and then objectify as art. (His cool, of course, may be pure bravado, even an act of self-romanticism, but I don't think it primarily is.)

But, despite their subjectivity, I trust Bergman's motives, which have a purity rare among film artists. His methods, on the other hand, are sometimes risky, deliberately puzzling, often frankly boring. In *Persona*, for example, there was one key scene in which the camera remained transfixed, in a close-up, throughout two identical, interminable speeches. I admired this daring attempt at austerity and his arrogance at forcing us to accept it—but I almost ran screaming from the theater.

In *Hour of the Wolf* Bergman is back to his more familiar tricks, mixing memories, visions and external reality in a deliberately confusing, if ultimately decipherable, way. There is a long dream sequence, perhaps the longest of the many he has shot, full of spectacular effects, including a long pan along the naked horizontal body of Ingrid Thulin. It is, on the whole, a more exciting film visually than *Persona*. Yet it seems something of a regression, a return to an easier, more kitchen-tested kind of magic making, instead of a development of that tight, highly charged but infinitely promising manner which he introduced last year. Perhaps *Persona* explained itself too little, but it left us caught up in a mystery, powerless to keep our thoughts from returning to it. *Hour of the Wolf*, though filled as always with those burning Bergman images of inner terror, explains too much (including, ironically, much of *Persona*) and thus allows us to escape from it relatively unscathed. But no matter how one evaluates it, the film further illuminates the dark and bloody ground of Ingmar Bergman's sensibility.

CHARLIE BUBBLES

ANDREW SARRIS

Charlie Bubbles is the most pleasant surprise of a year that has thus far been less surprising than disconcerting. First of all, the idea of Albert Finney doubling as star and director did not seem too promising, and not because there is any taboo against working both sides of the camera. Chaplin, Keaton, Welles, and Renoir come to mind immediately as impressive precedents for aspiring actor-directors. Even on a lower level of personal style, directing seems to bring out the better qualities of an actor. Gene Kelly was less of a ham in his own (and Donen's) musicals (*Singin' in the Rain, It's Always Fair Weather*) than in Minnelli's (*The Pirate*) or Sidney's (*Anchors Aweigh*), and Brando was less of a hog in the self-directed *One-Eyed Jacks* than in the Lumet-directed *The Fugitive Kind* and the Englund-directed *The Ugly American*. The real problem nowadays is that everyone including the leggy chorus girl in the *New Yorker* cartoon wants to be a director, with the result that aspiration too often exceeds inspiration.

The biggest surprise in *Charlie Bubbles* is that Finney's direction succeeds on its own terms as a tasteful stew of acting vignettes. Indeed, I'd have to go back to the Mercury Theatre casts of Orson Welles in *Citizen Kane* and *The Magnificent Ambersons* to find a comparable level of ensemble playing down to the smallest bits and pieces. Finney is certainly no Welles in the realm of intellectual and emotional expressiveness. As a work of art, *Charlie Bubbles* finally bursts into cop-out fantasy because its wholeness is unable to reconcile the perfection of its parts with any coherent attitude toward its subject. The film's ending leaves the audience up in the air literally and figuratively—literally because Finney's beleaguered Bubbles ascends a balloon *ex machina*, figuratively because the ascent forestalls an obligatory scene Shelagh Delaney neglected to write for Charlie and his estranged wife, Lottie (Billie Whitelaw).

Shelagh Delaney happens to be the girl who wrote *A Taste of Honey*, reportedly after becoming disgusted with the contrivances of a Terrence Rattigan play performed in a theater for which she worked as an usherette. It is natural for artists reacting against contrivance to let some air into characterizations. Unfortunately, it is equally natural for these artists to inflate individual characterizations at the expense of an over-all conception.

Albert Finney and Shelagh Delaney confront a familiar phenomenon of recent years in our popular culture—the movement of raw talent and energy from the north of England to the south. (In America and Italy, the analogous movement is from south to north.) Albert Finney's Charlie Bubbles is ostensibly a successful writer from the north who has settled in the sybaritic luxury of London, but the instant recognition of the "writer" in the film is more appropriate for an actor very much like Finney. The film begins very much like the standard satire of success. The setting is the murmuringly posh atmosphere of a London restaurant where Charlie meets with an agent and accountant to talk of roast beef and residuals. Charlie spots a less successful colleague named Smokey Pickle (Colin Blakely) dining indecorously with a wart-encrusted solicitor. Charlie and Smokey have barely said hello before they are spattering each other with the specialties of the house. Finney's *Tom Jones* fans chortle appreciatively at the anal level of the slapstick, satirically intercut with the discreetly disturbed expressions of the still-murmuring diners. The strange thing about the scene is Finney's extraordinary self-effacement. At first it seems only the modesty of an actor, and there is no end of that, but eventually the modesty of the actor is translated into the meaning of the character. Charlie Bubbles is not bored; he is tired. He is afflicted less with ennui than with downright exhaustion.

And so we have a double vision of Charlie's world, the satirical and the hallucinatory. The satire is cued by the kooky nomenclature—Charlie Bubbles and Smokey Pickle as the authors, Mr. and Mrs. Noseworthy as Charlie's devoted servants, Mr. and Mrs. Fettuchini as a slightly sinister movie couple, and Eliza Heyho as Liza Minnelli's sensitive rendering of the ugly Americaness in Charlie's cluttered life. But though the names suggest caricature, the characterizations do not. By forcing himself into the background of every scene, Finney functions like a solid double-bass player with a jazz trio. Every performer resonates through Finney's personable bulk and generous passivity. Finney's tact extends to his directing technique. He indulges in an occasional visual stunt like the closed-circuit television screens through which we see the childish disorder of Charlie's town-house existence, and a Felliniesque procession through the muddy bleakness of the industrial north. But even in these profoundly scenic sequences Finney's players are enhanced.

Nowhere is Finney gentler than in his scenes with Liza Minnelli, an ill-featured, ungainly girl who emerges triumphantly from the apparent humiliation of a sex scene during which her Eliza does not so much seduce the played-out Charlie as service him in the nether regions of his libido. By the time Finney is achieving new ecstasies of rapport with Billie Whitelaw as his casually earthy ex-wife and Timothy Garland as his emotionally crafty son Jack, Charlie's tiredness transcends any possible social or psychological interpretation. Satirical reality seems to sink into the swamplike realism of a dream. It is as if Charlie Bubbles dreamt the whole film in those few moments of semiwakefulness during which he was suspended between north and south, failure and success, innocence and guilt, hope and regret.

The beauty of the film is that it shifts imperceptibly from the Pickwickian to the Earwickian as attitudes flow into feelings. *Charlie Bubbles* falls short of greatness both because its feelings never coalesce into ideas and because its eponymous protagonist never wakes up long enough to resolve his relationships. Nonetheless a score of memorable performances must count for something on any ultimate scale of values. Albert Finney, Billie Whitelaw, and Alan Lake as a disconcertingly direct celebrity hound in an airman's uniform deserve special commendations.

RICHARD SCHICKEL

Here is Charlie Bubbles keeping an eye on things around the house: he has a television camera in every room and a nine-screen monitor in his study so he can see—and occasionally hector —friends and servants as they go about their work and play.

Here is Charlie taking his secretary and would-be mistress to visit his home town: he hardly ever gets out of his car or slows down to examine the landscape, preferring to keep aloof from the life that once he led.

And here is Charlie taking his son to a football match: they sit in a private booth and see the game through a glass dimly—cut off from the crowd, from the play, and from the possibility of partici-patory emotions.

Who is Charlie? What is responsible for his isolation? The rue-ful comedy that bears his ironically effervescent name dramatizes his situation with great simplicity. He is a writer, up from the working class of Manchester, who, in the course of becoming pre-maturely rich and famous, has mislaid a writer's basic tool—the capacity to feel and to respond. Now he must visit his estranged wife and son, whom he has set up on a farm outside his native city. His journey accidentally becomes an attempt—tight-lipped, mono-syllabic and grimly weary—to reestablish his connections with life, people, and his own history.

He fails—an act of will is no substitute for an act of faith—and is last seen loosing the few remaining lines that moor him to reality and drifting away from it all in a lovely, surprising, symbolic sequence that is daringly at odds stylistically with the naturalistic tone of the rest of the movie, yet just right as a climax.

Rightness, indeed, is the key to the film's success. It is, after all, no more than a series of minor incidents pegged to that simple, classic story line, a trip. Clumsily written or played, these vignettes might have been, like so many allegedly funny scenes in films these days, pointless and comic only by chance. But Shelagh Delaney's script has a way of lightly, precisely tapping the point of truth in each of them. Albert Finney and the rest of the cast have similarly good instincts, and they are handled by a new young director, name of Albert Finney, who has had the wit to find his own style and the confidence to stick to it. He has a fine, subtle eye for the absurdity of soft and vulnerable human beings trapped in the maze of hard, cold surfaces of modern life and moving with the speed of increasing desperation as they try to find something warm to the touch.

Movement implies displacement, and that is the film's true object. No one is where he is supposed to be. Charlie and his old North Country friend (Colin Blakely) don't belong in an expense-account restaurant in London, trying to relate by throwing food at each other. They don't fit in Charlie's house, either, for it is less a home than a repository for the gadgets with which modern man vainly tries to adapt to his electronic environment. On the other hand, as Charlie's trip proves, you truly can't go home again. The American girl (Liza Minnelli) who accompanies him is looking for her family's ancestral roots here, and all she finds is the rubble of reconstruction and a frigidly moderne hotel where she awkwardly offers herself to the indifferently receptive Charlie. As for his wife, beautifully played by the slightly, deliciously overripe Billie White-law, she is an urban type who likes the idea of farm life but has trouble coping with its practical aspects. Her son, in the true spirit of the times, lights up only when the telly does. Occasionally, to be sure, we glimpse someone who has resisted the lure of movement and stayed put, but these characters are the saddest of all, since stasis is a kind of living death.

So there is no way out, nowhere to go, nowhere to rest. We retain from *Charlie Bubbles* a series of images: human figures blurred as they hasten past themselves reflected in the glass and metal of their surroundings, occasionally frozen for an instant in a numb and terrible self-awareness. Laughter dies, gives way to a pity that does not purge, only discomfits. *Charlie Bubbles* is a modest thing, but, like all good work in the minor keys, it has a way of haunting the memory.

6

COMEDY AND SATIRE

THE ODD COUPLE and others

Wilfrid Sheed

For a veritable sirocco of hot air, a Hindenburg of deadly gases, ask a critic his theory of Comedy. Every critic has one, if you tickle him long enough, and it usually sounds like something that might go double for Everett Dirksen. We all believe in Comedy—true Comedy, that is, the comedy of Keaton and Fields, which was distinguished by —— (insert pet theory); we lament the passing of true Comedy, swear allegiance to the true Comic Spirit and shake our woolly pates over its decline.

I am in full agreement with all the above positions, being as stuffy about comedy as the next man; but, for all that, I would not lightly recommend to an impressionable youngster the diet of Leon Errol and Edgar Kennedy two-reelers, the slag from the Silver Age, that we used to get at the laff-movie-house in the Forties. He might get the mistaken impression that comedy still had a lot to learn in those days. The melancholy joke-milking, the endless double takes —these were *funny?* Well, yes—about as funny as kidnapping deans.

I was reminded of this by *The Party*, with Peter Sellers, which is about as close as we can now get to those two-reelers and is a lot better than most of them were. It has the trademark of old-fashioned social slapstick: the characters attend closely to their own business, as if nothing else were happening, until they are jarred to attention by some personal outrage; and after they have changed out of their wet clothes they return quietly to their grooves. The drunken butler, plowing solemnly through the inlaid pool, causes no comment; nor does he seem to surprise himself. He will not get any more drunk, nor any less drunk, so his part in society is fixed. The guests, meanwhile, are bent on their soup, maintaining civilization in the teeth of difficulties.

The one thing the old movie-makers did know is that two reels is more than enough for this stuff. Slapstick, even the best, is the most monotonous of forms, and *The Party* dissolves at last in dismal aquatics. (I don't get the falling-in-the-water joke and probably never will.) Peter Sellers does his Indian thing demurely, and for once his self-conscious underplaying is a kindness: it keeps the movie from palling for five minutes longer than nature intended.

One reel would be quite enough for *Inspector Clouseau*, but it might make a nice little reel. Alan Arkin is an expert physical comic, who easily passes the insane-concentration test: he plays to the subject, like a good monomaniac, and not to the audience. His practice of turning every foreign accent into Russian is, on the whole, sound—his interior life comes through as equal parts brute incomprehension and lively curiosity, and it is quite in order that, although raised in France, he would have acquired a foreign accent and missed the local one altogether.

The film winds down finally because the Arkin-joke has no other jokes to play with. Clouseau is a bungling detective for whom bungle-worthy situations must be continuously devised—which is like watching Pete Smith fall downstairs for two hours. (Pete Smith, medium-old fans will recall, made short films in the Forties that were long at ten minutes.) Present-day movies are generally cut to a certain length, whether designed to cover a giant or a midget idea, and comedy has suffered from this more than anyone. Once a joke has been made, it should not stand around grinning; Arkin is obliged to stretch his baggy pants to bursting while waiting for the vaudeville hook.

Movie comedy must expand, take in new themes or inflate the old one, or die. Stage comedy, on the other hand, can improvise within a Chinese box and never get any bigger. Thus, a play like *The Odd Couple* could simply state its business (Act One), twist it to the left (Act Two), and back to the right (Act Three), and everyone home to Scarsdale. But when it tries this on film, the theme simply gets weaker and weaker with each twist. (Since the same thing happened with *Luv, Barefoot in the Park,* and how many others, you would think someone would have learned something by now.)

But *The Odd Couple* has other troubles. It was a reasonably funny play, but always at the good pleasure of its actors. Two ex-husbands, goes the story, manage to re-create the awfulness of their respective marriages by rooming with each other. One is a slob, the other a fussbudget. Each must become steadily worse in recoil to the other. But there is a ceiling: the fussbudget cannot become an outright sissy; if he does, he is in a different kind of play.

On stage, Art Carney managed to function ferociously within these limits. He used the comic's classic weapon, insanity. His tidiness was not prissy but savage, maniacal, a ruthless fascist imposition of order, yet performed with a delicacy of movement quite mad in itself. One understood (and the play falls apart if one doesn't) how he and the slob could have been friends before their couplehood began, could have played poker together for years without plumbing the horror of each other's character. Carney's compulsion operates strictly within his own domestic setting, and mainly as a way of terrorizing his near ones. He probably doesn't even notice a spilled ashtray in other people's houses. Tidiness is a form of aggression which bores even its devotees when there is no one to fight with.

It goes without saying that Jack Lemmon, in the Rh-negative part, misses most of this. He has a gift for butchering good parts while managing to look intelligent, thus constituting Hollywood's abiding answer to the theater. His interpretation is plain fatuous, at once flighty and plodding. It seems that comedies of manners have a way of suffering in Hollywood, either because manners are simpler out there (how much can you do in a sport shirt?) or because the moguls feel that the average moviegoer eats off the floor before crawling, grunting, to his mattress.

Walter Matthau as the slob conveys the same elegance of feeling he conveyed on the stage. He knows who is master: the slump of his shoulders suggests a man forever waiting to be hit, as does the fast weave he uses for a walk. Sloppiness is a defensive tactic, requiring a sneaky stoicism. If you wait long enough, Mr. Clean will break his arm in the bathtub. It is worth any amount of suffering to see this. Suitably, Matthau is the one who is upset when the ménage breaks up: as a man of sensibility, he can become attached to even the ugliest situation. His friend, the blind effeminate fanatic, feels nothing and can batten on anybody.

The play said little of this. The movie says less.

Unintentional comedy is a form that has changed very little over the years. For instance, the recent *Interlude* is the very same movie that used to be called *Intermezzo* or *Late Prelude* or occasionally *Brief Rhapsody*: a rib-tickler chronicling the tragic love affair of an immensely talented musician and a fresh young sprig or broth (in the unlikely event it's set in Ireland) of a girl. Lines to expect are: "I think you'd better leave now," "I'll get my things," "Aren't we being unfair to Julia [Henry]?," "I don't care, I'm coming with you to Strasbourg [Tanglewood] [Bath]," "Rupert, please . . .," "Well, you've still got your music," "Yes—I know."

I'm not sure if any of these lines were actually spoken, because I was too busy admiring Oskar Werner's impeccably silly performance as Mr. Sensitive to take in much. Werner is ideal for these ladies'-magazine stories—he makes such a nice change from that coarse lout in the kitchen—and Virginia Maskell is a scream as his tortured wife (lines: "Is she very pretty? I don't want to know," "I'll get my things," etc.). Werner in fact displays as much feeling as a Mack truck, and the only proof we have of his genius is a series of enormous posters that follow him everywhere showing him glowering over his baton, but in the never-never land of *beat-me-Rudolph-but-don't-hurt-those-precious-hands* he is simply tops. I mention the film as a comedy sleeper. If you laughed at *Brief Encounter*, you will roar over this one.

In the same spirit of light summer hysteria, you might try *Blue*. Terrence Stamp has been reared by a bunch of toothy, desperate banditos, who have taught him to speak with a Southern accent for their own fiendish reasons—and it is certainly one of the most sublimely god-awful sounds y'all ever heard, ducks—and also to hate the wily white man. Alas for good intentions, Stamp falls athwart of Joanna Pettet (and that's exactly where he falls—right, plumb athwart), and, after a mess of heavy thinking and a-squinting and a-adjusting, he decides to defect to the Aryan devils. In the final take, he lugs the old bandit chief, who has always treated him like a son, across the old river to die; and I ask anyone who thinks that comedy is dead to glom this scene and see if it doesn't shake him a little bit more than somewhat.

To get back to the movies that are supposed to be funny: *Pru-*

dence and the Pill is the latest sex giggle out of England, a giggle that could pass for a death rattle in a lesser country. The sex revolution, such as it was, has here been domesticated and devitalized to the level of a muffins-and-marmalade middlebrow satire, full of mechanical high spirits, mechanical plot devices, and even a gamy old dowager to set things straight. The McGuffin (Hitchcock's word for a movie's excuse) is a three-minute spoken anecdote that should have stayed that way. Husband (David Niven) puts aspirin in the birth-pill bottle. So wife (Deborah Kerr) will have baby by other chap. *Flagrante delicto* and all that. Housemaid plunders pillbox and gets pregnant. Daughter—oh, forget it. Somebody had to do a funny pill film, and this is it, with tattered crinolines on. One can almost feel the elbow of the nineteenth-century commercial traveler crashing methodically into one's ribs as he tells "a good one" and hear the distant slapping of gaiters. There is even a mock-Dickensian ending, with everyone sporting a marvelous bouncing baby. Nature knows best, after all.

While poking thoughtfully among Granny's remains, down among the wax corsages and the used tea bags, one might also mention Noël Coward's *A Matter of Innocence*, which came and went this winter, leaving a slight trace of camphor and old knitting needles. Since this must have passed for high comedy once upon a time, it suggests that our ancestors had their problems in that area, too. It's all there, like Gatsby's neat, sad waltz, with a little Noël Coward wisdom about living your life when you're young and a little Noël Coward nastiness that takes it all back: live your own life, dearie, and become a tiresome old bitch, and, boomps-a-daisy, one of these days we'll write a song about you.

To end on a note someplace between platitude and confusion, the usual haunt of such discussions, Dudley Moore's *Thirty Is a Dangerous Age, Cynthia* is one of the most effective comedies seen recently, yet it is hard to say why. It appears to be modern, by virtue of jump cuts and over-all inconsequence, but is actually quite old-fashioned. It is a grab bag of familiar sequences—the private-eye parody, the Walter Mitty dreams of glory—strung on a preposterous story line, the way they used to do it. Its only distinguishing feature is perfection. Mr. Moore is a musician who has done his own score and his own comic choreography. And the consequence is a homogeneity of effect, a blend of movement and sound, that makes these dry clichés live. The Gordian knot is cut by genius, or the next thing to it. And this ultimately, when the spluttering is done and collars are loosened, seems to be one's theory of Comedy.

THE PRODUCERS

ARTHUR SCHLESINGER, JR.

The question before the house is: When can bad taste lead to good movies? There are certainly times when bad taste can be so outrageous, charming, and stylized that in some ghastly sense it works. I must confess myself, for example, a member of that very small minority which liked Billy Wilder's *Kiss Me, Stupid,* as well as of that somewhat larger minority entertained by *What's New Pussycat?* As old John Heywood used to put it, "Every man as he loveth, quoth the good man when he kissed the cow."

These reflections are incited by a terrible new film called *The Producers.* This film was written and directed by Mel Brooks, so the responsibility is clearly fixed. It seemed to me an almost flawless triumph of bad taste, unredeemed by charm or style. But I may be wrong. I had the uneasy impression that some of my colleagues in the screening room were already turning over in their minds rich phrases about the invention and audacity of Mel Brooks's black comedy.

Let me submit the evidence to the court. *The Producers* opens with a sequence in which Zero Mostel, playing a broken-down theatrical impresario, embraces a series of ladies in their sixties and seventies in the hope of extracting money from them for his next production. (One of the ladies, to her shame, is played by Estelle Winwood.) Funny? I gloomily consoled myself by supposing that the film had no alternative but to improve.

This was a miscalculation. The next sequence introduces a hysterical accountant, who, after considerable mincing and screaming, inadvertently shows the producer how, by overselling shares in his plays, he can make money so long as he confines himself to sure-fire flops. This leads to a frantic search for the worst play in the world —a drama comically entitled *Springtime for Hitler*, written by a still-devout Nazi—and for the worst director in the world, who makes his first appearance in drag. Finally a hippie is cast as Hitler. It will not surprise anyone who has followed me this far to learn that *Springtime for Hitler* becomes the biggest hit on Broadway.

Entrapped in this lulu is Zero Mostel, who does everything which gleaming eye, diabolical smile, overbearing truculence, and mock humility can do to justify his role. His accomplices include Gene Wilder as the accountant, Dick Shawn as the hippie, and a pretty girl named Lee Meredith. *The Producers* is warmly recommended for all those who regard the following things as hilarious: Hitler, Nazis, queers, hysterics, old ladies being pawed, and infantilism. In justice to Mr. Brooks, I should add that the film contains about four rather funny lines.

I LOVE YOU, ALICE B. TOKLAS

ARTHUR KNIGHT

The new Peter Sellers comedy, *I Love You, Alice B. Toklas*, is a picture that merely looks experimental, dealing as it does with the world of psychedelics, dropouts, and kooks. Actually, in both theme and treatment it bespeaks an utterly safe, conformist kind of experimentalism. When Sellers, playing a successful Los Angeles lawyer, joins up with the flower people through an altogether understandable infatuation with an elfin hippie, lovely Leigh Taylor-Young, we are invited to laugh at both him and them from a thoroughly bourgeois set of values. And if at the end, with a perhaps unconscious bow to *The Graduate*, Sellers races through the streets in search of "something better" than the middle-class respectability he seems doomed to return to, there is nothing to suggest in what preceded that he could or would recognize that "something better" even if it fell on him. The characterizations of the flower people are conventional, even comic-strip, but versatile Jo Van Fleet is marvelously funny in an updated version of the standard Jewish-mother bit.

CANDY

STEFAN KANFER

Experience teaches us never to trust anyone who is over-dirty; he is probably trying to hide something. In the case of *Candy*, the film-makers are trying to hide a number of things: lack of talent, wit, coherence. In its smirking promotion, *Candy* promotes itself as a piece of underground pornography that has miraculously reached the surface. It should have stayed under.

Candy is based on the Terry Southern–Mason Hoffenberg satirical novel in much the same way that an elephant might be based on a mouse. All that is left is a smear. Candy (Ewa Aulin), a teeny-bopper who seems to be mentally retarded, is molested by a series of dirty old men in odd cothing. They include a Mexican gardener (Ringo Starr), a poet (Richard Burton), a guru (Marlon Brando), a Minuteman general (Walter Matthau), a surgeon (James Coburn), and Candy's uncle and father—both played by John Astin. The attacks take place on a pool table and in a moving truck, a paratroop plane, a grand piano, a men's room, a police car, an Oriental temple, a Mercedes-Benz and a hospital room. In all cases, sex is represented by a lot of thrashing around under things like sheets, feathers, snow and water. When Candy does appear unclothed, she is coyly draped by her own tresses, à la Lady Godiva.

Having failed at titillation, the movie tries an onslaught of vulgarity. As if he had personally discovered the phallic symbol, director Christian Marquand presents a parade of hydrants, fingers, pointers and thermometers. Then he backs Candy up against a urinal, down on a toilet seat and up above a blood-soaked operating amphitheater. Yet with all his excesses, Marquand is a figure of refinement compared with scenarist Buck Henry (*The Graduate*), whose idea of humor is an aside to the heroine, "Why don't you put a meter on it and we'll all get rich?"

In its contempt for its audience, the film cannot be bothered with such niceties as acting. Men like Brando and Burton are never entirely inept, but, of all the performers, only Ewa Aulin in the title role comes off unstained—and that is because she is called upon only to look up, lie down and writhe her thighs. "Good Grief, it's Candy," says the ad for the film. The film itself says, Good Candy, it's Grief.

BARBARELLA

John Simon

A much less than tolerable entertainment is *Barbarella*. Granted, almost any film that starts with Jane Fonda in the nude is doomed to going downhill from there. But at least Miss Fonda, even if approximately clothed, remains omnipresent, lending grace, suavity, and a jocund toothsomeness to a foolish comic strip that emerges, in the movie version, a foolish comic strip. Terry Southern is the northernmost among some eight mostly French or Italian perpetrators of this science-fiction grotesque, a kind of Candy in the sky with zircons.

There are some interesting props and actors (in that order) involved, but they are put to flabby and self-indulgent use. Typical of Southern and of Roger Vadim, the director and Miss Fonda's husband, is the submersion of some vaguely funny lines and situations in masses of spurious chic and gutless parlor sadism. By the latter I mean a flaccid, jaded appeal to our baser appetites, always liberally doused with essence of cop-out, resulting in an elucubrated, anemic pornography. The only episode approaching true wit is one in which the cosmos-trotting heroine is to be tortured to death inside a pleasure machine, an orgasm organ; but that is a brazen plagia-

up eventually. Offer us incoherence, and we will tell you whether it is good incoherence. (In this case, it is lousy incoherence.) Call it nonlinear, and we will point out the lines for you. There is no such thing as formless art—any more than a thousand-pound woman is formless. It is just a matter of applying new measurements.

This scampering-dwarf aspect of criticism is tiresome for the people who wish to be left alone, to run their own fashion shows and prayer meetings and take up the collection without being heckled. But critics are masters of biologic adaptation and can follow you anywhere. If the object of your movie is simply to turn people on, all right, we'll judge it on that. We'll tell the fish whether it will turn them on satisfactorily or not. We'll also provide them with the names of the best nude cellists, the noblest soup cans, and the gooiest way to suck their thumbs, if that's what art is up to these days.

A movie like *You Are What You Eat* might retort, behind its hand, that a little pot is necessary for full appreciation and what would you guys know about that? Begging the question, we would observe that a little pot probably adds to the enjoyment of just about anything, including a blank TV screen, and that until we have an annual marijuana festival, and a panoply of accredited pot-head critics, we will just have to let that criterion go. It could be that *Lassie* would win such a festival paws down and *You Are, etc.* would finish nowhere. It could even be that the astounding success of Ed Sullivan and *The Sound of Music* can only be explained— But enough. Even critics do not engage in such necromantic conjecture.

The one interesting aspect of *You . . .* is the juxtaposition of the thumb business with much slathery tongue lolling and a brisk trade in Nazi helmets. Hippiedom has, like most movements, its fascist-infantile division, and the movie stumbles upon this—without for a moment indicating whether it is part of the expanded consciousness celebrated by the Reverend Yeah Yearh or an ugly regression which only a Norman O. Brown could love. *You . . .* is, though, for all its ineptitude and mental vacuity, a sincere piece of junk.

STAR!

ARTHUR SCHLESINGER, JR.

Other actresses were more beautiful than Gertrude Lawrence, or had better singing voices or greater dramatic range. But few have left, for my generation, such magical memories. I first saw her in *Nymph Errant*, a C. B. Cochran show with a Cole Porter score, at the Adelphi in London. It was—could it really have been? —thirty-four years ago. I was sixteen, and I still recall the curious enchantment of her performance. She died in 1952, and I suppose little is more unprofitable than exhorting the young about actresses they can no longer see. I can only say that Gertrude Lawrence was a rare one. She seemed invincibly sophisticated, but at the same time guyed her own sophistication. Her manner was infinitely romantic, but a mocking, satiric, sorrowful gaiety lurked behind every expression and every movement. Her "I love you" was the most subtly ambivalent of statements.

One shuddered to hear that *The Sound of Music* crowd—Robert Wise as director, Saul Chaplin as producer, Julie Andrews as star—had picked on this witty, spirited, stylish lady as the subject for their next bonanza after that ghastly saga of the Trapp family. The movies have given us too many feeble cinematic imitations of vivid players. It seemed preposterous to plunge Gertrude Lawrence, of all people, into a bath of lushly photographed and orchestrated saccharinity.

It is a pleasure to report that, whatever the mediocrities of the film, Julie Andrews has done something very close to justice to Miss Lawrence. Hers is a brilliant, indeed a stunning, performance. Liberated from the Trapps and Mary Poppins, she shows herself no longer the Mary Martin of the movies but astute, complex, and even sexy. She not only revives the astringencies she displayed long ago in *My Fair Lady* and *The Americanization of Emily*, but re-creates to an extraordinary degree the flair, excitement, and even physical appearance of Gertrude Lawrence.

Otherwise *Star!* is a routine, overblown musical, filled with the familiar stereotypes and falsities. Miss Lawrence, according to William Fairchild's implacably banal screenplay, traversed the same old course which every backstage beauty has gone through in every backstage film anyone has ever seen. It is an anthology of clichés, filled with such lines as "I want everything to last—all the excitement, all the good things."

It is sad to think that Robert Wise, who worked on *Citizen Kane* and *The Magnificent Ambersons* and as late as 1961 brought a certain visual tension to *West Side Story*, should have become such a hack. One finds it hard to believe in anything in *Star!*, apart from Julie Andrews. The private moments are straight out of the Sunday supplement; the alleged reenactments of great moments in musical comedy lack all plausibility; and the gay parties, as reproduced in the film, must have been among the most appalling in history.

Noël Coward, stiffly impersonated by Daniel Massey, is passable at the piano but all wrong when he attempts a scene from *Private Lives*. Richard Aldrich, who, for all I know, is a pleasant and unassuming man, comes off—evidently with his own permission—as a character of notable charmlessness and complacency. Even history is garbled: *Charlot's Revue* arrives in New York in 1924 without Beatrice Lillie.

Forget it, though. Gertrude Lawrence was marvelous, and so is Julie Andrews.

FINIAN'S RAINBOW

ARTHUR KNIGHT

Back in 1947, when *Finian's Rainbow* was the hottest ticket on Broadway, one of the charms of the show—quite apart from its lilting score and adroit lyrics—was the novelty of seeing a musical that seemed to be attacking racism head on. Its producers could also boast, quite properly, that theirs was the first Broadway production to employ a fully integrated chorus of singers and dancers. My, how progressive it all seemed some twenty years ago! My, how quaint it all appears today! How well-meaning! How simpleminded!

For the sad fact is that too much has happened in the intervening time; the ugly face of racism has come too close for anyone today to regard *Finian's* goodhearted, lighthearted magic as even a palliative to the problem. Wisely, the people at Warners have made no attempt to make us believe that it is. They have not updated it with references to Black Panthers or white supremacy, they have not sharpened the conflict or pointed the dialogue. They have left it just the lovely show it was—tuneful, well-intended, occasionally funny, always appealing.

The only changes they have made, so far as I can recall, are all for the better. The basic structure remains pretty much the same; after all, the screenplay is credited to E. Y. Harburg and Fred Saidy, who also wrote the show. Woody (Don Francks), the hero, has been made less wooden, less the stock labor organizer of the Thirties; and Henry (Al Freeman, Jr.) is now a research scientist temporarily forced into servitude to a reactionary Southern Senator. His slow-motion portage, à la Stepin Fetchit, of a glass of Bromo-Seltzer *must* be the comedic highlight of the entire film.

But best of all—the thing that makes *Finian's Rainbow* unique among contemporary musicals—is the canny utilization of its stellar cast. No one comes on like a star; each has been fitted neatly and completely into his own particular niche, and each serves himself best by serving the over-all pattern. Petula Clark, England's favorite "pops" singer, invests Ella Logan's old role with a beat and an accent that neither cancel out their creator nor sound like a hand-me-down imitation; Miss Clark is an authentic original in her own right. Tommy Steele, as is his wont, tends to oversell what David Wayne so gracefully shrugged away. But Fred Astaire, as Finian (a nonsinging role in the original), remains forever graceful and relaxed, never pushing for more than is required, never giving less than is due. His final shot, skipping jauntily off toward the horizon, has all the poignance of a Chaplin fadeout—plus the heartening assurance that it ain't necessarily so. By staying completely in its period, and doing everything supremely well, this *Finian's Rainbow* transcends time. Like Astaire himself, it seems ageless.

OLIVER!

JOSEPH MORGENSTERN

Oliver! redeems the whole rotten year. The most important thing about this musical version of *Oliver Twist* is pleasure, the sheer delight of a movie that can change the lives of kids who see it—for the better, for the better—and serve as a public bath for adults to luxuriate in, sing in, get cleansed in. The next most important thing is that the director, Carol Reed, the choreographer, Onna White, the fine cast and all the other artists who turned Dickens' novel and Lionel Bart's show into another new entity have also gone a long way toward redeeming the vitality of the movie musical as a species.

If a single word can suggest the essence of *Oliver!*, it is vitality. The film seldom flags, and when it does it renews itself almost instantly. The worst letdown is intermission. How many movies can you say that about? The break comes just when Oliver has made it from the teeming London markets to a placid Bloomsbury town house. But moments after the second half starts you find, in the "Who Will Buy?" sequence, that Reed and Miss White are just as good at catching us up in riches as in rags.

Most movies these days, and especially most movie musicals, leave a distinct impression that they've given you their all, barrel scrapings included. *Oliver!* gives a constant sense of life's super-abundance. Name anything good in the film and there always seems to be more where it came from: Oliver's strength and intelligence, Fagin's wit, Nancy's passion, the prodigal invention of such brilliant production numbers as "Food, Glorious Food," "You've Got to Pick a Pocket or Two," "I'd Do Anything," "Oom-Pah-Pah," "Who Will Buy?," and "Consider Yourself," in which Fagin's glue-fingered street phantoms sweep Oliver through John Box's wonderful sets like some Victorian version of the Red Guards.

And where did the good stuff come from to begin with? Dickens, of course, provided the original cornucopia, an inexhaustible supply of life in all its tumult. Lionel Bart provided a tunesmith's score, strong in the way a blacksmith's work is strong, but badly in need of complementary finesse that it never got in the American stage production. The score never got movement, either—the Broadway show was not choreographed, remarkably enough—and that is Miss White's great gift, a series of dances that not only move and sweep and build and swirl, but do so for sound dramatic reasons. Finally, with as much of an "of course" as for Dickens, the controlling taste and intelligence came from Reed, the director, who fused all his disparate parts into a whole.

Since Reed is the man who did *The Fallen Idol* and *A Kid for Two Farthings*, the perfection of his Oliver comes as no surprise. Played by an angelically beautiful boy named Mark Lester, Oliver is also smart and tough and has a terrible temper, and he and Jack Wild, as the Artful Dodger, sustain remarkably long takes and scenes together. Since Reed is also the man who did *Odd Man Out*, *The Third Man*, and *An Outcast of the Islands*, it's no surprise that his action sequences sing or that his attention to detail is sure, right down to Bill Sikes' hideous pit bulldog.

Yet surprises there are aplenty, and nothing from the past prepares you for them: the beauty of Oliver holding his porridge bowl up to Mr. Bumble (Harry Secombe) and saying, "Please, sir, I want some more"; the devastating simplicity of Oliver singing "Where Is Love?"; Fagin's entrance through a curtain of steam, like some nightmare Ninotchka; Ron Moody's warmth, humor and authentic nastiness in that character, a much richer one than Alec Guinness developed in David Lean's *Oliver Twist* twenty years ago; Shani Wallis' vibrant Nancy, a lover of life possessed by demons; and Oliver Reed's Bill Sikes, the meanest demon of them all. The spectrum of Dickens' reality has inevitably been filtered, this being a musical comedy and not a plea for social reform, but there's still plenty of shock and squalor too.

While few seams show in the production (and none in Oswald Morris' lovely color photography), *Oliver!* does have its faults. "It's a Fine Life" is a poor tune whose poor lyrics make unnecessary comments on the drama. Miss Wallis, rather then Nancy, seems to suffer a temporary loss of authority in "As Long as He Needs Me." Nancy's death scene doesn't work very well, even though Vernon Harris' screenplay has wisely transferred it from her bedroom to an off-camera corner of the Thames Embankment. These are small matters, however, in a film of such extraordinary grace and unity. Only time will tell if it is a great film, but it is certainly a great experience. Please, sir, I want some more.

8

VIOLENT GENRES

THE BRIDE WORE BLACK

Andrew Sarris

François Truffaut's *The Bride Wore Black* has been reviewed as if it were a filmed sequel to Truffaut's book on Alfred Hitchcock. But it isn't. Whereas Hitchcock is basically a genre director, Truffaut's temperament is closer to the sprawling humanism of Renoir. Of course, no director can memorize the life's work of another director without picking up a few tricks and ideas along the way. When Charles Denner's pathologically lecherous artist delicately poses Jeanne Moreau in the white tunic of Diana the huntress, the image of James Stewart adjusting Kim Novak's coiffure in Hitchcock's *Vertigo* comes immediately to mind with all its romantic reverberations. (The fact that Miss Moreau, like Miss Novak, is too substantial for the ethereal spirit of the illusion only heightens the resemblance.) Also, the mere fact that *The Bride Wore Black* is a violent melodrama with a soupçon of suspense is sufficient grounds for most critics to tag Truffaut with a Hitchcock label. However, even Renoir is not entirely a stranger to violent melodrama. The murders in *La Chienne, La Bête humaine, The Crime of Monsieur Lange* and *The Rules of the Game* are as memorable as any in the history of the cinema. But these murders do not make Renoir a genre director. Renoir's feeling for life flows over the violence like an inexhaustible torrent of tenderness. Whereas Renoir proudly sacrifices form (and art) for truth, Hitchcock salvages truth from an art that rigorously obeys the rules of the game. Truffaut breaks the rules of the genre without abandon-

162

ing the genre, and thus teeters precariously between Hitchcock and Renoir without committing himself entirely to either.

Truffaut begins *The Bride Wore Black* by plunging into the action before its premises have been established. Thus, the heroine has committed two murders and is well on her way to her third before the audience is informed of her motive. Truffaut's storytelling is thus anti-Hitchcockian in that it sacrifices suspense for mystification. Once the audience is implicated in the lyricism of Moreau's murderousness, it is too late to measure her motivation. *The Bride Wore Black* succeeds, therefore, as a *fait accompli*. Truffaut manages even to get away with a big hole in the plot. We are told that the heroine is tracking down five men who were involved in the prankishly accidental murder of her husband as he was descending the steps of the church with his bride on his arm, an overwhelmingly Orphic piece of sexual imagery reminiscent of a similar incident in Sam Fuller's *Forty Guns*. We see the five men playing cards in the hotel room and then joking about the long-range capabilities of a hunting rifle. We see one man load it for fun and another man fire it by accident. We see the bridegroom falling and falling and falling. We see the action in various speeds and colors until it is engraved on our minds with the reality of a recurring nightmare. But we are never told how the bride learned the identities of her bridegroom's murders. By simply showing us the murderers, Truffaut discharges his obligations to the genre. If he had wanted us to think more seriously about the premise of the plot, he would have told us much sooner. As it is, the director's procrastination is justified by the wildly unconvincing casting of Jeanne Moreau as a vengeful bride turned into a true *femme fatale*. Truffaut conceived Moreau's character as a Hawksian heroine divested of her sexual sophistication for the sake of the severe intelligence her revenge demanded. The result is a performance from Moreau so dully deadpan that the interest shifts inevitably to her male victims, all of whom rise to the challenge with vivid glimpses of life and desire on the brink of death.

Consequently, *The Bride Wore Black* derives its dramatic power from the irony of an illusion. The bride of vengeful death enters the lives of five men as a temptress. She is unreal, unconvincing, and discouragingly uncooperative, but it doesn't matter. Her victims will grasp at any straw that promises even a moment of pleas-

ure. Michael Bouquet's born loser is especially moving as an evocation of muddled middle-aged hopefulness in the presence of a
sexual fantasy come to life. If Moreau's character were at all real,
it would be impossible to forgive her for her mercilessness to this
particularly pathetic child of woman. But because of the displaced
sensibility of the film, the men are too real for the genre, and
Moreau too fantastic. Thus a second film emerges over the
smudged design of the first, a film more interesting than the first
because it is closer to Truffaut's true feelings. This second film
concerns the obsession of men with the ever-receding realities of
women.

What Truffaut has taken from William Irish's action novel is
the urgency of a melodramatic situation, the urgency without
which Truffaut's feelings would spill out over the edges of his
frames until more of him would be off screen than on. What
Truffaut has taken from Hitchcock is an adroitness in balancing
abruptness of action with a meandering for meaning so that every
characterization can be enriched with an intimation of inevitability. The difference between Truffaut and Hitchcock is the difference between a life style and a dream world. Truffaut's males are
derived from the director's sense of reality devoid of melodrama. If
Hitchcock and Irish had not intervened, Truffaut's lecherous males
would talk on night after night about all the women they'd laid
and about all the women they wanted to lay, until even their lechery would disintegrate in the lassitude of an uneventful life. By
contrast, Hitchcock's characters are designed expressly for their
genre functions in the sense that they correspond to conflicting
impulses in the director's personality. Hitchcock is what he is, and
Renoir is what he is, but Truffaut is still suspended between an art
of meaningful forms and a world of changing appearances. Still,
The Bride Wore Black is a film of undeniable if uncertain beauty,
by virtue of its director's critical intelligence in an era of mindless
lyricism.

BULLITT

Hollis Alpert

It never fails to surprise me to find film critics complaining about the lack of thought in American movies; with crystalline perception they tell us, in all the wisdom of their naïveté, that movies are made for commercial reasons, that, since they cost money, they are aimed at earning that money back. Since this state of affairs has been true since the days of *The Great Train Robbery,* one wonders what particular purpose is served by using that sort of critical yardstick. I find more interesting those who sense that film art sometimes develops out of and because of its restrictions, namely commercial considerations. The time is long overdue, it seems to me, when we must forget about "thought" in movies and concentrate on what makes them work or not work.

A case in point is the current *Bullitt,* financed by Warner Brothers–Seven Arts at a cost of $5,000,000 or so. Wherever the money went, we may be sure it did not go for anything resembling thought; they simply don't pay for that at Warner's or anywhere else. They paid about a fifth of it for Steve McQueen, and another fifth probably for an item called "studio overhead," and the remainder went into the various facets of production. Standard operating procedure these days, and yet *Bullitt* strikes me as one of the best movies I've seen this year: it has energy, drive, impact, and, above all, style.

How one attains that elusive last-mentioned quality is a matter of great and continuing concern to the professionals involved in movie-making. The scriptwriter, of course, can indicate some of it, but scripts tend to be dry documents. The script of *Bullitt* can't have been anything much. It has the same old nefarious "organization," the police detectives, the politically oriented district attorney, the pretty girl who sleeps with the detective. Mix the elements together and you've got a few dozen movies you've already seen. But add Peter Yates, the director, and William Fraker, the photographer, and Albert Brenner, the art director, and Frank Keller, the film editor, and the mixture then becomes unique.

Among them (with McQueen's expert participation) they have fashioned the most exciting fifteen minutes of cinema I've seen in I don't know how long—namely, an extended automobile sequence fraught with menace, chills, and a pit-of-the-stomach sense of participation. It takes us right back to the essentials of what first fascinated us in movies, but it is made more potent by sophisticated use of today's technology—and art. There may be a lack of thought in the sequence, but I have the nagging feeling that one might find meaning in it, for if it were merely visceral I doubt that it would have as much effect. Throughout the film one gets the sense that Peter Yates (and his accomplice, Mr. Fraker) are looking at the artifacts of this last third of the twentieth century with a clear but astonished vision. They show it to us real and also strange. Both are experts in the use of visual language. To simply term *Bullitt* "commercial" is to overlook the development of style, with all its implications.

TARGETS

PENELOPE GILLIATT

The Lady of Shalott looked at the river in her mirror, on and on. She was sitting at her loom, I think. ("Isn't anything going to happen?") Perhaps she threw her shuttle at some water voles, or imagined a combat to the death between fish. Everyone needs action. Stanislavski once said that the most interesting thing an actor can do on stage is fry an egg. Now, Peter Bogdanovich's *Targets* is supposed to be a polemic film in favor of gun control, but as you watch the central maniac's ghastly spree of sharpshooting, the repulsive thing is that you begin to look at it as if it were Julia Child slicing onions and cutting pastry on TV. The picture has a clumsy, diagrammatic plot (wanly acted, and fidgety to sit through) about the convergence of Boris Karloff, playing a Karloff-type aged star sickened by a career of blood, and Tim O'Kelly, as a clean-cut young man who goes berserk with a car-trunkful of guns. The sa-

lient and absurd truth about the experience of watching the film is
that you horribly want the assassin on the Los Angeles Freeway to
hit every far-off target in the heart, *because nothing else is happening.* You get impatient when his magnified finger presses the trigger of a perfectly aimed rifle and there isn't any ammunition left.
The dialogue scenes before the mayhem have been so void that you
have no sense that anyone in the film is alive. What you seem to be
watching is a technical job of work briskly done, like spring clean-
ing. Every time a person is killed through the madman's telescopic
sights, the action appears not as a murder but as a small achieved
task—another closet attacked and conquered by vacuum cleaner.
With nothing else going on, you are bound to fret when the bullet
misses. I don't believe for a second that this response lays bare any
ponderous truth about the violence latent in us all, blah blah. It is
simply that one psychically needs to see the event completed. In
better art, the strong natural lure of physical action is subsumed.
Hamlet roots out in you no great residual longing to see the sword
go home through the arras, because more interesting things are
happening. But a film like *Targets* turns us into a hall of brutalized
goons, gluttonous for neat, distant kills. The picture offers you a
filthy expertise by proxy. You become the surrogate technician. It
seems very nearly *your* finger on the trigger, *your* eye controlling
the sights, *you* dealing death at the far end of a telescopic rifle,
remote from motive or consequence.

I know the film was made in hard circumstances, on a small
budget, and it is only fair to say that the visual elements—as opposed to the performances—are skillfully commanded. But it
seems to me a fantastically foolish picture. How intellectually cha-
otic to make a gun-control parable so empty of any comprehension
of the people in it that the only response left to an audience is to
recline with a bag of popcorn and lust after a manly score of assassinations. Did Bogdanovich know what he was doing? Did he deliberately mean the film to demonstrate something about how anti-
thought all photographed action tends to be, how inhospitable to
sustained ideas the cinema is, how rabidly interesting it makes the
fitful and physical? Maybe. But, if so, the ironic point isn't detect-
able. There is no way to take a simple-minded film but simple-
mindedly. To get an audience to experience some primitive reaction and then to summon up the complex critical intelligence to in-
spect and disown that reaction needs the whole theatrical apparatus

of a Brecht production, keeping its brain, and yours, at full stretch. *Targets* innocently turns out to be plain rabble fodder, and you sit there munching it.

WILD 90

Hollis Alpert

We can all relax. Norman Mailer has approved the movies; he has actually gone and made one called *Wild 90*, thus revealing that the printed page is not sufficient to contain his large and spreading talent, which has now spilled over—"flushed" is perhaps the better word—onto the screen. This being a first film effort, we probably should not be overly severe in judging it. One the other hand, would Mr. Mailer be overly generous in judging a first novel that had no art, craft, wit, or purpose in being? Would he not, instead, suggest to so ungifted an author that he take up some other and more fitting pursuit, such as writing schlock screenplays? Well, I can't speak for Mr. Mailer; I can only speak for my own wounded sensibilities, having sat through ninety of the dullest, saddest, most boring minutes of my life. Add to those ninety the thirty it took me to get to the place of screening. I won't count the thirty it took me to get back, because they were filled with a blessed sense of relief.

Mailer is guilty, I'm afraid, of overstatement right in the beginning. There is his title. The ninety minutes to which it refers are not wild. They are noisy, and most of the noise is made by Mailer, who, as principal player in a turgid nondrama—presumably a turgid nonfiction nondrama—barks sometimes like a dog and sometimes like a seal. When something approaching human language emerges from the overmodulated sound track, it is invariably an obscenity or a string of obscenities. Poor Molly Bloom and her soliloquy are made to seem prissy and mid-Victorian by comparison. I, for one, haven't heard anything approaching it since I shared a barracks with some draftees during basic training. There's even the

same stale joke about a bird and some cow droppings; it gave me a
distinct sense of nostalgia to hear it.

But here I am implying that Mailer is solely responsible for those
ninety minutes, when the credits don't say he has *directed* the picture, they only say it's his; "Norman Mailer's *Wild 90*" doesn't
necessarily imply direction. But he is certainly the star, for we see
and hear him continually. He shadowboxes, stares fitfully at himself in a mirror, lovingly fondles a rifle, a pistol, and a submachine
gun, stomps an orange crate, and sadistically enrages a poor, bewil-
dered police dog. I forgot something: he also kisses a girl. You
haven't seen anything in the way of screen lovers until you see
Norman Mailer kiss a girl. The setting is a large, grimy room, a
kind of hideout for three mugs, of whom Mailer plays one, called
the Prince. As far as I was able to gather, they have knocked over a
string of grocery stores and are planning the next caper, another
grocery store. None of the three likes the others, and they all sit
around mumbling or yelling obscenities. Now and then someone
knocks at the door. When whoever it is enters, Mailer yells (barks,
rather) at them. They yell back. The police dog barks back—
understandably.

This goes on and on, while a man listed as D. A. Pennebaker
zooms in and out with a camera that appears to be held by a punch-
drunk writer. No reason for the zooms, or the close-ups, or for any
shot whatsoever. Toward the end, Mailer imperiously halts the
nonaction and incoherently barks directly to the audience, the
most egotistic moment of all, for he is clearly assuming that there
will be one. It seems he's sending up the CIA, or something like
that. Maybe it was the FBI. It would have helped to have subtitles.

I guess Mailer had fun making the movie, and maybe that does
justify its having been done. There's a distinct air of psychodrama
about it, of a therapeutic regurgitation for the participants. Maybe,
now that he has this movie out of his system, he can go back to his
typewriter, refreshed and released from writer's cramp. And you
certainly have to give him *some* kind of credit for this naked revelation of his personality—or at least certain aspects of his personality. A lady sitting next to me kept sighing through it. "How sad,
how sád, how sad," she sighed, she moaned, she wailed. I sensed
that she grieved for talent misused, for ego inflated, for the art of
letters mocked, the art of film excreted upon. Is not the obtaining
of this response a kind of triumph for Mailer, after all? But, if he

will excuse a vulgar paraphrase, it was not *Wild 90* this lady grieved for. She grieved for thee.

BEYOND THE LAW

STANLEY KAUFFMANN

I don't really want to review Norman Mailer's new film, but I'd like to say why. *Beyond the Law* is one more piece of almost maniacal self-indulgence, abetted by Mailer's idolatrous friends, without merit or interest except as it affords a peek, for those who care, into the private games of Mailer and pals pretending to be cops and criminals and hippies. (George Plimpton appears briefly as himself pretending to be the mayor who visits the police station where a lot of it happens. Alan Alda is better as Plimpton, in *Paper Lion*, than Plimpton is.)

Those who are dedicated to finding value in everything that Mailer does can find more of it here, I'm sure. Those who find something of *vérité* in every foot of film that's exposed by egotistical amateurs can write their reams about this picture's relevance to role-playing in modern life. Good luck to them. I take this film simply as a part of the price for having Mailer around. He splashes about, he jostles, he elbows, he irritates; in his ambition (announced at the last New York Film Festival) to be a Renaissance man, he overlooks one small detail: Leonardo didn't merely work in several fields, he was good in all of them. But Mailer is also the man who could write *Armies of the Night* and *Miami and the Siege of Chicago* in one year. Those books, particularly the first, are not exactly free of arrogance and solecism, but they are the outpourings of a potentially *large* writer who has at last found his moment. Ever since the Second World War, about which he wrote the best American novel, he has always been just out of step: a Depression child when the Depression mind-set no longer applied; a Jew when it became difficult to suffer in America for being Jewish; a white man when the drama became black; a middle-aged man when the action became young. With the Pentagon march last year and the political conventions this year, the man and the moment coincided, and as an author he became what he has always longed to be, an agonist-prophet of our time, embodying many of us in his ego, possessed by burning insight.

It's silly to wish he would stop making films, as it would be silly to wish he would stop writing his time-filling fiction or embarrassing articles like his defense of his friend Podhoretz' *Making It* in *Partisan Review*. One might as well wish that he would stop getting drunk in public. His films are part of the same urge, I think: a frenzy to grab at everything, every possibility of sensibility and power—which he tries to hide under the label "Renaissance man." I don't review his adolescent binges in life, and I don't see any reason to review his dreams-of-glory films. But after I saw *Beyond the Law* and was ready once again to write off Mailer as one more man exploded out of his head by the sheer size of contemporary experience, I read the Miami-Chicago book in *Harper's*. Here's a passage in which he explains why Chicago people remind him of the people in Brooklyn where he grew up:

> . . . they were simple, strong, warm-spirited, sly, rough, compassionate, jostling, tricky and extraordinarily good-natured because they had sex in their pockets, muscles on their backs, hot eats around the corner, neighborhoods which dripped with the sauce of local legend, and real city architecture, brownstones with different windows on every floor, vistas for miles of red-brick and two-family wood-frame houses with balconies and porches, runty stunted trees rich as farmland in their promise of tenderness, the first city evenings of spring, streets where kids played stickball and roller-hockey, lots of smoke and iron twilight. The clangor of the late nineteenth century, the very hope of greed, was in those streets. London one hundred years ago could not have looked much better.

O.K. If we have to have Mailer's films (he has just finished another) as part of the price of an author who can cascade like that, O.K.

WILL PENNY

ARTHUR KNIGHT

Onto the screen in the blue-cold moments before dawn rides a strange new hero for an American Western, although the familiar, craggy features are those of Charlton Heston. He is Will Penny, a range-weary, range-hardened saddle tramp who knows that his years of usefulness are fast nearing an end, and that somehow, for all his expertise with horse and rope, life has passed him by. There is no self-pity about the man, however, nor even a play for sympathy. Age is a fact of life, as much as the heat on the trail in summer or snow in the mountains in winter; one can only accept, and do the best he can.

For Will the test comes when, after being beaten, knifed, and left for dead by a gang of freebooters, he holes up in a cabin with a young woman (Joan Hackett) and her son. Although she is en route to California to join her husband on his pioneer farm, her enforced propinquity with the rugged ranch hand engenders first admiration, then love. By the end of the picture, while returning her love, Will realizes that it is far too late, that he is too old to settle down and start a farm or a ranch of his own. In a fadeout reminiscent of *Shane*, he rides toward the horizon, leaving behind the woman and the child, the only people in the world who recognize his value as a man.

All this is told with rare lack of adornment or sentimentality—albeit perhaps a few too many words—in Thomas S. Gries's action-filled script. Gries, who also directed *Will Penny*, obviously cares deeply not only about his character, but about the West itself, a way of life—and a breed of men—long since vanished. As a result, his film lacks most of the accouterments of the standard, standardized Western. There are no shoot-outs, no fancy dance-hall girls, no scraggle-beard comics, no hard-pressed heroic sheriffs (and no villainous ones, either). More than any film of recent years, it resembles a small-scale *Shane* in its appeal to the emotions, and the masterful *Ride the High Country* in its accenting of frontier authenticity.

For accurate comparisons, however, one must turn back to the stories of Bret Harte and the movies of William S. Hart, America's first great cowboy star. Both created a version of the West out of their own experiences, setting a handful of characters against the crude, raw, colorful background of the United States's territorial expansion in the last half of the nineteenth century. The marvel of *Will Penny* is that, a century after Bret Harte, half a century after Bill Hart, it achieves much of their same sense of this is the way it was.

The picture's tradition, to be precise, is the West, not the Western; and everyone connected with its production—the cast, Lucien Ballard for his evocative color photography, David Raksin for his always apposite score, and, of course, Mr. Gries—deserves thanks for so affectingly re-creating it for us.

WILD IN THE STREETS

JOSEPH MORGENSTERN

Before you can decode and digest the contents of American International's *Wild in the Streets,* you must accept the notion that an abysmally crude, cheap, incoherent, dishonest, contemptible motion picture made for no other motive than profit can nevertheless also have enormous brute force and considerable significance.

American International is the company that used to flood the youth market with inexpensive, almost absurdly innocent ghost stories (*I Was a Teen-age Werewolf*) and beach pictures (*How to Stuff a Wild Bikini*). In the past couple of years, however, the firm has been keeping up with its own cynical, astute reading of contemporary culture by offering kids such ominous trash as *The Wild Angels* (fascists on motorcycles) and *The Trip* (a lyrical tribute to lysergic acid). *Wild in the Streets,* then, is the latest in a lengthening line of shoddy goods that serves youth what it wants, or what adults think it wants, or what adults are willing to pretend it wants if there's enough money in the pretense.

Taken at face value as pop fantasy, this film is the inevitable, occasionally hilarious extension of the youth rebellion that is sweeping the world. A twenty-four-year-old-singer (Christopher Jones) becomes President of the United States. In a speech directed at the Eisenhower-LBJ generations he says, "What do you ask a sixty-year-old man? You ask him if he wants his wheelchair facing the sun or facing away from the sun." His twenty-five-year-old mistress (Diane Varsi) stands up from her newly won Congressional seat in a John Paul Jones hat and a vinyl vest, completely stoned and tapping a tambourine, to demand that the voting age be reduced to eighteen, or sixteen, or possibly fourteen. The legislation is pushed through after all the kids of the nation immobilize its streets and highways and dump LSD into the old folks' reservoirs.

Robert Thom's script makes some powerful appeals to the emotions, but rarely makes specific sense. Yet that is the point: the mindlessness is the message. *Wild in the Streets* is anti-Vietnam, antiwar, anti–foreign policy (*any* foreign policy), antirationalist (the President's "brain trust" consists of little lotus eaters, pot smokers and mind blowers) and, certainly, anti-youth. All adults are frauds or fools, but the youthocracy also finds its own form of fascism, setting up concentration camps to which all citizens are dispatched at the compulsory retirement age of thirty.

Unlike *Privilege*, which treated the same subject with a pretentious commitment to style, *Wild in the Streets* has the idiot courage, and therefore the power, of its crudity. It is a witch's brew prepared in the pressure cooker of commerce. It tries to have everything at least both ways: a blackshirted dictatorship that sends free grain to the world's hungry, an assassination attempt on a Kennedy-like President who is also a doddering demagogue by the time he is twenty-five. It is nothing substantial and everything urgent, and most of all it is an infinitely extensible shoe that fits white youth, Black Panthers, Red Guards, John Birchers, the poor, the disenfranchised, the powerless, anyone and any group cursed with want and doubly cursed with not knowing what to want.

WILFRID SHEED

Wild in the Streets is a Max Rafferty nightmare of what will happen to America if we keep on coddling those kids. What they will do is take over the country, is what they'll do (they'll outnumber us by 1974 or sometime, if you count toddlers and small boys too fat to move), and send us all off to old people's play camps. Since the movie's release coincided more or less with our spring riots, one imagines the nation's jumpier parents sending out for another two billion guns or so to preempt the first strike. Yet the cast includes such petition-signing liberals as Shelley Winters and Hal Holbrook. One wonders what they thought the film was saying and to whom.

Hollywood's hysterical fear of adolescents probably has something to do with having to drive bumper-to-bumper with them all day at speeds which make grownups nervous. Or something. But even allowing that our youths are all fascist beasts and political lunatics, and that they are capable of the degree of concentration and organization called for here, it requires a special Beverly Hills paranoia to suppose that they could jimmy political power from the adult world. Because, even if you got every infant to the polls and persuaded it not to vote for Daddy or Smokey the Bear, and even if they did all vote for the same pop singer (a miracle in itself), they would still not be able to run the country—for reasons too childish to go into.

Well, it's just a satire, says the movie. Didn't you see, we had Shelley Winters in there? But what, one wonders, is the point of this kind of satire? If kids do not have, and cannot have, the economic or physical power to take over the country, why pretend that they do? Why frighten a lot of aging homeowners needlessly with a rumble of straw teen-agers? Student rebellion is much too important and nuanced a question for witless caricature right now.

Aesthetically, silly satire is a bad form. You should believe what you're seeing while you're seeing it. Once you've gobbled down the premise, the rest should slide down back of it. But in this case the mind gags again and again. Our beloved political machinery is simplified out of sight: there are no delegates to be wooed, no convention; no coattails, no filimandering pork-busting, no Cook County voting machines; and it still seems incredible.

9

CLINICAL CASES

PRETTY POISON

JOSEPH MORGENSTERN

No matter how much of a marvel it may be, a movie that is maltreated at birth has little chance of making it later on. A truly marvelous thriller called *Pretty Poison* popped up recently after no advance publicity, almost no press previews, no first-run engagement and little critical support. Critics—and customers—tend to greet small, underprivileged films in the same way that teachers in slum schools tend to regard their pupils, as bad or dumb until proved otherwise.

Not that *Pretty Poison* looks small or underprivileged. It looks great, as a matter of fact. The film was shot in and around Great Barrington, Massachusetts, and David Quaid's incisive color photography heightens the sad beauty of an old New England mill town that has seen better days and almost forgotten them. Tony Perkins and Tuesday Weld give a pair of superb performances as a disturbed young loner and his bewitchingly innocent, twitchingly all-American honor-roll student and drum majorette of a girl friend. Lorenzo Semple, Jr.'s screenplay, based on a novel by Stephen Geller, sustains a level of wit and tension that few modern films aspire to, let alone achieve. And, wonder of wonders, the director of this modest, almost flawless entertainment is a thirty-one-year-old American, Noel Black, who had done *Skater-Dater*, a stylish short about kids on skateboards, but had never directed a feature film until producer Lawrence Turman put him to work on this one.

Pretty Poison starts with a beautifully sly-solemn scene in which

176

Perkins is about to be sprung from prison, or maybe from an insane asylum. "You're going out into a very real and very tough world," his earnest probation officer warns him. "It's got no place for fantasies." Quick cut to reality: Miss Weld in her majorette outfit, waving her baton to beat the band and giving a distinct impression that the film is up to something special.

And so it is. Perkins' fantasies are funny enough, but disturbingly sinister. At home in a trailer he listens furtively to short-wave radio. On the job in a chemical plant he watches red gunk being spewed into a river and broods about the pollution of the entire Eastern seaboard. Increasingly bent on mayhem, he snaps surreptitious shots of the factory with his little Minox, squints with a perpetual wind in his face, sets his jaw with schizoid valor and, posing as a CIA agent, enlists Miss Weld's help.

The marriage of their elegant performances and Semple's high-style dialogue must really have been made in heaven. Semple is the writer who set the tone for *Batman* on TV, and you can readily hear a common denominator in his ability to devise an artificial style and stick with it through thick or thin. In *Batman* it has generally been thin. Here, however, Semple leads us like lambs to the slaughter of a plot twist, turns parody on and off at will, and holds our interest as the story hustles its way to a slightly fuzzy but certainly serviceable denouement.

If the style is intriguing, the substance is no less so: pollution of our rivers, streams, and spirits, the fantasies America lives, guilt and innocence and the camouflage they wear. This is a lot for a ninety-minute movie to have on its mind, yet Black builds his scenes and directs his actors with great lucidity. He can pull off a big scene like the one between Miss Weld and her sexually competitive mother (Beverly Garland), but under his aegis even such minor characters as the probation officer (John Randolph) live intricate lives of their own.

Pretty Poison is a special film indeed, and Hollywood's financiers and merchandisers are struck even dumber than usual by the problems of selling special pictures. With no convictions of their own about its character, they picked the name of this one by taking a poll. Having settled on a conventionally lurid title, they certified its apparent shoddiness with squalid little newspaper ads. The film was ready to be released last July, but the producers were scared to death of the violence in it in the wake of two political assassinations. They waited, therefore, until the National Rifle Association had regained control of the country, and dumped it on the market without further ado. Unless the movie business is truly bent on self-destruction, a film like *Pretty Poison* deserves a return engagement in fine theaters that pride themselves on fine entertainment.

FIST IN HIS POCKET

STANLEY KAUFFMANN

Serious intent does not always result in serious work, even in talented hands. The young Italian Marco Bellocchio is certainly talented. His second film, *China Is Near*, with which he made his American debut, proved it. Now his first film, *Fist in His Pocket*, has arrived. It is excellently acted, and Bellocchio has directed with a wonderful modern impatience—impatience with irrelevant detail, mechanical transition, and conventional sentiments. But all the talents of cast and director spill out of the leaky script. Written by Bellocchio, it is intended as dark domestic tragedy; it ends almost as melodramatic parody.

An upper-middle-class family in a north-Italian villa. Winter. (It's not always bleak in northern Italy, but no young intellectual Italian director wants any suggestion of "O Sole Mio" in his work.) Mother, a widow, is fiftyish and blind. Four grown children: a lawyer (betrothed), an idle lovely girl, an epileptic son, and a demented son. The epileptic decides that, to free the eldest son, he will do away with all the others, including himself. A car crash on a particular trip would settle it, but he loses his nerve at the wholesale job and goes to work piecemeal. Subsequently he pushes Ma off a cliff and holds the loony under his bathwater. When Sis discovers this (after a spot of incest between her and the epileptic), she is shocked into a backward fall downstairs, cracks her spine, and is paralyzed. It all ends with the sister bedridden, helpless to aid the epileptic in the next room, who is writhing on the floor while a phonograph blares *La Traviata*. Violetta's penultimate note in Act One is prolonged on the sound track to finish the film with a scream.

This synopsis does Bellocchio no injustice, because what starts as Italianate Faulkner is soon so contrived in its dooms that it becomes a long gallery of grotesques, without much relation to us or to the demons in contemporary society. *China Is Near*, despite its dogged Godard imitations, is a much more relevant work. *Fist in His Pocket*, made earlier (1965), seems an overreaction to the sugar candy of most films. You can almost hear Bellocchio swearing to revenge himself for all the movie floss he had been forced to endure in his twenty-six years.

Yet it is finely executed. Three actors especially deserve mention. Lou Castel, the epileptic, is more than credible in perversity. Marino Mase, the oldest son, has strength and depth. The daughter, Paola Pitagora, is not only a good actress, she has one of the loveliest Italian faces on film record.

YOUNG TÖRLESS

Penelope Gilliatt

"What happens when one can torture or be tortured? I thought that worlds would crumble, and then I saw that they don't," says the hero of *Young Törless*, the first film by a young German director called Volker Schlöndorff. It comes from the Robert Musil novel of 1906, about a case of refined bullying in an upper-class academy in the days of Emperor Franz Josef. Some of Musil's notions about passive responsibility seem very modern, and the Sartre who wrote the introduction to Henri Alleg's account of torture in Algeria, *The Question*, would take his point about the obscure collusion that can exist between persecutor and victim. I suppose it is one of the standard bad dreams of adult life to be asked to give an account of oneself at an imaginary trial. For a child to have to endure it in reality, as a boy does in *Young Törless*, is a barbarism that could probably happen only at one of the traditional schools of the privileged. The viciousness of the German-speaking military academies during the period before the First World War has been eloquently written about. There is a racking picture of it in Sybille Bedford's novel A *Legacy*, and another in Rilke's short story "The Gym Period." Schlöndorff's film strikes me as more likable, more alert, and less overbearing than the Musil novel, which is sometimes dank and rather a knuckle-rapper about its insights. The movie was made with fine simplicity (in black and white, as it needed to be, though I daresay there was a fuss about the decision from the people who put up the money). Schlöndorff has worked as an assistant director with Louis Malle, Jean-Pierre Melville, and Alain Resnais, and his film has a lot of authority. There is an exceptionally absorbing score by Hans Werner Henze.

The easy victim of the story, called Basini, steals some money to pay back a debt exploited by a languorous tormentor. The theft lays him open, and an elite of wellborn louts decides to make him a slave, enacting musty rituals of mesmerism and performing physical torture on him in an attic decorated with corset advertisements. Törless, the bystander, watches without doing much, and his naïveté makes him spiritually an accomplice in atrocity, just as Basini's puzzled eagerness to please makes him lewdly interesting to terrorize and somewhat to blame. "There are no classes for the beginners in life," said Rilke, with stony truth. For the gulled who haven't yet grasped that most things are immoderately difficult, there aren't any lessons to help. The advanced little despots who do the torturing in *Young Törless* are better placed. Because they were grounded from birth in the idea that life is a power game, worth nothing unless it is won, they are instructed daily by the lesson of one another's society in the techniques of manipulation. Basini is a whey-faced boy who allures them by his capacity for putting up with anything. What begins in him as forbearance dwindles into compliance. His bafflement stamps him a born loser to the oligarchs, and so to be hated.

The school is ripe for him. Pretty-faced Nazis in embryo are tired of the minor sports of swallowing worms for bets and killing white mice. The comfortless life of the academy—no women, no music, icy walks, uniforms with scratchy military collars, meals brutalized by the rules of monkishness without the belief, secret lofts full of sadistic talismans where sex and punishment get forever confused—has bred one of the worst ethics the world can ever have known:

fidelity to a losing side is stupid, stupidity is something to kick, and kicking is funny, like poverty. "You know I haven't any money," writes Basini's mother in a letter that some stylish thug reads out for entertainment. Everyone roars obediently, and a wag tops the joke: "Not enough to keep a lover." The nobs of the school make constant wisecracks about sex. When Törless tries to stick up for Basini, who is dizzy after a terrible battering by a gang in a gym, the king of the jungle says, "One of his lovers, eh?"

Schlöndorff's film could be seen as a parable about Nazism and guilt by association, but that seems rather a trite idea of it. The most interesting thing about it—very rare in a movie—is the account it gives of the choices of opinion that stylize the architecture of an intellect.

CHARLY

Arthur Knight

On the surface, *Charly*, a new film lovingly directed by Ralph Nelson and knowingly written by Stirling Silliphant, would seem to have almost as many strikes against it as Charly, its ill-fated hero. Based on a TV play that was in turn based on a short novel by Daniel Keyes, *Flowers for Algernon*, it offers as its central character a mentally retarded young man who undergoes brain surgery, blossoms into a genius, then learns he is doomed to regress once more. Hardly the sort of thing to attract the Doris Day fans, one would suppose.

Cliff Robertson, who played Charly in the TV incarnation, fell in love with the role, acquired the film rights, and spent the next several years assembling his "package"—including co-star Claire Bloom. Ralph Nelson reports that when, after the success of his *Lilies of the Field*, United Artists asked if he had any other interesting, offbeat projects, he told them all about Charly—and was politely but firmly shown to the door. Oddly enough, it was Cinerama that finally backed the production.

The love, the dedication that went into the filming of *Charly* is evident in every aspect of the picture. There is a becoming modesty about it—not the penny-pinching variety, but the kind that purposely eschews big scenes or easy bids for sympathy. The Charly of the opening scenes is an overgrown kid, a butt for the cruel humor of the men at the bakery where he sweeps floors. At the clinic to which he is sent for observation, even a mouse can beat him in tracing a maze. Robertson characterizes him with slack mouth, glazed eye, sloping shoulders, and lurching walk. But Charly is eager to learn, and after he undergoes brain surgery his advancement is so rapid that soon he is lecturing to scientists. Perhaps the most fascinating part of the picture is to watch Robertson's subtle alterations of posture and expression as this change takes place.

A similar restraint and sensibility mark both the writing and the direction of the film. Although the kind of operation that Charly undergoes is still in the realm of science fiction, the film-makers made no attempt to gadget it up, realizing that the focus had to remain upon the man, not the machinery. Similarly, the love story, such as it is, is kept properly muted. Miss Bloom, as a clinical psychologist, responds warmly to the young man; but when he discovers that his phenomenal powers will be short-lived, he firmly rejects the girl and prepares to return to his vegetable state.

Ralph Nelson, obviously impressed by the multiscreen work he saw at Montreal's Expo, has invented an interesting technique that places side by side the two shots that normally would be intercut with each other; and Ravi Shankar has contributed a curiously apposite score that combines the Indian idiom with Western instrumentation. *Charly* represents experimentalism in the most positive sense of the word.

THE BOSTON STRANGLER

PHILIP T. HARTUNG

It would seem that the makers of *The Boston Strangler* were never quite certain how to handle the ticklish story of Albert De Salvo, the confessed murderer of thirteen women in and around

Boston in 1962–64, who is now an inmate of Walpole State Prison. De Salvo, extremely well played by Tony Curtis, who effectively catches the two personalities of this schizophrenic murderer, is not introduced until the movie is half over. The first part of the film concentrates on the shocked and frightened inhabitants of Boston as the murders mount, and on the efforts of the police to capture the obviously deranged perpetrator of these gory crimes. The Massachusetts Assistant Attorney General (played with his usual calm concern by Henry Fonda) is appointed to head the Strangler Bureau, whose staff goes to work on rounding up all the sex deviates in the Boston area. Quite a job, that—and for quite a while I thought the whole movie was turning into an exhibition of homos, fetishists and other perverts. The suggestion is that the Boston Strangler might be one of these men.

But no. Eventually we come to De Salvo, the quiet family man at home, the mad killer on the loose when he sneaks away from his job as a mechanic. He is finally caught by the hard-working police, especially one detective (George Kennedy), and then is questioned endlessly by the quiet but determined Fonda. The screenplay was written by Edward Anhalt from Gerold Frank's book; the direction was by Richard Fleischer, who runs the gamut from the sensationalism of the picture's first half to the calm resignation of the scenes with De Salvo that are crowded with psychiatric jargon and lectures on humanity and the treatment of the insane. I don't know how *The Boston Strangler* should have been made—if made at all. But I do know that one comes away from this version somewhat appalled but little wiser.

WILFRID SHEED

In a happier world, the critics would criticize and the moralists would moralize, and they could perhaps arrange to meet as seldom as possible. But in the present schlocky mess, the two tasks fall combined on the small moist brow of the reviewer, who is expected to cover every aspect of a movie, from intention to seating arrangements. So it is with a hollow groan that I slip into my cassock a moment and intone that *The Boston Strangler* is dirty pool, that movies should not bring in convictions before the courts do, and that a man with a living wife and children should be left to molder quietly in his asylum. I would not care to have been in their particular playground the day the film hit Boston.

Back safely in my baggy tweeds, I would say that, as a film, *The Boston Strangler* has been much underrated. The first two thirds make a good police-page movie: flat, groin-level observation of a city, much better than, say, *Madigan*, which hoked up its cops and robbers on basically conventional lines. (Imagine Pat O'Brien with a mistress and you're just about there.) *The Boston Strangler* also uses the split screen intelligently, to suggest multiple points of view, the essence of big-city movies.

To a cop's eye, all the world's a potential pervert, so you get a pretty maggoty vision of Boston. But I don't suppose it would surprise Cardinal Cushing much. To an elderly priest, all the world's a sinner too, but you don't carry on about it. This seemed to me the mood of the early vignettes, in which the first suspects are rounded up. They are shown for what they are, keeping as much dignity as they can, not swaggering or truckling more than they can help. One religious nut wants to confess general unworthiness, but the law doesn't cover it.

Then the focus narrows from the city to Tony Curtis, and hanky-panky sets in. We are shown the tastefully arranged corpses of various young ladies, but not of the Strangler's older victims. This dislocates our feelings about D'whatzit right off. Heroic efforts are made to make him seem like an incomparably charming fellow off the job. He is endowed with a luscious wife and two adorable children. By the time Henry Fonda goads him into collapse and confession, Fonda seems almost a cad, picking on this nice young man. We have lost all sense of the sick outrage that any investigator would have felt.

It is as if director Richard Fleischer wanted to make it up to the family for having shot the picture. But in that case, of course, he shouldn't have. You can't make a tactful movie about a mass murderer.

NO WAY TO TREAT A LADY and
Rod Steiger

STEFAN KANFER

Eyeing the widow and the wine, the priest broguishly in-
tones, "It's red like the blood He shed for you and me." Playfully
he proceeds to tickle her ribs until she shrieks with laughter. Then,
purpling like an eggplant, he chokes her to death and paints a lip-
stick kiss on her forehead.

The father image is only an illusion. The Roman collar is as big a
put-on as his accent and his wig. Under them is an effete, seething
schizoid (Rod Steiger) who can kill when he assumes an identity
other than his own. But who is he? New York's police assign a
green, gawky Jewish detective (George Segal) to find the answer.
After eyeballing the first victim, Segal promptly advances a pop-
psych theory to the press: the murderer, he argues, is a mother
hater who takes Mom for a slay ride every time he garrotes a
middle-aged lady.

The theory is not too far from the mark, but it elicits furious
denials from Steiger, who keeps taunting his pursuer by phone,
hanging up before the calls can be traced. Meanwhile, victim after
victim is fingered by the Manhattan strangler, who blithely pops
into new personae as easily as most men change ties. His disguises
range from the Irish priest to a German plumber to a homosexual
hairdresser. He even plays a prostitute in drag and throws in an
imitation of W. C. Fields on the brink of madness. But the killer's
ego is even more monumental than his talents. Eventually he over-
reaches by trying to do away with Segal's girl friend (Lee Remick),
then gets trapped in a theater, where the chase comes to its inevitably bloody conclusion.

Although murder and mental illness are hardly laughing matters,
director Jack Smight squeezes legitimate comedy from the corrosive camaraderie of Steiger and Segal in their hare-and-hound relationship. Not that the film is totally successful. Eileen Heckart, as

Segal's mom, aims at kosher salami but comes out Irish ham. And the end, heavy with Christian expiation, is as self-conscious as a Sunday-school morality play.

But Segal gives his best performance since *King Rat*, and Steiger offers the audience a cornucopia of characters and caricatures. Some are overplayed, while others are slighted, but consistency is beside the point: no other major American actor could have brought off this kind of multifaceted tour de force, which once was the exclusive property of Alec Guinness.

"I'm only forty-two," he explains. "Brando is forty-three, Paul Newman is forty-three, but I look like everybody's father." True enough. Although Rod Steiger's weight rises and falls with tidal regularity—and the demands of the role—he normally carries about 220 pounds of fat and gristle on his five-foot-ten frame. His hairline is almost a memory, and his jowls reflect years of studied attention to the pleasures of the table. Rod Steiger's worth has increased with his girth: his current fee is $500,000 a film, and most producers feel that the price is right for one of the most convincing character actors in Hollywood history.

Rodney Stephen Steiger is the kind of performer moviegoers seldom recognize on the street, and they tend to remember the role he created rather than the fact that he played it. Although a stratum of burly menace seems to underlie all his performances, there is uncommon variety in his characterizations: His recent range includes an evocation of Pope John XXIII in the semidocumentary *And There Came a Man*; Mr. Joyboy, the simpering mortician of *The Loved One*; the lascivious Komarovsky in *Doctor Zhivago*; and his favorite role, the guilt-racked Nazerman in *The Pawnbroker*.

Three times nominated for Academy Awards, Steiger won this year's Oscar for best male actor on the strength of his performance as the mulish redneck sheriff of *In the Heat of the Night*. It was a job of acting marked by a craftsman's meticulous attention to detail: the assured swagger of the small-town cop who knows he is the Law, the wobbly waddle in the sun that evokes languidity induced by oppressive heat. To achieve the effect, Steiger relied on his standard technique: total immersion. "I've never seen a man become a role so much," recalls director Norman Jewison. "Two weeks after we started the picture it was almost impossible to talk to Rod Steiger, because he was in a Southern dialect night and day."

Lurching from line to line, Steiger frequently ad-libbed his way through entire scenes—including most of a boozy encounter with Sidney Poitier in the sheriff's house. When the occasion calls for it, Steiger can stick to a script. In *The Mark* he played a psychiatrist and did not change a line—but improvised in other ways. Drawing on his five years of treatment in New York, he remembered two characteristics of his own analyst: "He had too many patients, and he was always exhausted." Steiger made the psychiatrist a chain-smoking, unshaven, love-haunted man—none of which was reflected in the screenplay.

Steiger is an actor who seems able to make the Method work. Born in Westhampton, Long Island, he quit high school at sixteen to join the Navy. When his hitch was up, he went to work for the Veterans Administration; a co-worker girl friend in Washington, D.C., got him interested in a local little-theater group. In due course, Steiger headed for Manhattan and the Actors Studio. He made his first hit as the original Marty on television, then scored in films as Marlon Brando's brother in *On the Waterfront,* for which he received his first Oscar nomination. Kept continually busy in movies, Steiger rarely has time for stage work. His longest run on Broadway was in the 1959 hit *Rashomon;* after the play closed, he married his co-star, Claire Bloom. Between assignments, the Steigers live in an antique-littered Manhattan apartment, where he dabbles in Sunday painting and writes occasional verse, none published so far.

Currently, the Steigers are in Hollywood to give one of their rare tandem performances. "We are planning to provide America's answer to the Burtons," says Steiger. "We are fighting back." Their vehicle is *The Illustrated Man,* a sci-fi thriller, in which Steiger plays a tattooed carnival roustabout whose dermatological decorations provide the starting points for separate stories. To play the part, Steiger underwent a ten-hour makeup session, getting himself covered from forehead to feet with multicolored intricate tattoos. Thinking ahead, Steiger is also reading up on Napoleon, whom he will portray later this year in *Waterloo.* He wants desperately to do the life of Dylan Thomas (but suspects that Richard Burton may have first crack at the role) and that of Ernest Hemingway. In any other actor, such ambitions could be put down as hubris, but for

Steiger it somehow seems natural. "There is no such thing as a straight part," he insists. "Every part you play is a character."

WARRENDALE

JOSEPH MORGENSTERN

Warrendale, a very nearly perfect documentary by Allan King, was made at a Canadian treatment center for emotionally disturbed children where the principal therapy is brute love.

Whenever, like young bonzes, the children are engulfed by their flammable passions, they are set upon by staff members and held in an unyielding embrace of locked arms and legs until the seizures are extinguished. Such tactics seem intolerably primitive at first, but slowly an explanation suggests itself. Warm, strong limbs surrounding a child who has a severe character disorder may give him desperately needed protection from the dark at the pit of his soul. Held tightly and safely as he screams bloody murder, the child can vent his dangerous emotions without actually committing bloody murder. Better still, he can begin to feel a crude kind of caring, a raw love that mere words could never convey to an orphan or the unwanted spawn of incompetent parents who has never before been loved, kissed, spoken to as if he really existed, or held by anything friendlier than a straitjacket.

Produced for the Canadian Broadcasting Corporation in 1966, Warrendale was subsequently banned by the CBC, and the BBC too, presumably because the children express themselves with all the considerable obscenity at their command. Factual information is inconspicuous by its absence: the film does not tell you in so many words that the Warrendale treatment is experimental or controversial; it lets you infer this. It does not tell you for a fact that most of these children were judged incurably disturbed before reaching Warrendale, that they are neither brain-damaged nor epileptic; it incites you to learn more for yourself outside the theater. You may be confused and repelled by the children's self-contradictory, terrifyingly antisocial behavior, but you sense that somehow, in their own involuted ways, they are fighting to be whole, that they are tough, intelligent, gifted survivalists in a world that treated them, before their arrival at Warrendale, as ordure.

An adventure of indescribable intensity, the film fashions its loose structure around one crucial event that occurred during the five weeks that producer-director King and his two-man camera crew spent at Warrendale. This was the sudden death of a staff cook named Dorothy, whose passing was particularly shattering to children with egos so small that they live in daily terror themselves of annihilation.

Moments after the fact of Dorothy's death is announced at a house meeting, kids are weeping, screaming, thrashing on the floor. Arms and legs are flying. Staff members are pouncing on them and wrestling them—not too calmly but never angrily—into quiescence. One teen-ager, perhaps the closest to health, takes an unpopular position by opting out of the communal grief because Dorothy, he says, didn't actually mean much to him. "I don't want nobody!" another girl screams. "I don't want nobody!" But she does. Therein lies the hope. So does a vividly intelligent boy, perilously close to an acceptance of himself as an acceptable human being, who still shouts a savagely obscene litany whenever he is menaced by kindness.

So does a drowsy girl-child, sucking at her bottle and surrounded by a staff member's arms, following a bedtime story with quietly flickering attention. ". . . And the princess whispered, 'You can climb up by using my hair. . .'" But the listener is not an infant. She is a fifteen-year-old girl whose emotional age swings more wildly than Tarzan on his vine. A short while later, when a gently humorous psychiatrist tries to convince the very same girl that her feelings are too precious to be dismissed, she replies with equally adult humor, "Dr. Fischer, you're going off your bloody nut!"

The pieces will not go together at first. Peter Pan is dead. Sugar, spice and everything nice is not what these kids are made of. But what, then, has gone into them? Beatings, anger, contempt, indifference, solitude. They are the unaffiliated of society. They belong to no one, subscribe to nothing but a Neanderthal principle of self-preservation. They are, unavoidably, us at our most desperate. And that is when the adventure of *Warrendale* grows nearly intolerable, when we begin to see more than a little of ourselves in these children, when we realize that they are simply more candid than we are in their biting, kicking, howling responses to frustration and unlove.

If only they *were* brain-damaged. How reassuring it would be to know that they have nothing in common with the more normally troubled children of normally broken homes, that they have nothing to teach us about the monster-babies of our slums who try to establish their existence by smashing and burning. How reassuring it would be to know that those titanic storms inside their skulls are only random short circuits and have no clinical connection with the daily aggressions of man against man, of nation against nation.

Or how reassuring it would be to know that some benign force could surround this whole, warring world in loving arms and locked legs and keep it from hurting itself.

STANLEY KAUFFMANN

Warrendale is so moving, so fascinating and fine, that I hesitate to say what's it's about. The moment I mention the subject, the reader will perhaps think that the film is noble and worthwhile but that he is willing to take its worth for granted and spare himself. This would be self-cheating—not of information or duty, but of humanity and, in a paradoxical way, of joy. *Warrendale* is a documentary about emotionally disturbed children. It is not a study, it is not propaganda. It is an *experience*, passionate and compassionate.

The title is the (former) name of a center in Ontario for disturbed children, not brain-damaged or mentally defective children. In 1966 a Canadian film-maker named Allan King was commissioned by the Canadian Broadcasting Corporation to make a film about the place. He spent a month getting acquainted with the children in House Two. Then he brought in his cameraman William Brayne and his sound man Russel Heise for about two weeks of similar visits. Then they shot film for five weeks in and around the house. Out of forty hours of footage, this hundred-minute film was edited by Peter Moseley. Hurrah—just plain, simple hurrah—for all of them.

Most feature films are made by men who first create or help

create or somehow acquire fictional scripts and then guide actors
and other artists to the fulfillment of the fiction. With a film like
Warrendale, nothing can be created except—a huge exception—
the confidence of the subjects. The film-makers have to know really
who their subjects are, and the subjects have to believe it. In short,
the prime requirement is not film talent as such, though these men
have enough, but empathy, communion, credibility. The most brilliant film-maker alive would have been powerless to make *Warrendale* without the confidence of those children (and the adult staff).
That confidence, in King and his colleagues, shines from the screen
—principally by virtue of the film's very existence.

It starts with the counselor of the house, a young woman named
Terry, waking the children one morning and having a tussle with a
teen-age girl who refuses to get up, who pulls the blankets over her
head and fights Terry. My reaction the first time I saw this film
(I've seen it twice) was that the girl was perfectly right: who
would want to get up when there was a camera grinding away in
the bedroom? And I began to warm up all my prejudices against
the intrusiveness of much *cinéma-vérité*. But it didn't take long to
see that my feeling was quite misplaced, that the girl's reaction was
(one might say) natural—she didn't want to get up just as naturally as if she and Terry had been alone. This is proved by the
spontaneity of all the other actions in the picture, including many
by that girl. The camera quite obviously became just another occupant of the house. At one point, one of the boys, blithely playing
Red Light with some of the other children in the street outside,
confides to the camera that he can see his friends' steps with his
back turned because of the reflections in the lens.

The basic Warrendale technique is "holding": when a child has
an emotional seizure, an outsize tantrum, one of the attendants—
sometimes two or three—pins his arms and legs and lets him rip.
Complete freedom of feeling is the essence, with restraint to keep
the child from hurting himself and to provide a sense of physical
contact, the *caring* of somebody else. We see this method used
frequently with these volatile children. But, crucially, a foreword
tells us that this is *not a documentary about a technique*, it is a
personal, selective record of an experience. I have no idea whether
the "holding" technique is good or bad therapy. I do know that
King's film about the place where it was used brought me close, in
a naked and tribal way, to five or six emotionally disturbed chil-

dren. It revealed not only the personalities but the worth of these children. There's a boy named Tony, about ten, splay-toothed and curly-haired, whose every second expression is "Fuck off," repeated in a pathetic defensive litany. When he's struggling in the counselors' arms during one of his tantrums, swearing furiously, I could only think, because of what I knew about him, even because of what he was doing at the moment and why he was doing it, "That's a *wonderful* kid. That's a terrific human being." King had led that boy onto film before then, had shown him playing and blushing and teasing and talking; now, because Tony was *present*, his tantrum seemed one of his ways to express an exceptional sensitivity.

The film merely presents some events in the life of the house. The central point is the sudden death of the relatively young Negro cook, a woman evidently dear to everyone. The chief counselor decides to announce it to all the children at once, and the resulting scene is heartbreaking—but not in a bedlam horror sense. Before the meeting one of the counselors asks the chief how they can explain the death to the kids when they don't understand it themselves. What we see with the children is this bafflement and fright *in extremis*. All the children feel various kinds of guilt for the cook's death. This, enormously amplified in them, is something that all of us feel at sudden death, particularly of the young: not directly responsible, as the children feel, but haunted by the sense that we ought to have been able to do *something*.

This experience is a model of the whole film. These children act out, in exaggerated and baroque ways, many feelings that other children, other people, feel and suppress or understand objectively and can control. These children have little objectivity or control, and they just let go: guilt about having been unloved in their homes, as if they had earned neglect, as if they were undeserving of this place and its care; fear to love because of the fear of loss of the beloved; unbridled anger at the teeming mysteries of just one ordinary modern day's existence. Society has not (or not yet) given them the means to control their fears and to invent answers as it has given to many adults and to the clergyman who presides over the cook's funeral.

Any film that is an impromptu record is likely to have roughnesses and omissions. For instance, it's clear that King was caught slightly short because the cook died early in the filming and he had only a little footage of her. (Understandably, he shifts her death to a point near the end of the film; strict chronology was not important, and the film would have run downhill if he had followed it.) Some of the sound could be clearer, some of the sequences fuller. A few of the children are left virtually unnoticed, like a pretty teenage girl, flirtatiously dressed, who sits in the background chewing gum and reading magazines while other children are threshing about in counselors' arms.

But much more bothersome are two extrinsic facts. The first is that the Canadian Broadcasting Corporation, having commissioned this film, refused to show it because it contains—often—the words "fuck" and "bullshit." I hope that at least some members of the CBC felt that this decision was a fucking disgrace. Would it have been impossible to show this utterly humane, basically ennobling film late at night, even if it meant canceling for one evening some acid-in-the-face private-eye thriller with scrubbed language?

Second is the fact that Warrendale has now changed hands and methods, largely (I'm told) because of controversy over this film. I'm as incompetent to comment on the political questions as the therapeutic. I do know that, watching this film and knowing that at least some of the children have been moved and are being treated differently, I felt that something warm and organic and nourishing had been hurt.

Last year we saw a documentary called *Titicut Follies*, made in a Massachusetts institution for the criminally insane, a picture that no doubt originated in a genuine impulse to expose oppressive conditions but that, I thought, began to get some gawking kicks out of showing them. I mention that picture only to assure those who saw it or who wouldn't see it that *Warrendale* has not the slightest resemblance to it. It is not an exposé, it is not a chamber of horrors. It is a *union* with some children who become very precious to us before the one hundred minutes are up. Partly this is because they are in themselves interesting and they are allowed—induced—to be *there*; partly it's because they seem to be us, under a distorting magnifying glass. Jean Renoir has called Allan King "a great artist" —not a bad compliment from a man who is a pretty fair artist himself. Inarguably, King has evoked those children's inner selves so powerfully on the screen that he has snared us up there, too.

10

ADAPTATIONS

Making Lawrence More Lawrentian (THE FOX)

PAULINE KAEL

If you're going to see a movie based on a book you think is worth reading, read the book first. You can never read the book with the same imaginative responsiveness to the author once you have seen the movie. The great French film critic André Bazin believed that even if movies vulgarized and distorted books they served a useful purpose, because they led people to read the books on which the movies were based. But when you read the book after seeing the movie, your mind is saturated with the actors and the images, and you tend to read in terms of the movie, ignoring characters and complexities that were not included in it, because they are not as vivid to you. At worst, the book becomes a souvenir of the movie, an extended reminiscence. (Girls read *Doctor Zhivago* so they can "see more" of Omar Sharif.) Bazin didn't live to find out that reading the book after seeing the movie would become such a mass-audience phenomenon that movies not based on novels would be "novelized" for additional revenue, nor to find out that college students, taking up "film as film," would increasingly reject the whole reading experience as passé. There is a new generation of moviegoers which believes that a movie is *sui generis* and that a critic is betraying a literary bias—and thus an incompetence at dealing with film as film—in bringing up a movie's literary origins. Last year Brendan Gill discussed this problem in relation to *Reflections in a Golden Eye*, and it recently came up in a symposium on movies at the New School for Social Research, where the participating critics were dumbfounded to discover that

194

some of the younger members of the audience did not believe that even Albert Camus' *The Stranger* was relevant to a discussion of Visconti's film version.

Even if one hadn't read D. H. Lawrence's *The Fox*, it would enter into a discussion of the movie version, because from the movie one would almost inevitably assume that Lawrence was to blame for what seems dated. There are moments in *The Fox*, as there are in *Reflections in a Golden Eye*, when one is likely to smile a little patronizingly at dear old D. H. Lawrence, as at poor little Carson McCullers. As the creaking Freudian wheels turn, one is tempted to say that nothing dates faster than the sex revelations of yesteryear. It wasn't until these movies were over that my head cleared and I realized that what had seemed so ploddingly literary that I had automatically blamed it on the original authors wasn't in the books at all. It seemed so "literary" just because it wasn't the author—wasn't Lawrence or McCullers—but an attempt to modernize or clarify the author and to "fill out" the author's material. Lawrence's 1923 novella, like McCullers' short novel of 1941, is still too subtle to be made into a movie aimed at a large audience without "bringing it up to date," which means bringing in the sexual platitudes that—in movies—are considered Freudian modernism. This has the odd result of making both these movies seem novelistic when they depart most from the novels.

The movie *The Fox* is about two young women—sickly, chattering, ultrafeminine Jill (Sandy Dennis) and dark, quiet, strong March (Anne Heywood)—who are trying, rather hopelessly, to run a chicken farm in Canada. A gentle but powerful man (Keir Dullea, in a fantasy portrait of Everywoman's dream) who used to live on their farm returns and puts things in order (thus demonstrating that farming is really man's work). But his proposal of marriage to March awakens the lesbianism dormant in the girls: Jill uses her weakness to make March feel protective, and the women become active (at least, kissing-in-bed) lesbians. Though he and March go out to a convenient little shack and shack up, Jill is still dependent on March; he eliminates Jill, in a scene of implausible and clumsy contrivance, by chopping down a tree so that it hits her. There is also some symbolism about a fox that March has somehow been unable to shoot, although it has been wrecking the girls' farming plans by raiding the hen coop; the man kills the fox and, of course, raids the hen coop himself. The symbolism

seems rather quaint and rather extraneous to this triangle—which
is pretty much *The Children's Hour* in a woodsy setting—and
rather confusing; the ads therefore explain that the fox is the "symbol of the male," and the trade press "clarifies" things even more
by explaining that the "shotgun, axe, carving knife, tree, pitchfork,
etc." are "phallic symbology." The movie (again like *Reflections*)
has a solemnly measured manner, which one might assume is the
result of following a "classic" in an honorably respectful but too
literal-minded way; one seems to wait for the next development
rather than enjoy what's going on.

But D. H. Lawrence's *The Fox* is a story about two spinsterish,
educated, and refined English ladies, approaching thirty, in the
year 1918; the ladies are, as people used to say, attached to each
other. The fox of the story does indeed represent the male to
March—but to a sexually repressed March. And the male who
comes into their lives, and whom March immediately identifies
with the fox, because of his smell and look, is a boy of twenty and,
instead of a nice farmer, primarily a hunter. And it's because he
is a hunter—in that same mystic sense of willing the death of his
prey which reappears in Norman Mailer's recent novel *Why Are
We in Vietnam?*—that he is able to kill the inconvenient Jill, doing so right in front of the poor girl's parents. (The parents are one
of those "details" that movies eliminate when they want to keep
certain characters sympathetic—in the same way that Perry and
Dick in the movie of *In Cold Blood* still kill four people but no
longer deliberately swerve their car to smash a dog.) This hunter-
boy, far from giving March a sexual sample of what she has been
missing, is rather afraid of so-much-woman, and at the end of the
story D. H. Lawrence undercuts the simple, "Lawrentian" male-
female stuff with some impassioned second thoughts about the
whole thing. Married to the boy, March is not the submissive female he had hoped for; she is independent and unsettled and unhappy. The fox may have outfoxed himself; he wishes he had left
the two women "to kill one another."

The central problem of *The Fox* as a movie is the problem of
adaptation. The adapters (Lewis John Carlino and Howard Koch)
are neither incompetent nor stupid, but is there a mass market for
a story about repressed spinsters in 1918? That being highly ques-
tionable, they have made *The Fox* a modern story. But you can
hardly make it modern without making it more explicit, and if it's

all spelled out, if everyone is sexually aware, if March is the kind of girl who sings a bawdy song like "Roll Me Over" and proceeds to roll around and thrash about in an experienced, if bewildering, way in that shack, you no longer need symbolism. The sex sequence not only makes the symbolism superfluous but disintegrates the characters, because if March is a swinger like this, if she isn't afraid of sex with men, what's she doing in the woods playing house with that frumpy little Jill? The force of the novella is in what Lawrence treats symbolically—the hidden power of sex in the women and the ambivalence of the male. The movie not only brings the hidden to the surface but resolves the male ambivalence in banal male strength. One kind of schoolgirl crush gives way to another. I wonder whether we could watch *The Fox* feeling so relaxed and patronizing about the author who used to be considered sensational if the man were still Lawrence's *boy?*

To take this a step further: My guess is that *The Fox* will meet with less critical opposition than *Reflections in a Golden Eye*, just because it is so sexually explicit that it is tame and "healthy," whereas the stifled homosexuality of Marlon Brando's duty-bound Major Penderton is grotesque and painful. Although Brando's character could hardly be taken as a cue to go and do likewise, *Reflections* was condemned; the ban became an embarrassment, because where but in the seminaries are there still any considerable number of *repressed* homosexuals? The scenes of Elizabeth Taylor and Brian Keith making love in the berry patch could hardly shock a modern audience, but the fat, ugly Major putting cold cream on his face, or preening himself at the mirror, or patting his hair nervously when he thinks he has a gentleman caller, is so ghastly that some members of the audience invariably cut themselves off from him by laughter. Lawrence's scared boy with a latent-lesbian bride might have made them laugh, too. Both these movies are about homosexual drives and how they lead to murder, and I think it's fair to say that neither of them would have been made even just a few years ago. And yet it's already too late to make these movies the way they have been done. *Reflections* has been furbished with *additional* fetishes, as if the original weren't Southern and Gothic enough. The horsewhipping that Elizabeth Taylor gives Brando— which doesn't appear in the book—is a new antique, and so is the conversation that follows, in which she explains that the whipping cleared the air and that he is more agreeable now, so that we are cued to crank out the Freudian explanation "Oh, yes, he wanted to be beaten," as we crank out "He hit the horse because . . ." There is much heavy cranking to do in both these movies.

Is there any reason, then, to see them instead of just reading the slender little books, with their glimpses of character, and an author's distinctive voice, and prose that carries one along? Despite everything that is laboriously wrong with *Reflections*, the visual style—like paintings made from photographs—is interesting, and the director, John Huston, and the actors were able to do some extraordinary things with Carson McCullers' conceptions. One cannot imagine earlier reigning idols of the screen (Gable? Tracy?) playing the Brando role, and though his performance doesn't completely come to life—maybe because the Major doesn't have much life in him, and Brando subdued is Brando partly wasted—it nevertheless shows our greatest actor in a serious, complex role, and there are moments when the performance *does* work and Brando shows how good he is. And when Brian Keith does, too. And Elizabeth Taylor is charming as a silly, sensual Southern "lady"—a relief from the movies in which Burton ostentatiously plays down to her and she valiantly tries to act up to him and they're both awful.

The Fox doesn't have such striking performances, and although it is probable that not very many rising young stars would care to risk the whining Sandy Dennis role, one might uncharitably point out that she had already made an acting style out of postnasal drip. *The Fox* is monumentally unimaginative, but it certainly has been mounted; the color photography is banally handsome, and there's a tricky Lalo Schifrin score to supply excitation. Maybe it is because the adapters and the director, Mark Rydell, are so plainly wrestling with Lawrence in terms of their commercial idea of honesty—making Lawrence more Lawrentian—that the movie has a simple-minded fascination. It's easy to sink into and soak up, and it may be a popular success, because many people will enjoy the sexy romance, which is pretentious enough to pass for a serious treatment of a classic. This would be no more foolish than to take a detective thriller like *In the Heat of the Night*—which is entertaining because it's a good racial joke about a black Sherlock Holmes and a shuffling redneck Watson—and inflate it to the status of important drama, as if that inflation were necessary for one to enjoy the picture. Lawrence once sent his Frieda a picture of Jonah and the whale, with the caption "Who is going to swallow whom?" This may have some small relevance to his unresolved novella. There's no doubt about the movie's swallowing the book; will moviegoers who then read the book be able to see Lawrence through the blubber?

No matter *how* a movie like *The Fox* might be done—even if it should be done with artistry, and even if Lawrence's conceptions should be retained—it would be unlikely to have the kind of impact that Lawrence's writing had when his books appeared. The movie of *The Stranger* is set in the correct period, the Thirties, but that doesn't help to relate it to what Camus' great modern statement of the concept of alienation meant in its period—which, conceptually, was the Forties. The picture might be more imaginative, the hero better cast, and so on, but how can the historical impact and importance of the novel be communicated when the idea of alienation has already become conventional—has been reduced to the cut-rate *Cool Hand Luke*? *The Stranger* is a beautiful movie, but it is not an "important" one; it functions on the screen not as a definitive new vision but as a simple story with intelligent overtones—a factual account of Meursault's last days, which, because of the impact the book was to have, now seems almost pre-alienation, a precursor of Camus. By the time *The Stranger* or a book by D. H. Lawrence is *filmed*, the book has already changed our lives, and the movie is just a famous story. Only if you know the book and what it meant, only if you have a sense of history, does the movie version suggest more, and help to bring back to you what the book represents. To be "important," a movie must deal with characters and situations, whether historical or modern, in terms of the greatest honesty possible in its time—what Lawrence and Camus did in their novels, and Carson McCullers did, on her own scale.

THE LION IN WINTER

PHILIP T. HARTUNG

The Lion in Winter is the year's best comedy. In portraying the intrigue and battle of intellects between King Henry II and Queen Eleanor of Aquitaine over which of their three sons should inherit Henry's throne, the film has some of the sharpest and wittiest lines to be heard on a sound track. And what's more, it has a superb cast to put the lines over brilliantly. I know that the critics will jump on *The Lion* and complain that it is too static at times and follows the original play too closely and even seems to divide itself into three acts. Similar complaints were made against *Who's Afraid of Virginia Woolf? The Lion* (with its bickering mainly between two people who realize before the finale that, in spite of the hateful things they have said, they have a certain love and respect for each other) resembles *Woolf* at times in its strong dialogue, bright wisecracks and angry tensions. James Goldman wrote the script from his original stage play, and if it is talky, the talk is interesting and character-revealing, as the King and his estranged wife, the three sons and two French house guests play the game of one-upmanship during their twenty-four hours together in the 1183 Christmas court at the damp, gloomy Castle of Chinon. The dialogue, often poetic in its choice of words and imagery, is an engaging mixture of medieval and modern. James Goldman is not writing a factual movie about the Plantagenets, but an interpretation in which he successfully combines their language and ours.

Visually Martin Poll's production of *The Lion in Winter* is a delight, not only for Douglas Slocombe's good color photography of the handsome costumes, outdoor scenes, and attractive (though no doubt very uncomfortable) old buildings that substituted for the Chinon Castle in the south of France, but also for the very photogenic cast, who look right in these costumes and sets and not like actors wandering through a historical pageant. Under director Anthony Harvey, this cast shines, even such comparative newcomers as the five young people who are the real pawns in Henry's and Eleanor's struggle to name the successor.

The picture belongs, of course, to Peter O'Toole and Katharine Hepburn, who have never been better than as the fiftyish King and his sixtyish Queen whom he has locked in another castle for the last ten years and now brings to Chinon for the Christmas row. O'Toole was also good as this same Henry II in *Becket*, but Henry was a younger, more dashing man thirteen years ago when he fought with his former friend, the Archbishop. Now O'Toole's Henry is graying, aging, still sincerely wanting to be a good king, but still willful and wanting things on his terms. He detests Eleanor, who favors Prince Richard as the next king, while Henry wants to leave his crown to the nitwit Prince John. Frustrated because none of his sons is worthy and because Eleanor won't cooperate in having their marriage annulled so Henry can marry his mistress, the French Princess Alais, the angry King spends most of his time raging; as a lion in winter, O'Toole rages well.

Katharine Hepburn doesn't have to rage as the lustrous Eleanor of Aquitaine. Her chiseled, freckled face is beautiful as she strives to put Henry in his place, reasons with deceitful Richard, turns John off with "Hush, dear, Mother's fighting," or tries not to show how she's suffering while watching Henry courting young Alais. Miss Hepburn is perfect at conveying Eleanor's brilliance, her disappointment with her sons, heartbreak ("How from where we started did we reach this Christmas?") and understanding ("We are all barbarians"). Her portrait of Eleanor stands as the performance of the year.

The young people in the next generation certainly deserve applause, too: Jane Merrow as Henry's quiet French mistress, who knows she's become a pawn; Timothy Dalton as her brother, the French King, who tells Henry about Richard's homosexual overtures and about the other two boys' conniving; Anthony Hopkins as Prince Richard, who makes you wonder why he was called the Lionhearted; Nigel Terry as the sneaky Prince John, who later became the villain in so many of the Robin Hood stories; John Castle as Prince Geoffrey, the brightest of the plotting sons, so efficient at scheming that you wonder why Henry didn't aim for him as successor. As we know from history, Eleanor won: Richard became king after Henry's death six years later. At the end of this well-

made movie, no one wins. For a few moments it looks as if Henry
is going to kill all three sons, who are drawing daggers against him.
But he knows he can't—which gives Eleanor an opportunity to get
in a last wisecrack, "Spare the rod and spoil the child." But it is
Henry who has the last word as he escorts his wife to the barge that
will return her to the castle prison: "I hope we never die." And
they laugh—and you laugh, too.

ARTHUR SCHLESINGER, JR.

When a film opens with a shot of drifting clouds and
when, a moment later, crossed swords are suddenly raised against
the placid sky, one recognizes a director with a firm grasp of cinematic cliché. When, as the film proceeds, scene after scene has
flames in the background—guttering candles or flaring torches or
roaring logs—when the tolling of bells serves as the punctuation
between scenes, and the sound of hidden choirs adds emotional
emphasis, one begins to acknowledge a master of banality.

But I do not want to give the director, Anthony Harvey, exclusive credit for the *Lion in Winter* debacle. Mr. Harvey made a
harsh and original film of *Dutchman* a year or two back, and he
may here simply be deferring to what he regards as the ritual of
historical drama. First responsibility must go to James Goldman,
who wrote both the original play and the screenplay.

The Lion in Winter, an episode in the lives of Henry II and
Eleanor of Aquitaine, takes place in 1183. The dialogue is very sub–
Christopher Fry (Henry to his girl: "Has my willow turned to
poison oak?"), interlarded with anachronisms: I rather doubt that
the word "motivated" was used very often in the twelfth century.
James Goldman, in addition, is a writer who tries to have it both
ways. Fearful after a "strong" dramatic scene that the sophisticated
members of his audience will snicker, he then tacks on a smart
modern crack. Thus, after a vicious fight with her husband and
sons Katharine Hepburn as Eleanor is required to say, "What family doesn't have its ups and downs?" or "Dear, dear, whatever shall
we do with Mother?" The actors can do very little with such material. Katharine Hepburn struggles valiantly and ends up a cross be-

tween Judith Anderson and Helen Hayes. *The Lion in Winter* is a
ludicrous film.

JOHN SIMON

James Goldman's *The Lion in Winter* was the kind of play
to delight Walter Kerr: vaguely literate, somewhat historical yet
saucily anachronistic, and as stuffed with suburbanly suburbane
epigrams as a Victorian sofa with horsehair. Henry II of England,
Eleanor of Aquitaine, and their three sons, using a French king
and princess for pawns, wrangle over succession to the throne and
disputed territorities; this is presented as TV domestic comedy, di-
lutedly Freudian and Shavian, and concentratedly middle-class
Jewish. The film version, from Goldman's own screenplay, sticks
closely to the original and suffocatingly in our craw.

The basic device, again, is the epigram, and a medieval royal
family doggedly brandishing not broadswords but thin witticisms
can be pretty funny—the wrong way. The two most quoted *mots*
are, "The year is 1183 and we are all barbarians," and (tossed off
after some particularly murderous scheming and counterscheming)
"Well, what family doesn't have its ups and downs?" The first is
the sort of thing we get in Shaw, Giraudoux, Anouilh, with the
difference that the anachronism there is not self-consciously wink-
ing at you but is slipped in almost unnoticeably. The second item
could come out of any post-Odetsian Jewish comedy, and the joke,
if any, derives as much from that as it does from the understate-
ment.

Nevertheless, to the casual glance this might not seem all that
different from, say, *Saint Joan* or *Judith*. But, of course, it is. In
discreetly modernizing medieval Europeans or ancient Hebrews,
Shaw and Giraudoux tried, without violating the spirit of those
peoples, to raise their language to literature, and their problems to
myths. Goldman, however, lowers the roughhewn dignity of the
Middle Ages to brittle cocktail-party chatter: "He came down from
Paris with a mind like Aristotle's and a form like sin"; "We vio-
lated all the Commandments like a shot. . . ." Clearly, the dialogue fares no better than the Decalogue. One gem that produces
especially knowing laughter is, "In a world where carpenters are

resurrected, everything is possible." Now, this is completely alien to the spirit of the twelfth century; but how can the twentieth feed on such dated schoolboy blasphemies?

And consider these further examples: "Henry's bed is *his* province," Eleanor declares; "he can people it with sheep for all I care —as I believe on occasion he does." Or this: *Eleanor:* "Have you found a way to sell everyone to everybody?" *Prince Geoffrey:* "Not yet, Mummy, but I'm working on it." Or: *Eleanor:* "When can I believe you, Henry?" *Henry:* "Always, even when I lie." If you ran out of peanuts, you might possibly serve this with the martinis, but when it comes marching at you in serried ranks waving pennants inscribed "Literature," "Drama," or "Film" and trying to puncture you like a tin of canned laughter . . . but there I go sounding like James Goldman. Anyway, no thanks.

If I make so much of the bad writing in *The Lion in Winter*, it is because this kind of pseudoliterate hack work seems to be on the upswing; what else is one to conclude after seeing within a short space *The Secret Ceremony, Negatives,* and this film, all in that genre of which Ben Hecht's *The Specter of the Rose* remains a supreme example? Goldman's script, moreover, can boast of a multiple echo. Thus Henry's "I am an old man in an empty place" reverberates with two lines from Eliot's "Gerontion," and Eleanor's "The sun was warmer then and we were every day together" comes from Jacques Prévert's chanson "Les Feuilles mortes": "*Le soleil [était] plus brûlant qu'aujourd'hui . . . Nous vivions tous les deux ensemble . . .*" "Sleep and dream of me with croutons," says Henry to one who would devour him; the trouble is that you cannot see the soup for the croutons.

Add to this the weightily inept direction of Anthony Harvey (remembered—would that he were not—for *Dutchman*), which mistakes boom-and-zoom–happy camera histrionics for liveliness and imagination. A typical sequence has Henry rattling up to the battlements of Chinon Castle, only to crumple there as the camera rises and rises to show us the king pitifully small from its eagle's-eye view. Simultaneously, John Barry's abominable score (a kind of Roseland Ballroom version of the Te Deum, complete with heavenly choir) soars to a pious crescendo, completing the image of man's puniness, especially when he gets involved in a film like this one.

But, obviously, no one has a feeling of slumming. Katharine

Hepburn conveys a profound sense of being immersed in Art perhaps even greater and more shattering than *Guess Who's Coming to Dinner*, and she sheds enough tears to erode the gold plating from a dozen Oscars. With the tears go assorted quavers of the chin, and since Miss Hepburn's voice even in carefree moments consists of an ambiguous rasp meant to suggest mischief, her Eleanor emerges a bundle of bravely packed-away miseries bursting at every seam. Yet if there is anything Eleanor of Aquitaine should not be, it is a cross between Willie the Weeper and Smilin' Thru. And there is the problem of playing opposite Peter O'Toole: this king and queen have an unnerving way of looking like King Oedipus and Queen Jocasta.

O'Toole's Henry is all hulking about, stomping around, harrumphing and Laughtoning it up: "tough" mannerisms, "shrewd" mannerisms, "lusty" mannerisms, with nary a characterization to hold them together—though this, needless to say, is equally the fault of the script. The three plotting sons seem to be rivals not so much for the throne of England as for the crown of Stock Performer of the Year. Jane Merrow, as Princess Alais, is considerably less apt and attractive than she was in *The Girl Getters*. Timothy Dalton provides the one performance well worth watching, turning the young French King into a complex, passionately and cunningly dedicated figure.

But I keep coming back to the inanities of the script. They extend from such low-level nonsense as Henry's having his mutinous sons guarded by one solitary soldier, when Eleanor and others of their faction are freely roaming the castle, to such advanced absurdities as having the cynical Henry overwhelmed by finding out about a homosexual liaison of an unfavorite son, or going to pieces over the discovery of his wife's long-past escapade with his late father. In terms of neither history nor plot nor character does this make sense—only a rather twisted twist of the plot.

Even the *Times* reviewer, not exactly remarkable for her astuteness, has noted the patent silliness of a much-reiterated device: a character will say or do something quite ordinary and inconsequential, only to have another proclaim exultantly that *he* has won, because that ordinary and inconsequential thing was just what he wanted the first fellow to say or do. I could add a thing or two about that, but won't—lest Goldman declare that this was precisely what he wanted to provoke me into doing.

ROMEO AND JULIET

PHILIP T. HARTUNG

When I saw the attractive Capulet house in attractive Verona this summer (I'm not name-dropping; this *does* have a point) I realized Franco Zeffirelli could not have made his *Romeo and Juliet* there. He was right to seek other locations to tell his version of Shakespeare's tale of the star-cross'd lovers and set it in mid-fifteenth-century Verona but photograph it in Tuscany and Umbria, where he found the lovely old church that is the scene for Friar Laurence's church and cell, the handsome Piccolomini Palace in Pienza, which becomes the spacious Capulet house, and the town of Gubbio, whose streets are exactly right for those vicious Montague–Capulet street fights and duels. These places and the exquisite interior sets built in Cinecittà studios are caught by Pasquale de Santis, whose beautiful color photography also does full justice to Danilo Donati's stunning Renaissance costumes and the large cast of leads and extras.

In spite of the fact that the two title players do not always come through with the beauty and depth of Shakespeare's poetry (and thus recall the old argument, should middle-aged, well-trained Jane Cowl or a correctly-aged youngster play Juliet?), seventeen-year-old Leonard Whiting and fifteen-year-old Olivia Hussey are excellent as Romeo and Juliet. While we miss the poetic readings, we are given instead the fresh good looks, the vitality, the tempestuous awakening of first real love of two teen-agers who have captured the spirit, if not always the real meanings, of the lines. In any case, Zeffirelli, who wrote the screenplay with Franco Brusati and Masolino d'Amico, was not adverse to changing some of the lines and even the action in interpreting the characters; but what he came up with is a robust, "now" *Romeo and Juliet* told in lively cinematic terms that would surely have impressed even the Bard himself (who indulged occasionally in popular touches to win the crowds).

More than ever before (even more than in the modern American counterpart called *West Side Story*) this *Romeo and Juliet* emphasizes the youth-versus-old-age theme, the budding newcomers versus the Establishment. This teen-age Romeo and Juliet, attractive youngsters who fall madly in love, are ready to rebel against their parents' rules and are frustrated again and again. It is interesting, however, as a religious note, that their rebellion does not extend to Friar Laurence (nicely played by Milo O'Shea) to whose good advice they listen and who marries them when he realizes the sincerity of their love and the extent of their passion. Perhaps this Romeo, the wiser and the older of the star-cross'd lovers, does not want to break entirely from his elders; then again, it is Juliet who has the domineering father who insists on her marrying the solid, well-familied Paris.

Also interesting in this version of the story, events even more moving than the tragic fate of the two lovers are those concerned with the other young men of Verona, the senseless street brawls that stem from the enmity between the two families. The film opens with one of these scenes, which wins the anger of the Prince of Verona (intelligently and sensitively played by Robert Stephens), who berates both Lords Montague and Capulet. Later comes that worse fight between Mercutio and Tybalt, whose characters are already well established. (Mercutio, played as an older hippie by John McEnery, started his Queen Mab speech almost unintelligibly and with a great deal of bouncing around and then settled down to allow the exquisite poetry to win us to him. Tybalt, played like a handsome bully by Michael York, succeeded in making us dislike him when he objects to Romeo's presence at the Capulet ball.) The Mercutio–Tybalt quarrel starts on a half-humorous note, becomes serious, and then deadly when the mortally wounded Mercutio tells off the fighting families with "A plague o' both your houses." All of which leads to the terrific fight between Romeo and Tybalt, brilliantly photographed by de Santis' hand-held camera, which draws us into the pursuit and dueling and stabbing. It is these fights, meaningless, violent and deadly, which move us to tears and make us realize the futility of war.

And if young people are drawn to this *Romeo and Juliet*, it is to be hoped that this lesson against war will interest them and remain with them as much as the touching story of the young lovers. But oldsters might pay attention to the lesson, too—and with it they will see some of the most beautiful scenes ever filmed, particularly the Capulet ball with its grand sweep, gorgeous costumes and close-ups of Renaissance faces that are art worthy of museums.

JOHN SIMON

A master of the phony (who has the advantage of coming from the land of baloney) has now emitted his film version of *Romeo and Juliet*. In his staging of the play for the Old Vic, Franco Zeffirelli at least had an idea: to convert Shakespeare into a precursor of Arthur Laurents and give us a kind of *West Side Story* minus the music. For three acts that worked quite well. In his film, Zeffirelli has no clear-cut idea, except perhaps to give us a *Romeo and Juliet* for teenyboppers and pederasts. For the delight of the former, we get a pair of lovers so young that their delivery of verse sags with puppy fat, and for the delectation of the latter we get fondly lingering shots of Romeo's bare bottom, and a relationship between the stripling Romeo and the older Mercutio (creepily played by John McEnery) that rivals in intimacy and tenderness the puppy love of Romeo and Juliet.

There is a reason for the theatrical adage that no one under forty can play Juliet properly. The girl may be nominally under fourteen, yet she represents, along with youthfulness, that fruition of the feminine principle that takes years of acting experience on top of years of experience in living to manifest itself. Certainly it is their youthful innocence that makes these lovers lyrical; but only ripe humanity, a sense of really meaning the poetry (not Shakespeare's greatest), can make them tragic. Olivia Hussey (despite a super-erogatory layer or two of actual puppy fat) and Leonard Whiting are attractive youngsters, but even if they were much better actors than they now are they could not make us believe their intenser gestures and expressions, their more piercing utterances. There is a gulf between the words and the faces, between unmarked, un-marred bodies and speeches lined with wisdom and puckered with wit—a gulf of audiovisual dissociation of sensibility.

As might be expected from Zeffirelli, he unleashes a great deal of centrifugality—some of it effective, much of it distracting—and a minimum of respect for the text. When the director cannot divert our attention by avalanches of movement, he resorts to cutting. Thus Juliet's two important soliloquies, "Gallop apace" and the potion-drinking speech, are omitted, as is the moving final exchange with Romeo, "O God, I have an ill-divining soul . . ." Cut, too, are such effective scenes as the wedding feast that turns into a funeral, and the important slaying of Paris, which alone justifies Friar Laurence's abandonment of the revived Juliet in the tomb.

One of the apter aspects of the film, besides Danilo Donati's convincing costumes and the generally sound art direction, is the editing by Reginald Mills. But three other cutters get an unusual tribute: Franco Brusati, Masolino d'Amico, and Zeffirelli himself are credited with something called "screenplay." This consists almost entirely of blue-penciling, though not quite; the "Come, vial" soliloquy, which goes on for some forty-five lines, has been rewritten by the scenarists in four words: "Love, give me strength!" I wonder how much each of the trio was paid for writing one and one-third words into Shakespeare. I discount the frightened mumblings of "No! No!" by various bystanders during the dueling scenes; surely Brusati, d'Amico, and Zeffirelli threw those in gratis.

The color cinematography of Pasquale de Santis is merely adequate, and Zeffirelli does not help much, with such hoary tricks as framing Friar Laurence's head during most of the potion-preparing scene with a retort curving hammily around the edges of the shot. Another slight disappointment is Nino Rota's music. Rota established himself as one of the great film composers with his work for early- and middle-period Fellini films, as well as other brilliant scores—e.g., for Visconti's *Rocco* and Clément's *This Angry Age*. Lately, however, he has declined. Though this score is better than what he did for Zeffirelli's *Shrew*, its simplistic main theme falls as short of Prokofiev (with whom, alas, it must compete) as Zeffirelli does of Shakespeare.

THE KILLING OF SISTER GEORGE

HAROLD CLURMAN

The Killing of Sister George may attract many people by its boldness. What was once a skillful comedy skating between mockery of television sweetness and bitchy humor in regard to female homosexuality has been converted in the film into "the shocking drama of a love triangle involving three women"—in other words, an explicit exploitation of its lesbian aspect. The word itself was never pronounced in the play; in the film the young girl says to her jealous mate, "Not every woman in the world is a lesbian," to which the reply is, "I am aware of that unfortunate fact." Common obscenities are delivered full blast, and there is a lengthy and minute sequence of an all-female seduction. For some this may betoken "liberation" and may thus be presumed to mark progress.

The Killing of Sister George is nevertheless a bad picture. The fun poked at television is dissipated in extended banality, and the love affair is basically uninteresting because we don't give a hoot for any of the ladies engaged in it: their "psychology," neatly limned in the play, becomes falsely pathetic, a mere pretense of sympathy through its frankness. The play's superficiality was one of its assets. The spurious seriousness of the picture spoils the comedy, while its brave assault on convention is little but hollow show.

Take for example the ending. "George," the discarded television actress who for years has played the role of a sort of mother figure in a suburban English community, is offered a job as the "voice-over" for a cow in an animated film. She is insulted and at first scorns the very idea. But, like the inveterate ham she is—she has to act—the lady begins to rehearse a dolorous "moo!" In the play—which has only one setting and only four characters—she sits alone in her room shortly after she has been abandoned by her girl friend (gone off with the TV-program supervisor, a discreet lesbian of resolutely correct bearing), and with tears in her eyes bellows the bovine cry. In the film she returns to the empty studio stage and proceeds to wreck it, and by the time she gets to the "moo" we have nearly forgotten its motivation. Both humor and pathos have been vitiated.

Beryl Reid, an admirably resourceful comedienne of considerable dramatic power, plays her part exactly as she did in the play. This means that she is too vehement in relation to the camera close-ups; she seems to be overacting, to the detriment of both comedy and drama. Susannah York as "George's" girl friend—the best-drawn character in the play—makes a valiant stab at her part, but is by nature unable to convey mental incapacity or moral depravity. Coral Browne is at her best in the sexual encounter with the younger woman, but she has been so directed as to deprive the role of the least hint of comedy—which was originally its chief attribute. For some reason, every face in the film looks as if it had been polished with glycerine. The music in the somber moments is not only trite but absurd.

The groundlings of every stripe will enjoy the sight of the real Gateways Club of London—a lesbian dive in full swing.

THE BIRTHDAY PARTY

HAROLD CLURMAN

The Birthday Party, archetypically commonplace in its details, is in effect a fantasia of fear and persecution. Not only is Stanley, its central figure, a failed pianist gone to seed, hiding from the world and haunted by fear, but so are his persecutors. Even the dull "landscape" outside the tatty little seaside boardinghouse where Stanley has sequestered himself has the look of a town stricken by some nameless ailment. The buildings are haggard, the sea seems dead, the streets are inert, the beach chairs ghostly. They are all dyed with the hue of mortality.

Both in their sixties, Peter and his wife, who own the lodgings, are drab and depressed; the man, a lowly worker, is honestly, forbearingly, resignedly squelched; the woman, chirpingly and childishly so. She is too dimwitted to fear anything except perhaps the

Grim Reaper himself; she lives in a cozy vacuum of inanity in which only remnants of kindly and uncomprehending womanhood still reside.

Stanley is in terror of those who ruined his career, "carved him up," and ultimately of being taken away by them, removed. When two strangers, Goldberg and McCann, come on the scene, Nemesis (or "Society") enters. Of the two, McCann, the muscle man, is a moron, in shivering awe of his superior, Goldberg. Goldberg is all glib good humor, schmaltzy sentiment, fierce will, gifted with an armory of clichés. He too is mad: his affable sangfroid, his fake ease collapse now and then into insane rage at a reminder by his inferior of antecedents for whom he harbors a muddled nostalgia. He is also idiotically hypochrondriac.

The two men's toying and teasing and their bewildering demands on Stanley to justify his existence—addressed in a battery of questions composed of everything from stupid quiz posers to metaphysical and scientific conumdrums—reduce Stanley to speechless impotence. The inquisitors haul him off a helpless victim. Where he is taken—to a sanitarium, a madhouse, a gang boss or a prison—does not matter: it signifies his doom. No one is strong enough to protest; most are too dumb to understand.

Harold Pinter's ear is so keen, his method so economic and so shrewdly stylized, balancing humdrum realistic notations with suggestions of unfathomable violence, that his play succeeds in being both funny and horrific. He is aided in this in the film by William Friedkin's direction. It is comprised of excellent camera work, the subtle use of color and environmental authenticity, the elimination of all sound except for the dialogue, and above all the acting.

The cast is truly remarkable. In the part of Goldberg, Sydney Tafler's trim and powerful physique acts: it stands for "solid respectability." His unctuous bonhomie, his treacherously winning smoothness which spills out in a delightful Anglo-Yiddish accent (without caricature), his latent savagery constitute an unforgettable portrait. Very nearly on the same level, though in a less complex part, is Patrick Magee as McCann. Anguished by his own brainlessness, murderously protective of his private insanities, and something of a sleepwalker in his own and his victim's nightmares, he too creates a memorable impression. Robert Shaw's Stanley, though rather too robust to appear utterly consumed by despair, and somewhat more acid than the character as written, conveys the feeling of a tormented person who might once have become a whole man. Dandy Nichols' housekeeper is almost too absolute in her low-grade innocence and mental deficiency. She achieves tenderness not through sentiment but through her total unawareness of practically everything except the presence of Stanley, the scratchy cub in her care.

This, then, is as fine a film version of the play as I can imagine. Yet I felt something lacking, despite the fact that it is better acted and directed than were either of the two stage productions I had seen. At first, I thought my slight demur had something to do with cuts Pinter had made in the text (for example, Stanley's peculiar proposal of "elopement" with Lulu the neighborhood cutie, as well as the indication that in the blindman's-buff scene at the party Stanley had begun to strangle her), but on afterthought I have come to suspect that there is something in the play's essential nature which makes it truer to itself on the stage than it can be in even so excellent a film. On the screen *The Birthday Party* becomes a suspense and horror story—albeit a very special one—with such cinematic tricks as the sudden switch to sputtering black-and-white flashes, wiping out all color; on the stage *The Birthday Party*, less ominous, is an inescapably living experience, life itself!

And this for a paradoxical reason: film by its very quiddity is always more specific, more "realistic" than the stage: the camera reveals everything. By its very unmistakable "thereness" the film dispels some of *The Birthday Party*'s allusiveness and "make-believe." On screen we behold mystery concretely; on stage it exists covertly, phantomlike, in the manner of a memory which tinctures a whole episode or period of our lives with its own suprasensible aura. That is why I sometimes wish that film-makers would cease adapting plays and novels and conceive their work directly.

WILFRID SHEED

The boomlet in Harold Pinter movies is hard to explain. Since his little chess games do not exhaust even the resources of a small stage (most of them could be played out in an egg crate), they constitute a dismal waste of a wide screen. *The Caretaker*, currently revived after an earlier snub, achieves some small sense of motion, mainly by busting from one room to another and back, and even out into a hastily thrown-in back yard: but *The Birthday Party* scarcely moves at all, scarcely breathes. A spurious car scene and a vista of deck chairs do not a movie make.

Beyond that, one exposure to Pinter's obsession every three years fulfills most minimum adult requirements. After which you find yourself saying, Yeah, yeah—nameless menace. *The B.P.*, one of his first plays, states more clearly than most what is on his nerves; the development of his art since then has consisted mainly of fuzzing his message and of burying it in different parts of the room.

The nameless menace this time around comes to you courtesy of an Irishman and a Jew—let's just call them the Judeo-Christian heritage, shall we? The scapegoat is a would-be musician (Robert Shaw) holed up in a boardinghouse far from home—let's call him the artist in the modern world and be done with it. The story consists of a visit by the J.-C. establishment (they can always find you when they want you), followed by a harrowing initiation ceremony, at the end of which, in perverse imitation of baptism, the artist is born again, as a brainwashed square. Hence the title.

So crass a use of symbols is not typical of Pinter. In fact, in his subsequent games of blindman's buff he has been known to leave the room altogether while the audience grapples with the grandfather clock. In his painful press conferences, alias dental extractions, he now insists that he has no meaning at all, no symbols, nothing, leave me alone. So, although the movie is passing dull, it is useful to have this early leak, before his defenses were complete.

Try it this way: Pinter was a Jewish evacuee from London in World War II. This meant that he had to face the problem of assimilation, by himself, in a series of strange settings, at an age when most boys are concentrating on the best way to keep up their pants. English class apprenticeship is brutal enough if you are born to it. To an outsider like Pinter, it has the extra horror of meaninglessness. In *The Birthday Party* he acts all this out. The nice lady who runs the boardinghouse sells him out; so does the girl lodger with whom he has enjoyed an infantile friendship. Well, he never trusted them, anyway; translated into adult terms, the artist-scapegoat is a proud suspicious child. He builds no alliances against his masters.

The only hope he has is some crack in the establishment. The Jew and the Irishman, brain and muscle, are joined only by panic and mutual necessity. It would take very little to pry them apart. But the victim does not have the key. Indeed, it is his presence that holds them together. That's how it goes with institutional life, from empires on down: the top people would probably kill each other if it weren't for the children.

It is not particularly effective to have all this worked out stiffly and laboriously on screen, despite good performances by Shaw, Patrick Magee and Dandy Nichols. Pinter himself has since gone further underground, where the self-pity is less visible, where you can't even be dead sure that he hasn't gone over to the master class himself. At those incredible press conferences he is gnomic, supercilious, timid, in such strange proportions that you can't tell whether he is picking on us or we are picking on him. He is both the new boy and the upper-school tyrant.

Victims have always loved the stage; pity, terror, and revenge, and nobody knows it's you. Pinter was an actor before he was a playwright. It is no accident that his plays are written in code and that he denies to the point of tedium having any intentions whatever; it is as if some big boy's hands were on his throat. "Is this meant to be me, Pinter? Is this supposed to be clever, Pinter?" And perhaps it is no accident that for camouflage, and possibly out of admiration too, he learned how to empathize with the bullies himself. In *The Caretaker*, a much better play, the roles are optically interchangeable, so that you scarcely know bottom from top. But this small man's judo had not been perfected by *The Birthday Party*, and the dramatic tension of his best work is missing.

Hollis Alpert

Why is it that a medium which demands looking at, which has such dizzying visual (and aural) possibilities, should so often be used for endless stretches of talk? Admittedly, it is dialogue rather than mere monotonous talk that Harold Pinter, whose *The Birthday Party* has just been filmed, specializes in— and I must say at once that I enjoy Pinter and his exercises in ambiguity; but I must also admit that, in spite of a certain admiration for *The Birthday Party* as a play, I did not enjoy it as a film. It goes on and on; it simply talks too much.

I tried an experiment. I closed my eyes. And suddenly the whole thing came to life. I visualized my own setting. The actors—Robert Shaw, Sidney Tafler, Patrick Magee among them—were plainly very good. But, worrying that I might be missing something, I opened my eyes, and there they were, the same people; they'd hardly moved at all. An angle had changed on the room, making me aware that rooms, by and large, are very dull cinematic places. The point is that *The Birthday Party*, give or take a few moments of ingenious camera work by the director, William Friedkin, might just as well have been recorded on stereo tape and sold for listening to in the home.

This, I know, is a very harsh thing to say about a movie, especially one such as *The Birthday Party*, which requires considerable dedication from all concerned even to get it into production. I have the guilty feeling that I ought to be more appreciative of the cultural benefit bestowed upon me; but I also have the feeling that there is something patronizing about bringing *The Birthday Party* to the screen in this talky form, as though movies, per se, are being dignified thereby.

The movie doesn't really happen; it offers us some people to watch and hear in a shabby English boardinghouse setting. The boarder (Robert Shaw) is a seedy, guilt-ridden fellow (is it sex, failure, the human condition?), who is visited by two strangers. They torment him verbally, ask him idiotic unanswerable questions, force him to sit down and stand up, and give him a "party." Then, eventually, they take him away, a tongue-tied idiot. The trivial becomes the terrible, and with it a certain wonder, a certain pity. The acting is there, the words are there, but the movie isn't.

WAR AND PEACE

PHILIP T. HARTUNG

The bigger the film and more epic the proportions (like *Gone with the Wind, Lawrence of Arabia, 2001, The Bible,* and various lives of Christ) the more the critics sharpen their quills to make war and peace among themselves in their reviews. The Russian *War and Peace* is the biggest and most epic. And, sure enough, the reviews have run the gamut, from "the greatest," "masterpiece" and "very good indeed," down to "ridiculous" and "failure." One wonders if all the critics saw the same picture. Most of the adverse criticism, however, is aimed at the dubbing. The Walter Reade Organization (which is releasing the film in this country with Satra) prepared the American version and decided to dub it rather than use subtitles—no doubt to win the largest possible audience for this movie that cost $100 million. Although this is the best dubbing I have ever heard (it was done under the supervision of Lee Kresel), dubbing still leaves much to be desired—the synchronization is never perfect; and the voices themselves, while good, have a certain sameness and flatness. Furthermore, hearing the original Russian would have added much to the feel and atmosphere of the picture.

I must say, however, that after the first twenty minutes I forgot about dubbing and its eccentricities and found myself concentrating on the gorgeous visuals and the story—and admiring the excellent costumes and sets, the good cast, the film's faithfulness to Tolstoy and the 1805–13 period. The wonder is that *War and Peace* could be made so well. Leo Tolstoy's lengthy book (considered by many to be *the* greatest novel) wanders all over the lot, has hundreds of characters, and covers a multitude of subjects in depicting the history and struggle of the Russian people. That this all-inclusive novel could have been condensed and captured in a movie is amazing; and no doubt first credit should go to Sergei Bondarchuk, who wrote the screenplay with Vasily Solovyov and directed the massive, sprawling film, which in spite of its size has unity. Many of Tolstoy's characters are missing, but the main members of the Rostov, Bolkonsky, Bezuhov, and Kuragin families are there, and it is their fortunes and misfortunes we follow in Moscow, in St. Petersburg, and on battlefields in Austria and Russia.

Under Bondarchuk's direction, these battle scenes have a sweep that is almost too beautiful in long shots and too cruelly detailed in close-ups. But they convey the horrors of war and emphasize again and again Tolstoy's antiwar themes. These themes recur not only in the exciting visuals but also in the discussions of Pierre and Andrei, who wonder, "If evil men can work together to get what they want, why can't good men?" The two close friends are expertly portrayed: Andrei by Vyacheslav Tihonov as the handsome, gallant, but haughty prince, and Pierre by director Bondarchuk, who is no doubt too old for the role but comes through charmingly as the rather sweet, gentle, gullible do-gooder. Both men are in love with Natasha, played by Ludmila Savelyeva, ballet dancer turned actress, with extraordinary beauty and grace as she ages during the story. The many supporting roles are also well played, and outstanding among them is the portrait of Kutuzov by Boris Zahava as the commander in chief of all the Russian armies, the man who wisely waited for Napoleon and the French to destroy themselves after the burning of Moscow.

As a big-scale spectacular, *War and Peace* is as exciting for its beauty and display as it is for its story. And as beautiful as the magnificent battle scenes are the elaborate social functions, particularly the ball at which Natasha and Andrei meet and fall in love. The assets in this Russian *War and Peace* far outshine its defects. The American version, which runs for six hours and thirteen minutes (one hour shorter than the Russian version), is being shown in two parts. I'd advise you to see the parts on two separate days. But, above all, I'd advise you to see *War and Peace*.

STANLEY KAUFFMANN

The new *War and Peace* is probably the longest film ever made. (*Made*, not just allowed to run on, like some of Andy Warhol's.) Production started in 1962; sections of it have already been released as separate entities in several countries. For the United States the Russians decided to release it en bloc—or en blockbuster. The American version, even after one hour was trimmed from the completed film, is in two parts totaling six hours and thirteen minutes. You buy tickets for both parts, to be seen on the same day or on different days, and you get an intermission within each part.

This is not the first film of *War and Peace*. The Russians themselves made a ten-reel version in 1915, and in 1956 King Vidor directed an Italo-American production with Audrey Hepburn as Natasha and Henry Fonda as Pierre. Vidor's film, which had some pretty pictures in it, ran a mere three and a half hours. The statistics on this newest version are in themselves statuesque: over $100 million (in rubles, I assume); 272 sets; 120,000 extras for the battle scenes; and so on. Inevitably it is in wide screen and color. The color is surprisingly mediocre.

Sergei Bondarchuk, the director, prepared the screen adaptation and also plays Pierre. He has been seen here previously in a poor film called *Fate of a Man* (1961), which, too, he directed. When one thinks, or tries to think, of the amount of work Bondarchuk has put into *War and Peace*, the result is so stupefying that compassion almost begins to tug at criticism. Certainly one fundamental compliment can be paid him. He has tried throughout to make a *film* of *War and Peace*, not merely to chronicle the novel on film. He has tried, with widely varying results, for intrinsic cinema language. Sometimes, as in the duel between Pierre and Dolohov, this leads merely to hammy tricks with the camera. Sometimes, as in the death of old Prince Bolkonsky, there is an approximation of art. The best scenes are, predictably, the spectacles: the ball at which Natasha meets Andrei (smeared though it is with anachronistic and overdone music), the wolf hunt, the burning of Moscow, and—above all—the battle of Borodino. With every kind of panoramic shot across and above the giant steppe (helicopters were used), with very long tracking shots, with regiments marching and countermarching, with cavalry companies charging and riderless bands of horses stampeding, this enormous battle makes the eyes start and the jaw drop.

But. A crucial but. It is not very moving. What we are chiefly conscious of, in this scene as in most of the big scenes, is the size of the endeavor. It is a fifty-ring circus, not a work of dramatic art. When Eisenstein filmed a gigantic scene, like the battle on the ice in *Alexander Nevsky*, there was never a split second that deviated from a driving artistic concept which was where the whole episode began and which was part of a large design. Bondarchuk is rather a dumb director, incapable of such concepts, yet earnest and ambitiously imitative, who simply labors on and on to impress us.

But he has labored so long that the experience of this film, as a whole, takes on a somewhat grotesque quality. Standards of art begin to drop by the wayside, and we begin to be conscious only of stamina—his and ours. Films were not meant to go on at such length. This is not true of novels, such as the one on which this picture is based, because novels do not require the reader's presence in a certain place at and for a specific time; he can read when and where he likes, controlling his own pace. The fact that the film of *War and Peace* is divided virtually in half does not help; in a way it hinders, because it means going *back*, on either that day or another, to take up the film again. In two different years I attended two cycles of *The Ring of the Nibelungs* at the Metropolitan, going back once a week for four weeks. It was a highly pleasurable experience both times, because all four of the music dramas are independent yet interacting works; each week between performances was a time of savoring and anticipation. But the two-hour dinner break on the one day that I saw all of *War and Peace* was like a breather in an arduous unfinished job. It did not convert the mammoth work into two separate but related three-hour films.

It might be argued that one sometimes sees two independent long films in a day (something I have often done), but two such pictures would not, throughout six hours, exude a sense of desperation at trying to cope with one of the longest and greatest works in literary history, a desperation that inevitably wearies the viewer.

All the dialogue has been dubbed. The English words match the Russian lip movements fairly well, and most of the voices are adequately cast (old Prince Bolkonsky is an egregious exception), but there is a dead studio sound to the process, an absence of liveness and of planes, and we can never quite forget that all the speech *is* dubbed. Obviously we can never forget the subtitles in a subtitled film, but we know we are watching an attempt to bring us an unimpaired original, which is considerable compensation. To judge the actors purely visually, Bondarchuk behaves adequately as Pierre, Vyacheslav Tihonov acts and looks like Valentino as Andrei, Irina Skobtseva is a seductive Helene, and Vasily Lanovoi is a handsome Kuragin. Ludmila Savelyeva, the Natasha, looks like three parts Sylvia Sidney to one part Audrey Hepburn; she is sprightly as a child, unconvincing as a woman.

Again there is the question that recurs whenever a great book is filmed: For whom was this picture made? Here the real answer is: For the Soviet government, to celebrate its fiftieth anniversary. Well, at least that is a more rational answer than can usually be given to the question. But what's in it for audiences? Those who know the novel will get only sporadic entertainment and will certainly not feel that they have "seen" the book. Those who do not know the novel may get somewhat more pleasure but probably less than they have had from many historical films made from more malleable sources. Certainly they will get small indication from this film as to why *War and Peace* is a better novel than *Ben Hur* or *Gone with the Wind*.

Richard Schickel

One emerges from *War and Peace* exhausted and irritable. Since the length of the movie has been well publicized—is, indeed, the chief reason for curiosity about it—the tired condition of one's blood neither surprises nor dismays. Oxygen or a modest amount of alcohol will soon set it to rights. The irritation is less easily dismissed, for one has the feeling that it is not entirely the fault of director Sergei Bondarchuk and his cast of thousands. The policies of the film's American distributors are more than a little to blame for the restlessness it induces.

They have treated *War and Peace* with a lack of respect usually accorded sleazy Italian sex-and-sandal epics designed for short runs at the bottom of the bill. They have cut it and dubbed it and thereby ruined whatever merit it may have had. Both of these practices are painfully common among movie businessmen, and since they betray a fundamental lack of respect for the artist and the uniqueness of his vision, they are reprehensible at any level; the worst B picture is entitled to fail on its own terms. When they are applied to something like *War and Peace*, a once-in-a-lifetime attempt to place on the screen a detailed, faithful rendering of a great work of literature that is also a national epic, a film that required five years of effort and unprecedented backing by the Russian government, these policies seem to me little short of demented.

As usually happens when anti-artists start snipping around, it is the continuity, the connective tissue that gives a film its rhythm and its inner logic, that goes. Some fifty minutes of it went, and the film you are being asked to pay up to $7.50 to see has a bad case of the jumps. Too often you are unsure of how—or why—a character got from here to there, and what the time sequence of events is. And if you commit yourself to a six-and-a-half-hour movie the day is shot, anyway—what difference does another hour or so make?

As for the dubbing, it has the familiar effect of alienating audience from characters. You get fixed on those lips so obviously not speaking the lines you are hearing, you get to brooding about those radio-station voices *reading* instead of *acting* their parts, and it becomes impossible to sustain identification with the figures on the screen. Subtitling is not a perfect solution to the language barrier, but it is relatively unobtrusive, does not deny actors the use of their voices, the basic tools of their art, does not tamper with an intrinsic part of a film's design.

In the circumstances it is difficult to offer an intelligent critique of Bondarchuk's work—and impossible to discuss his actors—but as a guess I would say it has its own deficiencies. Missing is Toltoy's fascinating theory of history, as well as the Christian message he was propagating in his novel (neither fits Marxist theory very well), and without this intellectual and moral underpinning the film lacks power and purpose. Its characters, all of whom had carefully calculated symbolic weights in the novel, now have little organic relationship to the historical background against which they are placed and neither illuminate nor are illuminated by it.

That pretty much leaves the big battle at Borodino and the burning of Moscow to sustain interest. Both have a certain sweep and grandeur, but Bondarchuk concentrates excessively on the movement of masses, rarely favoring us with the telling, humanizing details—the faces in the crowd—out of which such masters of film spectacle as Sergei Eisenstein have patiently and painstakingly built their great action sequences. In particular, the story's emotional pivot, the lost wandering of the saintly Pierre (played by Bondarchuk himself) through the hell of Borodino, lacks the intensity, the sense of growing terror and pity, that can only be created by careful detailing. The burning of the capital and Napoleon's retreat are handled with greater sureness—proof, I suppose, that over the long years of shooting, the director learned a great deal by doing. Still, the feeling that the human element has been mislaid in order to concentrate on large-scale logistics persists. It is a human enough failing, but coupled with the ideological myopia of the Russians and the commercial insensitivity of their American distributors it leads one to think *War and Peace* was not really worth all that time or money.

THE HEART IS A LONELY HUNTER

RICHARD SCHICKEL

The Heart Is a Lonely Hunter deals—symbolically, to be sure—with the death of God. In the beginning he is alive, if not completely well, having taken the ironic pseudonym of John Singer —ironic because he is a deaf mute—in a medium-sized Southern city. Touchingly alone and kindly, no Old Testament deity, he is doing his best to help an amazingly various collection of psychological and physical cripples adjust to, and sometimes overcome, the afflictions with which their existence is cursed. In the end, overcome by the death of a character who can only be seen as his "son," he withdraws from this effort, leaving to their chancy destinies all who have come to depend on his aid and comfort in the microcosmic universe he has created around himself.

Of them all, Spiro, the "son," is outwardly the most grievously flawed. Also a deaf mute, he is grossly fat, half-witted—a child man. And yet, despite his symbolic identity, he is not a sacrilege, for he has a divine innocence, a surpassing sweetness, measured against which everyone else must be found wanting. He is, moreover, the only soul with whom Singer's understanding and ability to communicate are complete. The depth of his despair over Spiro's loss is therefore understandable and, by analogy, implies an explanation for the long silence of God that is so familiar to modern man.

All of this suggests a rigidity of structure, an emphasis on a controlling metaphor that often leads, in films, to artistic lifelessness. Nothing could be farther from the truth. The movie-makers may have perhaps been more explicit about symbolic meaning than Carson McCullers was in the novel upon which the film is based; they may also have been a bit more sentimental in their treatment of characters than she; yet this is a very good movie, holding back its larger meaning until the final sequence—and then not insisting on it.

The film's true and abiding fascination lies in its exploration of

Singer's relationship with the people he draws to him, partly altruistically, partly to assuage his terrible loneliness. They are all wondrously alive, difficult, self-contradictory. Among them are a drifter, drunk on cheap booze and cheap self-pity; a proud, dying Negro doctor and his embittered daughter, tragically misunderstanding each other; and, most important, a girl inching her way, her painful shyness deepened by bewilderment over the sudden crippling of her father and the poverty it causes, toward the strength and wisdom she will need to survive as a woman. Singer at least partially wins his battles for these lost souls. Their outward circumstances remain unaltered, but it is clear that his example—and none, of course, is more afflicted than he—gives them faith of a kind that will help them through the new trials which, as human beings, they will inevitably face.

Much of the credit for their uncanny ability to engage rather than repel, in their sadness and occasional grotesquerie, must go to the actors, three in particular. A newcomer, Sondra Locke, perfectly captures the gawky grace of a romantic adolescent trying to cope with unromantic reality. Chuck McCann (until recently host of a kiddie TV show in New York) is superb as Spiro. On his show he frequently impersonated Oliver Hardy, and his obvious feeling for mime has paid off in a lovely bit of work, full of the sudden frets and humors of a man hopelessly imprisoned in silence and misunderstanding. Finally, there is Alan Arkin as Singer. I have spoken before of his enormous gift for mime. In *Inspector Clouseau* he used it for comedy; here he uses it for serious purposes, although he deftly touches the edge of his character with humor. Singer's central tension is between his natural shyness and his desperate need to reach out and touch people whose inclination is to avoid one so afflicted. Arkin's ability to convey this endless inner struggle—and a great deal besides—effortlessly, modestly, with minimal attention being directed at the tour de force he is accomplishing, strikes me as a model of the screen actor's art.

One wishes to take nothing away from Thomas C. Ryan's sensible, low-pitched adaptation or from the skillful (if conventional) direction of Robert Ellis Miller, but in the end this is an actor's picture. Despite the larger meanings which give it resonance, *The Heart Is a Lonely Hunter* is essentially a study of real people responding to real pressures. They, not ideas, not metaphors, move one first to tears, then to understanding, not merely of themselves but of the entire human condition.

THE FIXER

RICHARD SCHICKEL

Ever since *The Fixer* was previewed in New York, I have noticed a number of chic opinion-makers putting on their crocodile-tear–stained faces and asking the working press to join them in pitying, censuring, and generally putting down director John Frankenheimer's film version of Bernard Malamud's latest novel.

There are some problems with the film, to be sure. It is based, as you perhaps know, on the historical case of one Mendel Beiliss (here called Yakov Bok), a Jew who was wrongly imprisoned for a preposterous crime, the "ritual murder" of a Gentile child in turn-of-the-century Kiev, during one of those waves of anti-Semitism that have periodically swept Russia. He spent years in prison merely awaiting his trial, and during those years he was systematically tormented, humiliated, abused in an effort to make him confess to the charges against him. The film records those years in all their horror, and many of its detractors tell me they regard this exploration of unrelieved misery as an irrelevant and boring exercise. Still others have expressed dismay at Frankenheimer's lack of stylistic venturesomeness. The film, they say, has an old-fashioned look, as if the last ten wonderful years in the cinema had never happened. Finally, it is claimed that the accents of the cast, mostly English, exist very oddly and uneasily in the carefully reconstructed (in Hungary) environment of czarist Russia.

Of these criticisms, only the last seems to me to have the slightest validity. That Yakov's time in jail was unpleasant, and that the movie is unrelenting in spelling out the details of that unpleasantness, cannot be denied. But there is no attempt to exploit them for merely sensational effect. They are dramatically necessary for a story that is an uplifting hymn to the human spirit. As to the question of style, it seems to me a form of cultural blindness to insist that because the new way of making a movie can be rewarding and/or delightful, it is the *only* way of making a movie. In this particular case, it would have been ridiculous. Malamud's novel deliberately attempted to recapture the spirit of the nineteenth-century novel and an archetypal simplicity which is what Frankenheimer obviously—and successfully—matched.

I suppose there is some validity to the criticism about diction, particularly in the case of Alan Bates's Yakov. I have no idea what an English vocal equivalent of a Russian-Jewish peasant would be, but I am pretty certain it would not be moderated North-of-England-workingman. Yet even this flaw must be considered within the context of the many fine things Bates does in this rich role —rich since Yakov Bok is the last man in the world you would expect to stand up to slow and endless torture. He is introduced as an apolitical and unreligious man, interested merely in getting along as best he can without making trouble. Anything but a born hero, he is devious, even rather cowardly—a very ordinary man. Bates gives us this basic character with wonderful ease and humor, and, for me at least, by the time he entered upon his agony I had quite forgotten my initial discomfort about his accent.

In prison, Bates becomes not merely a man exhibiting grace under pressure, but one exhibiting a much rarer capacity to grow intellectually and spiritually. For about two hours we are locked in a cell with Bates-Bok, who must, virtually alone, hold our attention. We must believe that each descent into despair, each flight into hysteria, each physical and emotional blow may shatter him. At the same time we must believe that somehow he is finding, not in ideology, not in faith, but somewhere in himself, in his guts, the strength to go on. We must believe in the likelihood of his defeat and the possibility of his victory, and Bates makes us do so in a performance of range and control.

In the process he gives us what may be a definitive portrayal of the psychology of an increasingly common figure in our time: the survivor, the man who mysteriously, miraculously finds a way to draw upon his own basic human instincts—capacities unknown to himself until he is forced to test them—to defeat those who would oppress him. It seems to me that a movie that seriously, sensitively probes at this central existential enigma must not be judged in niggling terms. What we have in *The Fixer* is not primarily a problem in the aesthetics of the cinema, but a splendid humanistic document, worthy of your closest attention.

ARTHUR SCHLESINGER, JR.

The Fixer—or at least the hour and a half I could abide of it—is worse than ludicrous; it is repellent. It is odd that this should be so. Bernard Malamud's novel about the Jew falsely accused of ritual murder in imperial Russia was strong and serious. John Frankenheimer has shown brilliant narrative control and drive in other films. The cast (Alan Bates, Dirk Bogarde, Hugh Griffith, David Warner) is good. But everything has gone wrong. It was a mistake, I think, to shoot a somber tale like this in cheerful color; nor did making it in Hungary bring it closer to Kiev than if it had been made in Culver City. The medley of accents—Cockney, BBC, East Side New York, Eastern European—is distracting. The confusion of tone is even worse.

The film begins with a thunderous scene of a pogrom shot in Frankenheimer's best bravura style. Suddenly the mood shifts to *Fiddler on the Roof*—gentle ghetto tailors uttering aphorisms; the hero speaking a Jacobowskylike soliloquy while pondering whether or not to sleep with a Russian girl. Then a child is found murdered; the hero is arrested; and the rest of the film, as far as I could endure it, is beatings, torture, degradation, and fairly unrelieved sadism.

The Fixer is made with evident contempt for its audience. The screenplay, by that old Popular Front hack Dalton Trumbo, mingles sentimental cliché, sententious nonprofundities, fake social concern, and a prurient relish in violence. This is a totally false film, devoid of a breath of human life or truth.

THE SEA GULL

ARTHUR SCHLESINGER, JR.

My youngest son sometimes talks about "dignified-type movies." By this he means films which, with due reverence, copy a classic work or event already fully realized in another medium—a notable novel or play or historical event. *David Copperfield, Henry V, Wilson* were all dignified-type movies. Such movies rate little space in histories of the art. Often they are great bores.

Yet, every once in a while a dignified-type movie succeeds in evoking the quality of the work or event from which it is derived. Sidney Lumet did this in *Long Day's Journey Into Night;* he has now done it again with *The Sea Gull.* Lumet is a serious and gifted director of uneven taste. When he is on his own, as in *The Pawnbroker,* the results may be mixed. When he accepts the discipline of O'Neill or Chekhov, the result is likely to be more powerful than, say, the latest chef d'oeuvre of Robert Aldrich.

"Behind the door of every contented, happy man," Chekhov once wrote, "there ought to be someone standing with a little hammer and continually reminding him with a knock that there are unhappy people, that however happy he may be, life will sooner or later show him its claws, and trouble will come to him . . . and then no one will see or hear him, just as now he neither sees nor hears others." Chekhov invented a new form of dramatic art to render this sense that "what is terrible in life goes on somewhere behind the scenes." He moved Western drama beyond the architectonics of the "well-made" play into the evanescence and duplicity of human life.

In *The Sea Gull* an aging actress pays summer visits to her brother and son on a country estate. On one occasion she brings with her Trigorin, a successful novelist. Nina, a free and innocent girl on a neighboring estate, falls in love with Trigorin. As Trigorin lightly consumes and rejects Nina, so the actress all her life has consumed and rejected her son, who loves Nina. The victims are destroyed, the sophisticates continue on their way.

Shot in delicate color beside a misty Swedish lake, the film admirably reproduces Chekhov's mixture of humor and melancholy. It follows the play faithfully, scene by scene; there is no attempt to portray what Chekhov kept as offstage action—Nina and Trigorin in Moscow, for example. Lumet gives the story a slightly Freudian twist, suggesting that the son's crisis lay more in his relationship to his mother than to Nina. I am not sure that Chekhov intended to have this point made so sharply, but it is a permissible reading of the text.

Chekhov requires ensemble acting, and here Sidney Lumet's touch falters. Vanessa Redgrave is a lovely, precise, and moving Nina; no actress around attains stunning effects with less apparent effort. Denholm Elliott and Harry Andrews are just right. But James Mason's Trigorin is a bit stagy and contrived (no doubt Trigorin was, too); and Simone Signoret, playing the actress as if out of Maupassant, and David Warner, playing her son as if out of John Osborne, are out of cadence with the rest.

"Shakespeare's plays are bad enough," Tolstoy once said to Chekhov, "but yours are even worse"—a salutary reminder of how foolish great men can be. Fortunately Chekhov persisted in doing his thing, and now Lumet has done well enough by Chekhov. For this reviewer, *The Sea Gull* seems likely to offer a far more satisfying aesthetic—if noncinematic—experience than most other films of the month put together.

JOHN SIMON

Chekhov was the musician of boredom. No one, not even Beckett, has drawn such recondite harmonies and such subtle discords from the motions, utterances, and silences of boredom. Frustrated lives palpitating in concert, hurling unsolicited gifts and demands at one another, misunderstanding or understanding one another too well, and hurting either way, they talk and live right past one another. Dialogues are not so much conversations as reciprocally embarrassing confessions colliding in mid-air, and the atmosphere is so smoky with frustration that joy cannot grow in it. Yet sapling joys do shoot up from time to time, only to wither swiftly and sheepishly.

That is the basic quality of *The Sea Gull*, and even if Sidney Lumet had captured it in his film version, it would probably have made for a cumbrous, oppressive film. But he captures nothing of the sort. Lumet's boredom is one that settles viscously on the viewer, who cares not a straw for Lumet's straw men; whereas Chekhov's people, properly interpreted on the stage, are as fascinating as a juggling act in which the balls are continually dropped until one hangs on every move of the bizarre, unhappy prestidigitators in the hope that one of their tricks might succeed.

Part of the trouble is the medium itself. The stage always affords full view of the arena of fumbles; every unsuccessful move can be seen in all its ramifications. Or, more precisely, the stage always shows you the space between the actors, the small but sufficient abyss into which their enterprises hurtle. The camera—except as handled by a master, which Lumet categorically is not—cannot capture the hollowness of space, the oppressive immovableness of a seemingly harmless enclosure, stasis settling on everything like a fine, corrosive dust. Then again, a filmed play requires inventiveness in camera setups, a sharp feeling for montage, and self-effacing camera movements, lest, given the sparseness of action, one become aware of technical overcompensation. But Lumet is either too dazzled or too crudely confident to be at home in art.

And, of course, there must be performances. Performances that can make demanding stage roles survive this transplanting into alien ground. Even from good actors, though, Lumet can extract glutinous or shrill, colorless or desperate performances. Least excusable here is the casting of Simone Signoret as Arkadina. While most of the actors speak in well-tailored English accents, Miss Signoret putters or sloshes about in a *débraillé* French one (not a stylish one à la Charles Boyer) that is often incomprehensible. Her appearance has also become hard to take, especially when the text has her remark on how well she has kept her figure, and her acting is unsubtle—in part, I suppose, from exhaustion from her bouts with English.

As Trigorin, James Mason acts dazed, uncomfortable, constrained. Yet that is the opposite of what characterizes this successful second-rate writer: postures of existential despair, affectations of bluff simplicity, and, underneath, complacency; if the actor is very great, he may be able also to show the genuine sense of emptiness at the core. Mason maintains an all-purpose remoteness, relieved only by faint but rather too genuine yearning, and makes Trigorin uninteresting.

Vanessa Redgrave is—by now, at any rate—too much of a raw-boned thirtyish English governess to pass for the vulnerably young, sweetly tremulous Nina. A jaw like hers could take all of fate's punches; and how could poetry, except perhaps Edwin Markham's, live under that backward-sloping forehead? Her innocence comes across studied, and she pathetically lacks pathos. Her fourth-act scene (which loses much by being shot outdoors) remains wholly unmoving. Even if Lumet was trying to adhere to Chekhov's designation of the play as a "comedy," that surely means a sad comedy of absurd waste, and it is better for Nina to err on the side of Ophelia than on that of a budding Madwoman of Chaillot. As Konstantin, David Warner tries hard to compensate for his lack of sensitive looks and personal charm; what comes out is not a young Aleksandr Blok but a young blockhead with pretensions.

Harry Andrews is an unshaded, frenetic Sorin, Eileen Herlie a flat Paulina. While Kathleen Widdoes acts Masha well enough, the aura of smugness and prissiness that always surrounds this actress erects a sympathy barrier. Alfred Lynch is a believable Medvedenko, but Ronald Radd a noisy cliché of a Shamrayev. Perhaps the worst performance (after Signoret's) is Denholm Elliott's Dorn. Elliott, who can be brilliant as a roué, a weakling, or a bounder, simply cannot cope with the decent, weary doctor—a sympathetic and perceptive man gone stale with age and provincial drudgery. His wig, moreover, makes him look like some villainous marquis at the court of Louis XV or, equally inappropriately, a diabolical Mark Twain.

It is not so much a question of individual shortcomings, however, as of what these actors jointly undo. Here Lumet is most to blame. And what preposterous directorial ideas he has! At the beginning, Masha and Medvedenko, totally out of period and character, are shown rolling around in the tall grass; as Masha adjusts her disarrayed undergarments, she declares that she wears black out of mourning for her life. Or, at the end, how stupid to cut that great line "The fact is, Konstantin has shot himself," and substitute a view of Treplev's bloody body—just like the sea gull's!—floating in the lake, then have Dorn enter the drawing room ominous and silent, and have a slow circular panning shot (a favorite Lumetian device) around the lotto table, where each face registers a different yet obvious expression. A long hammy silence, then blackout. No! It is that awkward, whispered last line—with its "the fact is," and to Trigorin, of all people—that is needed; and the lotto players playing on as if nothing had happened.

Gerry Fisher's color photography, at least in the print on display at the Plaza Theatre, is rather poor; it looks like hand-tinted film, the faces mostly heliotrope, and nature a washed-out bluish green or greenish blue. The interiors are better. The Swedish house and lake used work in quite nicely, although one never gets a sense of exactly who lives in that house and exactly where. The translation by Moura Budberg is all right, but it has been carefully pruned of literary or cultural references that might puzzle the customers of less pivileged neighborhood theaters. As I myself was leaving the Plaza, a woman was explaining portentously, "Unrequited love!" That may have been her own, unabetted cloddishness, but I cannot help feeling that Lumet's unrequited love for "Art" encourages such vulgar errors.

II:

REFLECTIONS

THE GRADUATE MAKES OUT

Hollis Alpert

From a window of my apartment I have a view of a movie house on Manhattan's East Side, where, ever since last December, *The Graduate* has attracted long lines of patrons. During some of the coldest winter weekends, the lines extended around the corner all the way down the block, much like those at the Radio City Music Hall during holiday periods—except that the people waiting for the next showing were not family groups but mostly young people in their teens and early twenties. One night when it was eight degrees outside I passed the line and noticed how little they seemed to be bothered by the weather; they stomped their feet, they made cheerful chatter; it was as though they all knew they were going to see something good, something made for *them*. There were other cinemas nearby, but no one waited outside in the cold. *The Graduate* was the film to see.

It still is, although now, with the warm weather, I notice that older people have begun to intermix with the young crowd. Either *The Graduate* has begun to reach deep into that amorphous audience that makes the large hits or the elders have become curious about the movie their offspring have been going to see again and again. For that is what has been happening. *The Graduate* is not merely a success; it has become a phenomenon of multiple attendance by young people.

Letters from youthful admirers of the movie have been pouring in on Dustin Hoffman, the talented thirty-year-old actor who plays the unprepossessing twenty-one-year-old Benjamin Braddock. A

235

strong theme of identification with Benjamin's particular parental and societal hang-ups runs through these letters, as it also does in the letters to Mike Nichols, the director with an uncanny knack for forging hits. They've been writing to Joseph E. Levine, who backed and has been presenting the film. One boy from Dallas wrote Levine, bragging that he had seen *The Graduate* more than any of his friends, no less than fifteen times.

I have seen *The Graduate* three times—once at a preview, twice with audiences—thus satisfying, I hope, the Columbia graduate student who questioned my qualifications to assess the film after only one viewing. "But you must see it at *least* three times," she told me at a brunch given by her literature professor. "You see, it has meanings and nuances you don't get on just one viewing." She, and many others in her age group, cultishly attach all sorts of significance to the most minor of details. In the film's opening moments, for example, Benjamin is seen in the cabin of a huge jet, blank-faced among rows of blank faces. "Ladies and gentlemen," the captain's voice announces, "we are about to begin our descent into Los Angeles." My graduate student interpreted this as symbolic of Benjamin's arrival in purgatory. Close to the end of the film, Benjamin is seen in an antiseptic church, outlined against a glass partition, his arms spread out. Many have interpreted this as suggesting a crucifixion theme, an interpretation, I have it on good authority, that was far from the minds of Mr. Nichols and Mr. Hoffman.

Viewers have made much of the symbolic use of glass and water in the film, signifying Benjamin's inability to get through, to communicate with the generation that has produced him. He peers through the glass of a tank at captive fish. At poolside, and in the pool, he looks out at his parents and their friends through the glass mask of a diving suit. At other times it is through sunglasses that he sees a home environment grown somewhat strange. Surely, Benjamin is alienated, but what is so odd here is that the generation-gappers who love the film regard this sense of estrangement as natural and normal, given the times and the middle-class values espoused by Benjamin's family and friends.

Hollywood has made strenuous attempts to appeal to the young film audience in the past, from Andy Hardy to Elvis Presley. There have been bikini beach parties, rock-'n'-roll orgies, Annette Funicello, and Peter Fonda on LSD, but the coin taken in from these

usually cheap and sleazy quickies has been but a pittance compared
to the returns from *The Graduate*. I need cite only the fact that
The Graduate has already taken in more than $35,000,000 at the
box office, after playing in only 350 of this country's theaters. Marlon Brando, the revered James Dean, and Presley never came near
doing that. But this film, without the so-called stars for security,
has now done better, financially speaking, than all but a dozen
films of the past, and it still has thousands of drive-ins to play
throughout the summer; it has yet to open anywhere abroad; and
there are still those lines in front of the theater I see through my
window. It is quite possible that *The Graduate* will become one of
the three or four most profitable pictures *ever* made, perhaps as
profitable as *The Sound of Music*, which has done so sensationally
well that some critics renamed it *The Sound of Money*.

But how can these two industry landmarks be equated? *The
Graduate* would appear to be squarely attacking all that *The
Sound of Music* affirms so prettily: sugary sentiment, the sanctity
of vows, whether religious or marital, the righteous rearing of chil-
dren, melody over the mountains. The one has the well-scrubbed
Julie Andrews and a dozen or so cute kids, all of them singing the
Rodgers and Hammerstein lush gush as though it were the equal of
Handel's *Messiah*. The other has the appealing but unhandsome
Dustin Hoffman, Anne Bancroft playing a dissatisfied, alcoholic
bitch of a wife, and a musical score by Paul Simon (performed by
Simon and Garfunkel) that, contrasted with *The Sound of
Music*'s sentimental reverence, chants, "And the people bowed and
prayed/To the neon god they made . . ." Yet a somewhat similar
pattern of attendance has been noted about both films. The young
audiences go to see *The Graduate* again and again. Housewives,
matrons, women's clubbers went to see *The Sound of Music* again
and again. We must hypothesize, then, that in this period of selective filmgoing there are at least two huge American audiences there
for the right picture, one made up of the seventeens to the twenty-
fives, the other of the over-thirty-fives. The Motion Picture Association now advertises its more adult fare as "suggested for mature
audiences," but one wonders which is the more mature.

I have encountered some members of my generation—let us
loosely call it the over-forties—who haven't liked *The Graduate*.
More than that, it made them angry. It was almost as though they
felt themselves personally attacked, and it has occurred to me that

their reaction is less objective and critical than emotional and, possibly, subliminal. These friends do worry about their children, they have brought them up well, given them opportunities of education and aesthetic development, and they are quite certain they have managed to establish communication with their young. Their wives don't drink or seduce the neighbor's son. What's all this business about honesty and truth in *The Graduate?* The cards have been stacked against the middle-class parent and in favor of the rebellious "now" generation. They darkly hint at the commercial motives of Levine, Nichols, and company, who, it's true, hoped to come through at the box office, but had not the faintest notion they would come through so handsomely.

But *The Graduate* was not meant as an attack on a generation; it merely tells a *story*, as effectively as the makers knew how to do it. To understand the story it is necessary, however, to understand that Benjamin Braddock belongs to a milieu that has been termed the affluent society. He has never known financial insecurity—he has grown up among gadgets, among cars and swimming pools— and this he has taken so much for granted that it literally has no meaning for him. His parents, on the other hand, have presumably known hard times; they know the value, for them, of money, of material success, of things. When Benjamin comes of age, literally and symbolically, he finds himself vaguely rejecting all that his parents hold so dear. He finds himself a kind of object, the proud result of proper rearing, a reward of his parents' struggle in his behalf. Somehow, he feels, this is wrong, but he doesn't yet know what is right. What guides and counselors does he have? "Ben, I want to say one word to you, just one word," a friend of the family breathes in his ear at a welcome-home party. Benjamin awaits the word, among clinking glasses holding machine-made ice and good bourbon and Scotch. "Plastics," the fellow says, imparting the great secret to success in our time. "There is a great future in plastics." The young audiences howl, at least they did when I was there, and they're on the side of Benjamin and the movie, which pokes fun at the plastic society and those who believe in it.

It is also interesting that while Benjamin tunes out for a while, he doesn't turn on. He neither joins nor identifies with the hippies, the yippies, or the weirdies; he is still thoroughly middle-class, affluent variety. As he lazes purposelessly in the California sun his thoughts turn heavily to those of sex with Mrs. Robinson, whose frustrating marriage has borne her only one good result, her lovely daughter, Elaine. Elaine will soon have the benefits of her young womanhood, while the mother will sink into her bitter middle age. Unconscious envy on Mrs. Robinson's part turns into willful determination, and she reveals herself in her nudity to Benjamin's unwilling gaze. He first runs from her as from the very devil; after all, there are the proprieties, not to mention the taboos.

But then he backs into the affair with Mrs. Robinson, who uses him for the sex she doesn't get from Mr. Robinson. In only one moment does she allow Benjamin to reach her; their intimacy is, literally, skin deep. When Benjamin stupidly assumes that affection is necessary in a furtive affair, the surprised Mrs. Robinson expels cigarette smoke into his mouth. She too is aware of and insistent on the taboos; Benjamin is never, ever to take Elaine out, for she assumes that by her actions she has cheapened both Benjamin and herself.

And, of course, he does, forced into it by his unaware parents. Some critics have felt that the film breaks in two around this point, that the first half is a "seriocomedy" and the second a kind of campus romance with a chase finale. But this criticism seems to overlook the unifying fact of its all being viewed and experienced through Benjamin, who is in a process of muddle, change, and development. He is a truth-seeker, trying to cut through to some acceptable level of meaning. He even tells the truth to the outraged Mr. Robinson about the affair with Mrs. Robinson: "We got into bed with each other. But it was nothing. It was nothing at all. We might—we might just as well have been shaking hands."

One of the great appeals of the film to the young, and to the young in heart of all ages, is Benjamin's honesty. The most important thing in common between Elaine and Benjamin is that they share the urge to see honestly and clearly. But Elaine's emotions are still unstable. She allows herself to be rushed into a hasty, secret marriage with an available suitor, appropriately enough a medical student, a candidate for surgeondom.

It is the ending of the film that has annoyed some, and delighted many others. If it were not for the ending, I doubt that The Graduate would have aroused as much enthusiastic favor as it has among the somewhat inchoately rebellious young. The distraught Benjamin, madly seeking his lost Elaine—the pure, the good, the holy—manages to reach the church, but not (as is invariably the case in a

Doris Day movie) in time, upon which his hoarse, despairing appeal causes Elaine to leave her newly wedded groom and the assembled relatives, and to take a bus to nowhere in particular with Benjamin. To hold off the outraged parents, the attendants, and the minister, Benjamin grabs a large golden cross and swings it menacingly, then uses it as a makeshift padlock on the church doors.

Curiously enough, the writer of the novel on which the film is based, Charles Webb, who was not much more than Benjamin's age at the time of writing, had fashioned a different ending—not *very* different, but crucial nevertheless. Benjamin, in the book, did arrive at the church in time, and there was no further "moral transgression" on his part involved, except, perhaps, for that bit of cross-wielding. It turns out that Mr. Webb was disturbed by the changed ending. He wrote a letter to *The New Republic*, complaining about critic Stanley Kauffmann's laudatory interpretation of the film, and particularly by what Kauffmann had approvingly termed the "film's moral stance." "As a moral person," Webb wrote, "he [Benjamin] does not disrespect the institution of marriage. In the book the strength of the climax is that his moral attitudes make it necessary for him to reach the girl before she becomes the wife of somebody else, which he does. In the film version it makes no difference whether he gets there in time or not. As such, there is little difference between his relationship to Mrs. Robinson and his relationship to Elaine, both of them being essentially immoral."

However, it does make a great deal of difference that in the film he does not get there in time, and the audiences have taken delight in just that fact. This film-bred, film-loving generation has seen that the ending is aimed, in a double-barreled kind of way, at what might be called general moral complacency in America, and also at Hollywood morality, which, from time immemorial, has felt it necessary to approve only the sexual love that occurs during the state of marriage, and that, up until only a decade ago, took place in twin beds, with at least one foot of the man on the floor.

Not only does Mr. Webb, in his letter, equate morality with marriage licenses, he overlooks the fact that even in his novel Elaine would already have taken out a marriage license by the time Benjamin reached her. And there is a thing called consummation. The Nichols ending (relatively little story tampering was done otherwise) is a bold stroke that not only is effective but gives the story more meaning. We now see clearly Mrs. Robinson's tragedy, that she was unable to break out of the hollow formality, the prosperous smothering surface of her own marriage. "It's too late," she screams at her daughter, who is about to head for Benjamin. Upon which Elaine, seeing it all clearly for the first time, screams triumphantly back, "Not for *me*."

But if that old Production Code has been forsaken, if Doris Day has at last been soundly spanked for her virginal sins, hasn't morality triumphed after all? Of course it has. Mike Nichols, perhaps without fully realizing it, has lined up old Hollywood with avantgarde Hollywood. He has contrived a truly moral ending, and a most positive one at that. Honesty wins the day. Sex without love has been put in its place. Ancient taboos have been struck down. Material values have been shown to be hollow. As uninhibited and refreshing as *The Graduate* is, we are still left in fantasy land. "Most of us," a friend of mine ruefully commented, "still miss the bus."

On the other hand, perhaps the reason this newly mature generation has taken so to *The Graduate* is that it thinks, assumes, imagines it can make the bus. Mike Nichols told of meeting, recently, one of the leaders of the Columbia University rebellion. The student had loved *The Graduate*, as had his associates in rebellion. "In a way," he told Nichols, "it was what the strike was all about. Those kids had the nerve, they felt the necessity, to break the rules."

The Graduate represents a breakthrough of sorts in the Hollywood scheme of things, aside from its fine acting, its technical accomplishment, its vastly entertaining qualities. For it has taken aim, satirically, at the very establishment that produces most of our movies, mocked the morals and values it has long lived by. It is a final irony that it has thereby gained the large young audience it has been seeking and has been rewarded by a shower of gold.

BURTON AND TAYLOR MUST GO

WILFRID SHEED

The latest thing in divinity—and you get there by drawing a straight line through Aristotle, Daniel Boorstin, and Oleg Cassini —is the contemplation of pure celebrity: celebrity, that is, for its own sweet sake, unmarred by talent or achievement or any distinguishing feature whatever. Let the Duke of Whatsit be our prototype, right? In this field, less is much, much more. If the pure celebrity is an author, he can write ten bad books in a row and lose nothing—or ten good books in a row and gain nothing. But, ideally, he will stop writing altogether and become a simple object or totem, more ghastly with each passing year.

The purest celebrities we have in show business, in this strictly technical sense, are probably Mr. and Mrs. Burton. Not that they are inactive, good gracious no, but there is an unearthly stillness about their joint career. They have never made an especially good movie, and probably never will. *Virginia Woolf*, their tiny triumph, was done far better on the stage by Arthur Hill and Uta Hagen; and no one ever thought of making a pure celebrity out of Arthur Hill.

It would be easy simply to say that the Burtons have Star Quality, the ability to get to those lonely people of medium height and sandy hair and cause them to rip your clothes and try to kill you; but this lets us off the hook too lightly. For the Burtons have, on close observation, very little Star Quality. Richard Burton was once a promising actor. End of anecdote. Of Elizabeth Taylor there is even less to be said. Their appeal is thus startlingly pure, unqualified, dependent on nothing—therefore likely to endure a long time.

The curiously dead, airless quality of their movies is just right for the timeless contemplation of celebrity. But before poking into that, we might take a swift Toynbee-esque look at how it happened. The cult got under way with a couple of broken marriages, his first, her nth—hardly apocalyptic by Hollywood standards; like the death of Adonis, once you've seen one you've seen them all. But these broken marriages came at a nexus of great nonevents— Eddie Fisher and Debbie Reynolds and the filming of *Cleopatra* in Rome. In the toy-fish world of gossip, these were the hundred days that shook the world, the two that made a Revolution, the twelve days of Christmas: moments of cultural surge and clash, when history heaves up and gives birth. Nothing can stop an idea, however trivial, whose time has come. And that's about how it was with Taylor and Burton.

It might have been hoped at first that the fusion of these two aging civilizations—1940's M-G-M and England's Old Vic—might have done what Greek philosophy and Hebrew religion did for each other, rather than just another Austro-Hungarian fritz. Miss Taylor had, of course, peaked alarmingly early, around twelve, in *National Velvet*. One remembers most fondly following her doings in those chatty Leo the Lion ads. If the authorial voice may break with honest emotion for a moment, I myself once clipped her picture, booted and spurred for the Grand National, from one of the magazines. When I was twenty-one, she would be nineteen—so if Princess Margaret couldn't clear a Catholic with Parliament . . .

As history records, the race was not to the swift. Miss Taylor threw in her formidable lot with Nicky Hilton and then someone else, and then someone else again. She was now the most beautiful girl in the world, but no more so than hundreds of others. The face in the old photo had more character, more promise than this. She had survived better than the other doomed children of M-G-M, Judy Garland and Mickey Rooney, at least so far as the eye could see. But that's all—just survived.

Her voice is the tipoff to how little a major-studio upbringing can leave you with. Every great star I can think of has had a memorable voice, whether it be a silly one like Monroe's or a kinky one like Grant's, or a love object in itself like Jean Arthur's or Carole Lombard's. But I defy anyone, pausing now for needed rest and reflection, to remember Elizabeth Taylor's voice at all; defy, with all timidity, the most gifted mimic to recall it to you.

It is a voice that began life in an elocution class. Its native notes are "mass-media Standard." Raised in the land of the regionless nonaccent, southern California, it now has no edges at all, no resonance, no crust of local experience to convey. With such a voice, bleached out and colorless, flat performances are almost a certainty: and these we got, in *Butterfield* 8 and A *Place in the Sun* and other pre-Burton so-sos.

One solution in a case like that is to resort to flamboyance. Just as a pleasant, basically neutral figure like George Plimpton can become interesting simply by doing interesting things, so middle-period Taylor began to make a name as a heller and cusser (cussing, though, always in that voice). She switched her gossip holdings from the reserved Michael Wilding to the booming Mike Todd. And so on. No one would suggest that these moves were planned tactically. Public fact and private truth are not necessarily connected. What you see through the side of the bowl tells you nothing about what the fish are thinking. Still, the lives of the stars are the only common myths we have, our own little Helens and Clytemnestras, and we have to make the best of them.

In this world of public myth, Richard Burton was an inspired choice for the next stopping place. He not only had voice enough for two, but his persona as irresistible Welshman beefed up her reputation for flamboyance. Burton was more than willing to help on all fronts, with those incredible interviews, criticizing her legs and bust (earthy plain talk, none of your press-agent claptrap) and praising her wonderful fire and honesty. He also added automatic class to the operation, with his famous feeling for poetry, which Miss Taylor was said to share, instinctively as it were. (For Todd she had become Jewish, for Burton something a little more Celtic. What the hell?) If anything was going to revive the spark of the old Van Johnson era and build a new legend for this gallant Leo the Lion relic, it was a match with Burton.

From a publicity angle, the coup worked out just fine. The orbit, once you get your celebrities up off the pad, takes care of itself and lasts the lifetime of the first witnesses, who see that star up there long after the light has gone out. Culturally, things have not worked out so well; better than Lee Radziwill, infinitely better than, say, the Windsors doing *Macbeth*, but still not so well.

What went wrong? In Miss Taylor's case, the answer is suitably simple. It seems that the acting help just arrived too late. As a child she had been drilled in the insipid techniques of the Hollywood Forties, and she cannot shake them now in any kind of role. They have tried to exploit her fiery, earthy womanliness again and again in *The Sandpiper* and *The Taming of the Shrew* and *Boom*, but every time it comes out air and water, because she hasn't the idiosyncrasy of voice and manner that colorful women have in real life. She can shout and lunge about with the best of them, but this isn't interesting, just noisy. One thinks of the jolly German emcee cutting off the neckties of the guests. There is nothing drearier than eccentricity without wit or personality.

Likewise, when they try, as in *The VIP's* or, in a different way, *Doctor Faustus,* to bring out her regal, dignified qualities, nothing answers there either. Her dignity is simply stiff and ladylike, a little girl on her best behavior. (As for her woman of smoldering sexuality in *The Comedians,* one can only cry, in memory of the old days, "Get a horse.") Her offscreen personality may have developed in all these directions and more. But her acting closed up shop long ago, as one's handwriting does or one's walk, and she cannot do anything with it, short of contortion and shrillness. Even a frontal assault on her voice problem (in a couple of movies she has tried foreign accents) has been repulsed. The timbre is unmistakably made in Hollywood.

The Burton question is a little more complicated. He maintains a sly, self-mocking manner, as of one who is up to something. In the movies he makes with Liz, he seems not to be trying, almost as if he were embarrassed. He seems often to be thrusting the scene at his wife, to see what she is able to do with it. A sense of "Don't blame me" prevails.

Whether his acting is still there is not always easy to tell. In *The Comedians* he was so listless as to suggest sleepwalking. Was this interpretation or veiled protest? In either event, he has been relying on this style rather too heavily lately. In nonclassical parts, he is quickly becoming a byword in dullness, simply because he plays everything down so low that it doesn't count.

In classic parts, he is clearly something else. He reads poetry well, although with an undifferentiated "feeling" that seems to apply equally to all the poems he reads. His acting range even here consists mainly of louder and softer. Yet given good enough language to keep him awake, he can still move you. When the language is bad, his voice becomes a solemn tin drum.

One sometimes gets a feeling, from outside the bowl, that he is instructing his wife as they go along, helping her through her scenes rather than concentrating on his own. The element of slight competition by which acting teams are ignited to greatness is altogether missing. Even in *The Taming of the Shrew,* all is horseplay. The message, not so very subliminal, is that they're only kidding, that they love each other very much, whatever you may have read in Walter Winchell.

Whether husbands and wives should ever act together is a question they probably mull over for hours at the Lambs (and bless their woolly heads for that). But surely couples shouldn't act together when the differential in talent is as great as this. Mr. Burton may be very good (although promising actors are as common as world's most beautiful women), but he is not good enough, either at acting or at acting tactics, to carry a subaverage film actress like Miss Taylor through whole movies; they simply fall down on top of each other.

Meanwhile, we have the prospect of many more classics fumbled through and rendered slightly boring, interspersed with outright junk like *Boom*. Richard Burton's knack for reading poetry has perhaps led him to overrate his own literary taste. At least, his choice of contemporary scripts has been medium to awful. *The Milk Train Doesn't Stop Here Anymore*, on which *Boom* is based, is not only one of Tennessee Williams' very worst plays, but one in which the leading actress is obliged to make a campy fool of herself throughout—hardly the role for Miss Taylor at this ever delicate stage of her career.

Not that it matters. Their celebrity selves are beyond the power of their acting selves to harm. Perched at their lecterns, perched in their sailboat, passing eternally through New York dripping quotes: transcendence, the nearest thing to doing nothing at all. The Duke plays golf, they make movies. It doesn't matter. Nobody keeps score. Might have been quite good if he'd taken it up in earnest. Might have been quite bad too. We'll never know. Great zest for living, though. Grand to have him with us. Zest. Fun. Grand.

Of course, there is always one other possibility: that what a thousand bleating critics have failed to do the iron laws of history may one day do for them—namely, split the megacelebrity back into its component parts. For some time now we have been getting hard rumors (as opposed to the usual soft gossip) that an astronomic convulsion is already in the works—new groupings, new names to memorize.

If so, will Miss Taylor continue to wrestle with Thespis, or devote herself to good works, or simply become a force for world peace?

Will Burton find another Eliza Doolittle, to try to make a silk purse out of?

Is there a place for Mickey Rooney in all of this?

If you find these questions trivial, you may have a point. But until someone learns how to build a better celebrity—and this would probably involve taking a hard look at Earl Wilson, Sheilah Graham and the whole press-agent corps—these are the ones we've got, and we must learn to enjoy them. And before you start that toneless whimper, that "Why? Why must I? What's happened to this country, anyway?," etc., you might remind yourself that so far, at least, the condition is only mildly hereditary over here. Did you ever try reading about the Dutch royal family? (Oh, you did? And you preferred it? I see.)

THE STUDENT MOVIE-MAKERS

STEFAN KANFER

Blood seeped through the student's shirt as he lay writhing on a suburban street in Evanston, Illinois. Sirens screamed as an ambulance rushed to the scene, emergency bandages and tourniquets held at the ready. A policeman ran toward the accident—and then stopped in horror and anger. Glaring at the onlooker with the camera, who made no attempt to help the sufferer, he roared, "What do you think you're doing?" "Making a movie," came the mild reply. Suddenly aware that the blood looked suspiciously like ketchup, the cop sighed, "Everybody's making a movie."

Well, almost everybody. The incident happened a few blocks from Northwestern University; both the cameraman and his ketchup-doused victim were undergraduates at the school. But the scene could have been almost anywhere in the United States. Students in college, high school, and now, in some cases, even grade school are turning to films as a form of artistic self-expression as naturally as Eskimos turn to soapstone carving.

Dozens of U.S. high schools now offer at least a rudimentary course in film appreciation, while more than one hundred colleges and universities have movie-making as an accepted part of their curriculums. Even where no classes are available, students by the hundreds are forming their own film clubs and making movies with hand-held eight-millimeter cameras, portable tape recorders, and the unpaid acting services of hammy classmates or wary adults.

The reason for this celluloid explosion is the widespread conviction among young people that film is the most vital modern art form. Jean Cocteau believed that movies could never become a true art until the materials to make them were as inexpensive as pencil and paper. The era he predicted is rapidly arriving. Students can now make a short film for as little as twenty-five dollars, and a workable sixteen-millimeter camera can be had for as little as forty dollars. McLuhan-age educators, moreover, welcome this form of creative endeavor. Some foresee the day when film training will be an accepted and universal part of education. Says Father John Culkin, head of Fordham's Center for Communications, "Students ought to be learning the fundamentals in grade school—early high school at the latest—so that when they finally get to college they have an opportunity to blossom out, without worrying about the mechanics."

Student film-making approaches professional quality and quantity at the college level, where three big universities clearly outstrip the rest: the University of Southern California, the University of California at Los Angeles, and New York University. All three have full-scale curriculums leading to bachelor's and master's degrees, professional-level studios, sophisticated faculty guidance. At U.S.C., for example, resident teachers of the school's 350 cinema majors include Hollywood directors King Vidor and Norman Taurog, while Jerry Lewis is an "adjunct professor." U.C.L.A., which has an enrollment of over three hundred, is about to complete a $2,500,000 film-production center, including several tons of first-quality equipment purchased at an auction from the old Hal Roach Studios. Twenty-five hundred miles away, the N.Y.U. film school (enrollment 250) lacks the advantages of California sunshine and nearby Hollywood expertise, but it does have a top-flight staff of twenty-seven, headed by Robert Saudek, one-time producer of TV's *Omnibus*.

All three schools have been around long enough (U.S.C., the nation's oldest, was founded in 1929) to have developed more or less distinctive styles of their own. U.C.L.A. favors and encourages free-form experimentation. Movie-makers at rival U.S.C. try to put a high professional gloss on their products and are very Hollywood-conscious, so much so that one professor recently complained about the plethora of student parodies of *Bonnie and Clyde*. N.Y.U. students, by contrast, tend to turn out deliberately rough-hewn works with the grainy look of neorealistic *cinéma-vérité* documentaries—a reflection, perhaps, of the fact that most of their films are shot on location in the streets of nearby Greenwich Village.

In some cities, children are learning to make movies at the same time that they are mastering the ABC's. In Lexington, Massachusetts, for example, Yvonne Andersen, thirty-six, runs an extracurricular workshop where children aged five to twelve are introduced to the rudiments of animated film. Their work shows a freedom, verve, and humor that Disney might have admired. Their short subjects (four minutes maximum) range from settings of favorite nursery rhymes to imaginative moralistic fables like *The Amazing Colossal Man*, written and produced by a dozen workshoppers. In this no-nonsense parable, suspicious earthlings annihilate a peace envoy from outer space.

More typical—and more demanding—is the once-a-week film class at Northern Valley Regional High School in Demarest, New Jersey. Taught by English teacher Rodney Sheratsky and documentary-film maker Eric Camiel, the course includes aesthetic theory, film history, and exercises in cinematography, cutting, and editing. Students, most of whom borrow their parents' eight-millimeter equipment, are required to make one filmlet a week, which is subjected by Camiel to scathing professional criticism. He can be high in his praise for efforts that show both imagination and care, and many do. One of his students this year did a four-minute movie on the theme of pregnancy, using dense filtered colors, quick cuts and even a touch of underground technique: he doctored the film stock with scratches to help create an abstract effect. The point is not that any of the students are embryonic Eisensteins, says Sheratsky, but that "these kids, all of them, are thinking film."

Students who think film best have at least one chance every year to display their wares to professional scrutiny at the annual National Student Film Festival. Jointly sponsored by the National Student Association, the Motion Picture Association of America, and Manhattan's Lincoln Center for the Performing Arts, the festival last month showed entries from thirty-seven colleges, which were judged by a panel that included directors Norman Jewison (*In the Heat of the Night*) and Irving Kershner (*The Flim Flam Man*) and producer Philip Leacock (*Gunsmoke*). The prizewinners in the contest's four major categories:

Drama: *THX 1138 4EB*, by George Lucas, twenty-three, of U.S.C., is a sci-fi chiller that looks at a cowardly new world where two varieties of humanoids, the "erosbods" and "clinicbods," wander through dark corridors and light-pierced concrete caverns in pursuit of the only truly human character, "THX" (sex pronounced with a lisp). A vision of 1984, it evoked in fifteen minutes a future world in which man is enslaved by computers and TV monitors. Although portentous in theme, *THX* impressed the judges with its technical virtuosity: Lucas shot his future-oriented film entirely in present-day Los Angeles—much as Jean-Luc Godard, one of his cinematic heroes, shot the nightmare-future *Alphaville* entirely in contemporary Paris.

Animation: *Marcello, I'm So Bored*, by John Milius, twenty-three, of U.S.C., begins with an epigraph from the late Errol Flynn, "I believe I'm a very colorful character in a rather drab age." It then flashes through a quick-cutting kaleidoscope of mindless pleasure-seekers—motorcyclists, teeny-boppers, discotheque dancers—accompanied by a sound track of sighs and despairing screams. One judge saw in the eight-minute film a viable cinematic equivalent of pop art.

Documentary: In *Kienholz on Exhibit*, by June Steel of U.C.L.A., the camera roams for a leisurely twenty-one minutes over an exhibit at the Los Angeles County Museum by sculptor Edward Kienholz. Then an off-camera interviewer deftly questions a series of museumgoers, whose reactions are even more of a social comment than the artist's work. A pair of sclerotic city elders label the show disgusting; an appreciative young Negro in a golfing hat sizes up the exhibit as "it's, like, sad."

Experimental: *Cut*, by Chris Parker of the University of Iowa, is a difficult abstract work, with no apparent plot or sequence, which talks elliptically of Greek myths and their significance to film-makers: "Film is like the snake, the worm Ourobouros, and like all continuous forms can be symbolic of evil." Montages of images cascade across the screen for twenty-one minutes while narrator Parker reads the directions from the script ("Medium Shot: Wife on Ferris wheel, seat five. Close-up wife's frightened face . . .") in order to remind viewers that they are watching a film. The chaos is astonishingly well photographed and edited—and, far more than most of the other entries, displays a debt to the nonstyles and non-goals of the cinematic underground.

On the strength of his first prize in the current festival, U.C.L.A.'s Lucas has been given a contact to expand THX into a full-length film under the guidance of Warners–Seven Arts producer Francis Ford Coppola (You're a Big Boy Now), who graduated from U.C.L.A. in 1967. That kind of instant success is the exception. The rule is instant obscurity. A case in point is Marty Scorsese, twenty-five, an N.Y.U. film-school graduate whose It's Not Just You, Murray won a first prize at the 1965 student festival—and might well be the best university movie ever made. A fourteen-minute comic synopsis of low-class urban life that is vaguely reminiscent of Fellini's work, Murray is the picaresque tale of a vulpine con man who rises from petty-ante rum-runner to gunsel for "the Mob." The film had a brief Manhattan-art-house booking, and Scorsese was able to raise $24,000 for a ninety-five-minute feature titled I Call First. Evocative of Marty, it cuts off a slice of life about an Italian-American bank teller who falls in love with a girl he meets on the Staten Island ferry, deserts her when he discovers that she was once raped, and returns to the vulgar bachelor world of his street-corner cronies. Flawed and immature in plot and structure, First nonetheless has an exact sense of the Lower Manhattan milieu and some authentic and hard-edged dialogue—but almost no commercial possibilities. Scorsese, who put up $6,000 of his own savings to direct the movie, is now filming TV commercials in London.

Like the products of the underground-film world, campus movies are something of an acquired taste—which is one good reason why they have a limited commercial future. More than that, the bulk of them are simply the exuberant and untalented posturings of youth, which have no more claim to lasting attention than the sophomore poems and short stories turned out every year by aspiring collegiate Salingers and Updikes. Occasionally, of course, a student like Coppola will graduate to the ranks of Hollywood professionals. In the long run, though, the contemporary enthusiasm for student films is likely to turn out a far greater number of enlightened appreciators than new creators. That in itself could be a big boon to movies; whether cinema grows as an art form depends largely upon whether film-educated audiences demand better things of it.

THE LATE SHOW AS HISTORY

STEFAN KANFER

This week in the United States of 1968, a Negro waiter will shuffle off, mumbling, "Yassuh, I'se hurrin' fas' as I know how." An angry Indian will vow, "Many white eyes will die!" A Marine sergeant will cry, "Come on, let's get the yellowbellies!"

Such quaint language endures in the movies from the Thirties and Forties that unreel on television with the steady persistence of an arterial throb. Ranging back to the baby talkies, late-show films represent what Jean Cocteau called the "petrified fountain of thought." Ghosts of America's past, they evoke the naïveté, exuberance, and problems of a simpler society. To middle-aged Americans, they can also be embarrassments with commercials. Did the public truly love those painful Blondie pictures so much that Hollywood made twenty-eight of them? How did Turhan Bey ever become a star? Did anyone really take Errol Flynn seriously in *Desperate Journey*, after he sabotaged German munitions plants, hijacked a Nazi bomber, and shouted, "Now for Australia and a crack at those Japs!"?

Says producer Billy Wilder, "A bad play folds, and is forgotten, but in pictures we don't bury our dead. When you think it's out of your system, your daughter sees it on television and says: 'My father is an idiot.' "

Most children are not related to film directors, however, and to them movies on TV are an integral part of their epoch; they are growing up with a borrowed nostalgia for a time they never knew. The once-irretrievable past has become as salable as a personality poster, as audible as a Fred Astaire LP. The late show is ransacked for trivia questions and recherché clichés.

With more than 13,000 films waiting to be rerun on television, old movies have become America's National Museum of Pop Art, the biggest repository of cultural artifacts outside the Smithsonian Institution. On TV, of course, the movies are tiny, like warriors who have become trophies of a head-shrinking tribe. Despite this diminution, despite faded prints and commercials perforating climactic scenes, old flicks remain more compelling than most of the shows that surround them. Films may go in one era and out the other, but even the flattest Tarzan epic or the corniest war saga offers a series of clues to history. Like a paleontologist reconstructing a Brontosaurus from a vertebra and two teeth, the patient late-show viewer can reconstruct some of the main currents of American thought.

The old movies almost always portrayed U.S. dreams—and thus, indirectly, realities. Just as the peasant tales retold by the Grimm brothers spoke of common maidens who could spin gold from straw, Hollywood created its own folk stories from the yearnings of 1930s audiences. *If I Had a Million*, for example, tells of a quirky financier who sends million-dollar checks to strangers. A colorless clerk played by Charles Laughton receives his check in the mail, goes to the president of his company, sticks out his tongue and delivers a loud Bronx cheer. Blackout. In those precarious years, the vicarious thrill of giving a razz to the boss was irresistible—to say nothing of the complex moral that a nobody can suddenly acquire the money that can't buy happiness.

With a celebrated conscience that writhed with guilt beside the swimming pool, Hollywood writers sang a song of social significance. The loner of the Thirties film—Gary Cooper, Cary Grant, Jimmy Stewart—always triumphed against Big Money, amid settings of dreamlike luxury cluttered with butlers, white pianos, and canopied beds. Like animated editorial cartoons, their opposition was always a vested—and usually watch-chained—interest on the order of Edward Arnold. The heroine—Barbara Stanwyck or Jean Arthur—spoke with a catch in her throat that accented her vulnerability. But she had a whim of iron, and when she urged John Doe or Mr. Smith to Washington, the nation's laws were rewritten on the spot. As the Girl Friday, she was the flip, half-emancipated helpmeet to the strong but bumbling American Male.

In those films, passion was expressed with a kiss or a cheek-to-cheek dance. Yet, in retrospect, they often seem sexier than some of today's celebrated shockers. What made Mae West's *double-entendres* titillating was that they really had double meanings; current cinematic sex jokes have but one unmistakable point.

Today, children constitute one of the most militant majorities in America. And since a threat cannot be cute, the late-show screen child seems like a kid who has stayed up past his bedtime. During the Depression parents somehow found their children easier to get along with, perhaps because they had a sense of sharing a common crisis. Children seemed comforting, or at least cheering. Hollywood fostered Jackie Cooper, Frankie Darro, Mickey Rooney, Our Gang and the apotheosis of innocence, Shirley Temple. "I class myself with Rin-Tin-Tin," she later said, referring to such films as *Bright Eyes* and *Curly Top*. "At the end of the Depression, people were perhaps looking for something to cheer them up. They fell in love with a dog and a little girl—it won't happen again."

That love was not universal. Only a changed America could drive the Temple from the money changers, but even in the Thirties a bulbous misanthrope named W. C. Fields declared that "no man who hates small dogs and children can be all bad." Fields had a following that identified with his constant character, the put-upon male who could neither support nor desert his yapping family. This original style of explosive comedy arose from humanity under pressure—a kind of pressure that affluence has released, perhaps forever. The Marx Brothers, for example, remain as inseparable from the Thirties and Forties as F.D.R. More than any other stars, they bridge vaudeville, the silents, the talkies, and TV itself. But Fields, who always blew his cool, exerts an appeal rivaled only by Bogart, who never blew his. Both men nurse a surly integrity and loathing for any Establishment except the neighborhood bar—attitudes that delight today's young cynical idealists.

If the late show has a single classic hero, it is the outlaw with the gun. *Bonnie and Clyde* has its obvious origins in the old gangster films; there were fifty in 1931 alone. *Little Caesar, Scarface,* and *Smart Money* mirror the hostile hustle of Prohibition years and parody Horatio Alger by putting the happy ending in the middle, then massacring the criminal-hero in the end. The private eye too was a fixture of the time. Alone, armed only with a wisecrack and a .38, he faced the forces of evil and escaped intact. Today, the hero has joined the organization; like everyone else, 007 has an employee number.

Nor is that the only alteration. Today the prefix "anti" precedes such terms as "hero" and "war." In the Forties, those words stood naked and unembarrassed as Hollywood took the entire American melting pot and put it into uniform: "Here are the volunteers, sir—Jorgenson, O'Brien, Goldberg, Van Jones, Milwitzski . . ." A generation of war heroes seemed to spring to life from the recruiting posters: Alan Ladd, Gregory Peck, Van Johnson, William Holden. Not until the late Fifties were leading men, like Rod Steiger, allowed to act humanly scared again.

The war also simplified villains even more than heroes. Before Pearl Harbor, the heavy was a foxy seducer, a neurotic thug, or a fastidious mastermind ("I despise violence, but my assistant Hugo . . ."). The wartime villain was a wicked, witless German or a Japanese with Coke-bottle lenses on his sinister glasses. All this continued through the cold-war Fifties with their Slavic bad guys. Now the dominant heavies are a polyglot crew, their lunacy more important than their lineage.

Probably the most striking changes in American attitudes are reflected in the film progression of the teen-ager and the Negro. Before James Dean met Freud in Rebel Without a Cause (1955), adolescence in the movies was the period between acne and marriage. To modern teen-agers, Henry Aldrich seems as remote as Henry VIII. In a day when, in certain quarters at least, "student" is synonymous with "riot," nothing is more anachronistic than a conference in Dad's study or the dutiful screech "Coming, Mother!" It seems inconceivable that Louis B. Mayer's fondest memories were of the Andy Hardy films. "In one," he recalled, "Andy's mother was dying—and they showed him standing outside the door. Standing. I told them: 'Don't you know that an American boy like that will get down on his knees and pray?' They listened—the biggest thing in the picture."

Just about the only benefit today's Negroes can trace to the standard Hollywood product is the current Black Power slogan "Ungawa!," a fake African chant from a Tarzan picture. Even in

1950 reruns, Negroes are chuckleheaded or criminal. In mystery pictures it is a Negro who discovers the corpse and scampers away shouting "Feets, do yo' stuff!" Says the comic, "I don't want any dark innuendos." Chirps the chauffeur, "Anybody call me?" Even such all-black musicals as *Stormy Weather* and *Cabin in the Sky* patronized as they provided employment. "It's been a long journey to this moment," said Sidney Poitier when he received his Oscar for *Lilies of the Field* in 1963. But his was only the last lap. The first million miles were traveled by Eddie Anderson, Stepin Fetchit, Willie Best, Butterfly McQueen, and other gifted actors whose long ride in the back of the bus can be seen again every week on television.

With the new liberalities of the current cinema, such antique prejudices seem laughable—almost as laughable as the Sixties movies will be to late-show fans of the Seventies and Eighties. Then as now, viewers equipped with 20-20 hindsight will perceive the depressed, desolated land that bled through the Thirties films, the hunger for absolutes and the shrill patriotism that surrounded the war and cold war of the Forties. They will recognize the erosion of supposedly permanent mores and attitudes that characterized the late Fifties and early Sixties. They will survey the clichés of this period—the alienation bit, the under-thirty thing, the unromantic sex kick—and will realize that, no matter how laughable, these stereotypes too reflect a troubled reality. The hippie scene and the identity crisis will no doubt someday assume an air of innocence and cherished worth along with the Front Porch, the Soda Fountain, and the Family, which now warm the nostalgia of late-night retrospection. Hollywood, which liked to see itself as Everyman's Scheherazade, has also been his Cassandra; the two roles are inseparable.

FILM FOSSILS

Perhaps the foremost collector of film trivia is Harry Purvis, a Canadian writer whose catalogue, which appears irregularly in *TV Guide*, includes the following:

"Must you always think like a marshal? Can't you think like a human being just this once?" Dorothy Malone to Ronald Reagan in *Law and Order*.

"Why me? You have the pick of my brother's harem." Lucille Ball to Raymond Burr in *The Magic Carpet*.

"How long do you think I could hold on to my job if it got out that I had a transparent offspring?" Philip Abbott to Diane Brewster in *The Invisible Boy*.

"So, a lowborn blacksmith is the famous Desert Hawk." Yvonne De Carlo to Richard Greene in *The Desert Hawk*.

"You're wasting your time on the major. He's a fighting machine, a soldier's soldier, with no time for weakness." Bing Russell to Jewell Lain in *Suicide Battalion*.

"This girl's of a different race, of a different world. You've got your friends, your position." C. Aubrey Smith to Leslie Howard in *Never the Twain Shall Meet*.

"As a psychologist as well as a zookeeper, I believe it is better to face an emotion than to lock it up inside you." Karl Malden to Patricia Medina in *Phantom of the Rue Morgue*.

"You don't belong to any man now—you belong to Broadway." Adolphe Menjou to Katharine Hepburn in *Morning Glory*.

"I wonder what you'd look like dressed." Maureen O'Sullivan to Johnny Weissmuller in *Tarzan the Ape Man*.

L'AFFAIRE LANGLOIS

ARTHUR KNIGHT

Although no barricades have yet appeared in the streets, L'Affaire Langlois is currently rocking Paris like nothing since L'Affaire Dreyfus some sixty years ago. Each day, prominently featured on page one, the press summarizes the latest developments. The air is bitter with denunciations of France's Ministry of Culture, which is alternately portrayed as either the instigator or the scapegoat in the recent ouster of Henri Langlois from his post as director of the pioneering, world-respected Cinémathèque Française. Pickets demonstrating by the hundreds in support of Langlois have been clubbed and pummeled by the police, even while police chiefs send notes of good wishes and good advice to Langlois himself.

It all began on February 9, when Langlois, who founded the Cinémathèque (with Georges Franju) as a private enterprise in 1935, was summarily notified that he and his entire staff of sixty had been dismissed and a new director, Pierre Barbin, appointed in his place. Within hours, the new administration appeared at the Cinémathèque offices in the Rue de Courcelles, ordered everyone out of the building, and proceeded to change the locks on the doors. "It was like Germany in 1933," recalled Lotte Eisner, Langlois's able curator of archives. "I was then working on a Czech-owned paper in Berlin. One afternoon the Nazis came in and simply took over everything. That evening I left for Paris."

No small part of the alarm registered by both the public and the press in discussions of the Cinémathèque case springs from a growing suspicion that "it can happen here." For all the esteem that the French people may feel for *"le grand* Charles," there is also a growing resentment of his autocratic ways, and an awareness that his government is spreading its bureaucratic control over all aspects of French life. Significantly, as of the present writing no one has yet so much as dared bring the Langlois dismissal directly to de Gaulle's attention; and many feel, since de Gaulle is notoriously uninterested in film, that he has never even heard about it.

On the other hand, probably nowhere else in the world is the film medium held in such high regard as in France, nor has a film museum so firmly embedded itself in the affections of the people. Through daily showings of its vast collection at the three theaters operated by the Cinémathèque in Paris, as well as through dozens of *ciné-clubs* organized all over France, Langlois has created an extraordinary awareness of cinema as a cultural force and an artistic heritage. Indeed, many of today's leading French directors—Chabrol, Demy, Godard, Truffaut—proudly call themselves "sons of the Cinémathèque" and claim it as their school and the cornerstone of their careers. All of them have assumed an active role in organizing the various recent "manifestations" against the widely unpopular change in administration.

On the most overt level, these demonstrations have taken the form of mass picketing outside the sprawling Palais de Chaillot, which houses both the Cinémathèque's collection and its largest theater. (The Palais was promptly closed down by Barbin and his group, inspiring one agile partisan to scramble up the façade and write "Ex-" before the inscription "Musée de Cinéma.") On a more potent level, Chabrol, Demy, Truffaut, and many others organized informal "committees of correspondence" to urge individual film-makers and studios all over the world to bar further screenings of any titles they may control in the Cinémathèque collection until Langlois is reinstated.

Moreover, their campaign has been accorded an overwhelmingly favorable reception. Dozens of top American directors, including John Ford, George Stevens, King Vidor, and Fred Zinnemann, responded by cabling their support for Langlois; and most of the leading American film companies have already put the Cinémathèque on notice to cease and desist from future showings. In no less impressive numbers, film-makers on the far side of the Iron Curtain have taken similar action.

The official reasons given for Langlois's dismissal include the charges that he is a poor administrator, that many of the films in his collection have seriously deteriorated, and that he has failed to keep a full catalogue of his archive holdings—all of which Langlois, a fiftyish, portly, Buddhalike individual, would readily concede. But he counters by charging that when, three years ago, the Ministry of Culture finally got around to appointing an administrative officer to work with him, they selected a man without any experience whatsoever in museum affairs; that his repeated requests over the years for additional funds to preserve the collection had consistently fallen on deaf ears; and that, because of copyrights and other legal complications, no film curators anywhere in the world would dare to publish a full listing of the contents of their collections.

What is more to the point, Langlois feels, there are now strong forces in the state-owned TV network who would like to use the Cinémathèque's films as a source of inexpensive program material. Langlois has steadfastly blocked this—in part because he believes that films should properly be seen in a movie house, more importantly because he is aware that the moment this happened the Cinémathèque would be in immediate danger of losing vast sections of its collection to those producers and distributors who actually control the commercial rights in the films. Barbin, on the other hand, has no such compunctions; his first official act, after shutting down the Cinémathèque's theaters, was to begin an inventory of the archives with just that purpose in mind.

To Barbin's consternation—and this may well be the saving of the Cinémathèque—he soon discovered that many of the films in the collection had not been assigned to the Cinémathèque at all, but to Langlois personally. Over the long years that saw the transformation of the Cinémathèque from a wholly private organization into a nationally subsidized institution, Langlois and the Cinémathèque Française remained virtually synonymous.

Even now, plans are afoot to open a new Cinémathèque in Paris with Langlois at its head, should the Ministry of Culture refuse to rescind its order. A luxurious town house has already been made available for this purpose, and innumerable assurances of support have been forthcoming. Langlois has even received offers from several institutions abroad—from other museums aware of his lifelong devotion to film and of his incredible flair for arranging and mounting memorable gallery exhibits. But Langlois, a professional Parisian, merely smiles a heavy-lidded, Buddha smile, lifts a pudgy forefinger, and declares, with a conscious bow to Marshall McLuhan, "Today the man who holds the image holds the power."

What he implies is that this is why his government, fearful of powers it does not control, has stripped him of his position. But what he also implies is that his reinstatement is inevitable, because others around the world also recognize the power of the image and trust him to continue to use it impartially, and with taste and discretion. Until that day arrives, however, "L'Affaire Langlois" seems bound to continue unabated in France, with repercussions throughout the rest of the film-loving world. For the basic purpose of Langlois's perfervid supporters is to prevent the cinema, that international art form, from becoming subverted to the whims of bureaucrats or the political interests of an increasingly totalitarian state.

OSCAR WILES

ANDREW SARRIS

The shadow of Martin Luther King hovered like a very bad special effect over the fortieth annual awards presentations of the Academy of Motion Picture Arts and Sciences. After a week of America's hypocritical reaction to its own Passion Play, Oscar was hardly obliged to provide the same old resounding rhetoric on the same old good intentions. The historicity of one man's dream was too complex a subject for the histrionics of an industry's fantasy. Hollywood has always been at its worst and its most pretentious at those moments when it chose to jut out its noble profile of social responsibility. Besides, what point is there in an actor repenting after Edith Head has designed his sackcloth and ashes?

Elmer Bernstein began the proceedings with a "tribute" to Max Steiner, said tribute consisting of a mangled medley from the sound tracks of *Gone with the Wind*, *Now Voyager*, and *A Summer Place*. Oscar's orchestra under Bernstein's baton provided the tinniest sounding music this side of Minsky's. How I longed for Jack E. Leonard to harangue the conductor and his noise-makers! Instead, Gregory Peck, the liberals' retort to Ronald Reagan, spoke with awkward sincerity about Martin Luther King and the race, color, creed bit.

Peck then presented the perennial master of ceremonies, Bob Hope, a performer so suffused with presence that I sometimes long for his absence. As it was, the tastelessness of his gags knew no bounds. There were jokes about the inconvenience caused by postponing the telecast from Monday to Wednesday, jokes about the President's decision not to run, an elaborate routine based on the pun of one kind of bombing in Hanoi and another in Hollywood, another pun on Oscar night for Hope being considered Passover, a joke about the telecast being transmitted to Cuba by National Airlines, a joke about the gold drain and de Gaulle, and the usual prurience about dirty movies and Dame Edith Evans wearing a mini-skirt and *Tom Jones* winning the 4-H award if it came out today, and other bits of levity too numerous and too horrendous to mention.

Carol Channing, that feeble invention of the gossip columnists, was introduced to present the "sound" award, and *In the Heat of the Night* had the first of its five prizes. The other nominees had been *Camelot, The Dirty Dozen, Doctor Dolittle,* and *Thoroughly Modern Millie.* The criteria for this particular honor baffle me more than most. The level of theatrical projection being what it is today, I usually settle for being able to hear the dialogue.

Patty Duke, the beautifully anguished duckling of *The Miracle Worker* now transformed into the silly goose of *Valley of the Dolls,* presented the award for best supporting actor to George Kennedy in *Cool Hand Luke.* I had first noticed Kennedy as the stuttering villain in Henry Hathaway's *The Sons of Katie Elder.* Kennedy strikes me as one of those real-life people who turn to acting relatively late in life to fulfill their frustrated fantasies and then give everything they have and are to their roles. Florence Bates was this way. Also such interesting athlete-actor types as Max Baer, Elroy Hirsch, and Bill Dickey. I preferred Michael J. Pollard in *Bonnie and Clyde,* and when neither he nor Gene Hackman won I suspected that *Bonnie and Clyde* had just about had it for the evening. George Kennedy's acceptance speech set the tone for the evening as warm, brimming gratitude stopping just short of maudlinity.

Bob Hope then introduced Louis Armstrong to blow a little, sweat a little, and croak a little over a song called "The Bare Necessities." The staging might be described as Posthumous Disney if it were not otherwise so incredibly indescribable. Katharine Hepburn was then introduced on a film clip summarizing Oscar's first ten years. Miss Hepburn was the only one of this year's nineteen living acting nominees not present at the Oscar telecast. The film clip reminded us that Miss Hepburn had won her only Oscar in the same decade that Spencer Tracy had won his first of two, and right then and there I began to have a strong hunch that Hepburn, Tracy, and *Guess Who's Coming to Dinner* might still be heard from.

Dustin Hoffman and Katharine Ross came up to the rostrum with that very special tenseness all the nominees were to exhibit during the evening. They presented the cinematography award to *Bonnie and Clyde* over *Camelot, Doctor Dolittle, The Graduate,* and *In Cold Blood*. The National Society of Film Critics had given the photography award to Haskell Wexler for *In the Heat of the Night*, and he wasn't even nominated by the Academy. I thought Surtees (*The Graduate*) and Conrad Hall (*In Cold Blood*) were on a par with Guffey and Wexler, but it looked like a split evening.

I began to lose track of the awards as the procession of performers became more fascinating. Macdonald Carey and Diahann Carroll struggled with Bob Hope and an unruly rostrum that seemed to have sunk into the floor. Hope's professionalism was tested and not found wanting, but nothing in the evening up to that time had prepared us for the surreal spectacle of Martha Raye reading and mugging her way through a message from General Westmoreland congratulating the motion-picture industry for entertaining the troops in Vietnam. We were mercifully spared the sight of Miss Raye's green beret, jungle fatigues, and jump boots, a costume that once made page one of *The Village Voice* in the days before Stephanie Harrington became fashion coordinator.

A film clip from *The Graduate* was shown on the screen. It was the sequence in which Anne Bancroft warns Dustin Hoffman not to date Katharine Ross. Hoffman runs upstairs to tell the daughter about his relationship with the mother, but before he can get it out, Bancroft pops her head in the doorway, and Ross, seeing her wet as Hoffman is wet, realizes the truth and reacts with pain and violence. As Hoffman leaves, Bancroft says goodbye in close-up, and the camera zooms back to show her huddled in the corner joining two white walls. It is at that precise moment that Mike Nichols strains to become Michelangelo Nichols by sacrificing an emotion for an effect. As much as I admire his handling of the three players, I deplore his stylistic eclecticism. Still, I thought that Ross, Bancroft, and Hoffman would have been perceptive choices for Oscars, but they were all doomed to disappointment for a bewildering variety of reasons.

A singer called Lainie Kazan came on to sing "The Eyes of Love" from *Banning*, and for a few seconds I thought that the sound on my set had gone off, but it turned out that Miss Kazan was merely a saloon columnist's conception of a song stylist, all style and no song, all manner and no method. Barbara Rush introduced the maxi-midi skirt to the ceremony, and I suddenly hated *Bonnie and Clyde* for encouraging such a monstrosity. Robert Morse seemed as impish as ever, but I had almost forgotten that he existed. *The Anderson Platoon* won the award for best feature documentary. I would have voted for *Don't Look Back*, which wasn't even nominated. *The Redwoods* won for short subject, and I suddenly wondered if this would influence Ronald Reagan not to chop down redwoods that stood in the path of superhighways, and then I realized that Governor Reagan was conspicuous by his absence, an act of tastefulness I would not have expected of him. Nixon has been very silent lately, too. Are the Republicans preparing to harvest a windfall of white backlash votes, or what?

Olivia de Havilland spoke about the second decade of Oscar in a manner now established as one-half gushy and one-half perfunctory. The receding crane shot of the wounded in Atlanta still looked impressive, but as much as I love Vivien Leigh, this was one evening I could have done without the climactic shot of the Confederate flag. The projectionist achieved what amounted to a jump freeze as he almost jammed the projector trying to get the racist standard off the screen. An example more of thoughtlessness than heartlessness. The Oscarcast was trapped by its conflicting functions, on the one hand honoring its past achievements, and on the other paying tribute to a fallen leader of a people abused and humiliated by Hollywood movies for more than half a century. To love any aspect of America's past is to acknowledge complicity in America's racism, and Hollywood is hardly the only sinner in this regard. Still, I think the most eloquent memorial to Martin Luther King would have been the uncomfortably ambiguous Mammy of the late Hattie McDaniel in her celebrated staircase scene in *Gone with the Wind*. That was where we were, on a fake staircase in a fake Atlanta, and this is where it's at, in a real cemetery in a real Atlanta.

Eva Marie Saint awarded the prize for Costume Design to someone from *Camelot* who sported the first Nehru jacket to break Edith Head's hegemony. (Mini-skirts and turtlenecks were her other taboos.) Unfortunately decorum in costuming was degenerating into monotony. Natalie Wood gave out a special-effects award. Elke Sommer materalized in all her sensual splendor with Richard Crenna, and I must confess that Miss Sommer makes me pine for the days when actresses exuded more glamour than talent. Against my better judgment, of course. A musical group called Brazil 66 defied description with a split-level presentation of Burt Bacharach's "The Look of Love" from *Casino Royale*. There must be at least a hundred musical groups with more talent than Brazil 66, but with the Academy membership overloaded with senior citizens there is little hope for the newer sounds of folk and rock.

Walter Matthau presented the supporting award to Estelle Parsons, who had flown from her play in New York to be present for the ceremony. I preferred Katharine Ross, but Miss Parsons was undeniably more effective in *Bonnie and Clyde* than in *The Seven Descents of Myrtle*, which I had the misfortune of seeing. But how times had changed! Back in 1950, half the Oscar nominees seemed to be hanging around New York during the ceremony. The theater was the big thing for an actor; the movies were just big money.

Grace Kelly summed up the third decade in Oscar's history from her palace in Monaco, which seemed more like the background for a professional screen test. Can Our Gal Grace really find happiness as a postcard princess after having been a movie queen? The film-editing award went to *In the Heat of the Night*. A very knowledgeable film critic once told me that the film-editing award is the tip-off on the ultimate Oscar for best picture, but I later discovered that the editing and best-picture awards have coincided less than fifty percent of the time. Angela Lansbury received a standing ovation for a moderately professional rendition of "Thoroughly Modern Millie." She wasn't all that good, but her predecessors would have had difficulty making *Ted Mack's Amateur Hour*, though Satchmo might make it on nostalgia and personality.

The Jean Hersholt Award went to Gregory Peck, who proceeded to invite contributions to the Martin Luther King, Jr., Memorial Committee in Atlanta, Georgia. The evening was concluding on a liberal note. Hal Ashby dedicated his editing award to "peace," Rod Steiger accepted his best-acting award from Audrey Hepburn and assured Sidney Poitier, "We *Shall* Overcome." For his part, Poitier expressed genuine pleasure over announcing the best-actress award to Katharine Hepburn (for one of the weakest performances she had given in thirty-five years of movie acting).

As the evening dribbled to a close, Hope snapped off his best line: "I've never seen six hours whiz by so fast." Angie Dickinson and Gene Kelly and Shirley Jones and Rock Hudson and Leslie Caron entered and exited with a whimper. Sammy Davis, Jr., concluded the musical festivities with a Rex Harrison number from *Doctor Dolittle*, a bizarre idea in itself made more so by a lack of talent in Sammy so variable as to be confused with versatility. He can't sing, he can't dance, he can't act, and he can't tell jokes, but his confidence is infinity itself.

One moment lingers in my mind: Robert Wise very graciously introducing Alfred Hitchcock as the winner of this year's Irving J. Thalberg Award as if to acknowledge the ridiculous irony of the gesture with helpless good-will, and then Master Alfred himself accepting the honor with ironic brevity and then thinking better of it almost in an unconscious surge of emotion as he tried to add "Thank you very much" to his earlier "Thank you," but only fluffing the line as only the worst actors would fluff it if they relied on spontaneous improvisation instead of prerehearsal. I remember also the curious way Claire Bloom stared at the self-absorption of Rod Steiger at his moment of imminent triumph. Where does art leave off and life begin in the gaze of a beautiful woman? The separation is probably never complete. Mike Nichols accepted his own award with the heartfelt sincerity he once satirized in his salad days on the debunking circuit.

The show was awful and dull at the same time, the awards only moderately surprising. Some people had tried to build up suspense for *Bonnie and Clyde* and *The Graduate,* but I have a feeling that the Academy was looking for an excuse to rap these two films for their assorted audacities, and the New York Film Critics' Circle gave them that excuse. Although he didn't win an award, Sidney Poitier dominated the proceedings and the year generally as the embodiment of a fantasy, perhaps even a dream, of interracial understanding. For all his limitations in this limitless issue, he somehow seemed more appropriate to this tragic moment in history than any mere actor could be expected to be.

ABOUT THE CONTRIBUTORS

HOLLIS ALPERT is a film critic for *Saturday Review*. The author of four novels; a collection of essays, *The Dreams and the Dreamer*; and a biography, *The Barrymores*, he has taught at New York University and Pratt Institute.

HAROLD CLURMAN is theater and film critic for *The Nation*, and Visiting Professor at Hunter College. An active stage director, he was one of the co-founders of The Group Theatre and has been a film producer and director. He received the George Jean Nathan Prize for Dramatic Criticism in 1958, and the Sang Prize for Dramatic Criticism from Knox College in 1968. His published works include *The Fervent Years, Lies Like Truth, The Naked Image*. He has written articles for *The New York Times*, the London *Observer*, *Harper's Bazaar, Partisan Review*, and others.

PENELOPE GILLIATT, film critic of *The New Yorker*, was formerly film critic of the London *Observer*. She has written two novels, *One by One* and *A State of Change*. A book of her short stories is entitled *Come Back if It Doesn't Get Better*.

PHILIP T. HARTUNG, film critic of *Commonweal*, has contributed articles on film for the *Encyclopedia Americana* Annuals and *The Book of Knowledge* Annuals. He has also reviewed movies for *Woman's Home Companion, Charm, Scholastic Magazines*, and *Esquire*.

PAULINE KAEL reviews movies regularly for *The New Yorker* and has been a movie critic on the *New Republic* and *McCall's*. She has written film criticism for *Partisan Review, Sight and Sound, At-*

lantic Monthly, and *Harper's Bazaar*, and is the author of two critical collections, *I Lost It at the Movies* and *Kiss Kiss Bang Bang*.

STEFAN KANFER is film critic of *Time* magazine. He has contributed articles to *Life*, *Harper's Bazaar*, *Esquire*, *Atlantic Monthly* and *Playbill*.

STANLEY KAUFFMANN is the film critic of the *New Republic* and one of its literary critics. He is the author of *A World on Film* and has been a Visiting Professor in the Yale School of Drama.

ARTHUR KNIGHT is a film critic for *Saturday Review*, a professor in the Cinema Department of the University of Southern California, and a member of the board of trustees of the American Film Institute. He is the author of *The Liveliest Art* and co-author with Hollis Alpert of *The History of Sex in the Cinema* and has contributed to the *Encyclopaedia Britannica* and *Collier's Encyclopedia*.

JOSEPH MORGENSTERN is the film critic of *Newsweek*. He has been a reporter for *The New York Times* and a film and drama critic for the New York *Herald Tribune*. His novel, *World Champion*, was published this year.

ANDREW SARRIS is film critic of the *Village Voice*, Associate Professor of Cinema at Columbia University, a member of the Program Committee of the New York Film Festival at Lincoln Center, and a Guggenheim Fellow. His books include *The Films of Josef von Sternberg*, *Interviews with Film Directors*, *The American Cinema: Directors and Directions 1929–1968*, *Films of the Thirties*, and *The Films of John Ford*.

RICHARD SCHICKEL is film critic for *Life* magazine. His books on movies include *The Disney Version*, *The Stars*, and *Movies: The History of an Art and Institution*. He was co-editor of the first volume in this series, *Film 67/68*, and his most recent work was *The World of Goya*, a biography of the painter.

ARTHUR SCHLESINGER, JR., who formerly reviewed films for *Show* magazine, is now a reviewer for *Vogue*. He is also a historian and writer.

WILFRID SHEED is film critic of *Esquire*, book editor of *Commonweal*, and former drama critic of the latter magazine. A frequent book reviewer for *The New York Times Book Review*, he is the author of five novels, the most recent of which is *The Blacking Factory*.

JOHN SIMON is film critic of the *New Leader* and drama critic of *New York* magazine and the *Hudson Review*. He has taught at Harvard, the University of Washington, M.I.T., and Bard, and is the author of two books of criticism, *Acid Test* and *Private Screenings*. He was the winner of a Polk Award in criticism for his articles in the *New Leader* in 1968.

INDEX

Abbott, Philip, 257
Academy Awards, 186, 261–66
Academy of Motion Picture Arts
    and Sciences, 261–66
Addams, Charles, 51
Addison, John, 93
Affaire Langlois, L', 257–60
Albee, Edward, 46, 77
Alda, Alan, 170
Aldrich, Henry, 255
Aldrich, Richard, 157
Aldrich, Robert, 228
Alexander Nevsky, 91, 219
Alfie, 81
Alleg, Henri, 179
Allen, Dede, 117
Alpert, Hollis, 29–31, 57–60,
    113–15, 165–66, 168–70, 215–
    216, 235–41, 267
Alphaville, 250
Amazing Colossal Man, The, 249
Americanization of Emily, The,
    156
Amico, Masolino d', 206, 209
Andersen, Yvonne, 249
Anderson, Eddie, 256
Anderson, Judith, 203
Anderson Platoon, The, 98, 102,
    264
Andersson, Bibi, 40
Andrews, Harry, 229, 231
Andrews, Julie, 156, 157, 237
And Then Came a Man, 186
Andy Hardy, 236, 255

Anhalt, Edward, 183
Antonioni, Michelangelo, 79, 115
Apra, Pierluigi, 80
Aragon, Louis, 67
Arkin, Alan, 143, 224
Armies of the Night (Mailer),
    170
Armstrong, Louis, 262, 265
Arnold, Edward, 253
Artaud, Antonin, 67
Arthur, Jean, 243, 253
Ashby, Hal, 265
Astaire, Fred, 158, 253
Astin, John, 149
Aulin, Ewa, 149, 150
Aurthur, Robert Alan, 88
Autant-Lara, Claude, 45

Bacharach, Burt, 264
Baer, Max, 262
Balcony, The, 46, 48
Ball, Lucille, 257
Ballard, Lucien, 173
Balthazar, 69
Bancroft, Anne, 237, 263
Band of Outsiders, 39
Banning, 263
Barbarella, 150–51
Barbin, Pierre, 258, 259, 260
Barefoot in the Park, 143
Barry, John, 204
Bart, Lionel, 159, 160
Bates, Alan, 228, 229
Batman, 177

269

Bazin, André, 194
Beatles, 152, 153, 154
Becket, 201
Bedford, Sybille, 180
Before the Revolution, 78, 81
Beiliss, Mendel, 225
Belle de Jour, 43–49, 123
Bellocchio, Marco, 76–81, 82, 83, 178, 179
Belmondo, Jean-Paul, 39
Benefit of the Doubt, The, 100
Ben Hur, 221
Bennett, Jill, 89, 90
Bergman, Ingmar, 23, 24, 25, 30, 31, 32, 40, 78, 130, 131, 132, 133, 134, 135, 136
Berlin Film Festival, 37
Bernstein, Elmer, 261
Bertolucci, Bernardo, 38, 78–79, 81
Best, Willie, 256
Bête humaine, La, 162
Bey, Turhan, 252
Beyond the Law, 170–71
Bible, The, 216
Birthday Party, The, 211–16
Björnstrand, Gunnar, 29
Black, Noel, 176, 177
Blackmer, Sidney, 52
Blakely, Colin, 138, 140
Bloom, Claire, 181, 182, 187, 266
Blow-up, 115
Blue, 145
Boffety, Jean, 121–22
Bofors Gun, The, 92
Bogdanovich, Peter, 166, 167
Bogarde, Dirk, 227
Bogart, Humphrey, 254
Bondarchuk, Sergei, 217, 218, 219, 220, 221, 222
Bonnie and Clyde, 43, 68, 70, 112, 113, 117, 249, 254, 262, 263, 265, 266
Boom, 244, 246

Boston Strangler, The, 182–85
Boulle, Pierre, 64
Bouquet, Michael, 164
Box, John, 159
Boyer, Charles, 230
Bradbury, Ray, 63
Brando, Marlon, 137, 149, 150, 186, 187, 197, 198, 237
Brasseur, Claude, 39
Brayne, William, 190
Brazil 66 (musical group), 264–265
Breathless, 35, 38, 39, 69, 72
Brecht, Bertolt, 38, 71, 95, 168
Brenner, Albert, 165
Brewster, Diane, 257
Bride Wore Black, The, 162–64
Bridges, Beau, 87
Brief Encounter, 145
Bright Eyes, 254
Brook, Peter, 100
Brooks, Mel, 147, 148
Brown, Jim, 88
Brown, Norman O., 155
Browne, Coral, 211
Browne, Roscoe Lee, 85
Brusati, Franco, 207, 209
Budberg, Moura, 232
Bullitt, 165–66
Buñuel, Luis, 39, 43, 45, 46, 47, 48, 49, 123
Burns, Mark, 90
Burr, Raymond, 257
Burton, Richard, 149, 150, 187, 198, 242–47
Butterfield 8, 244
Byron, Stuart, 74

Cabin in the Sky, 256
Caine, Michael, 81
Camelot, 262, 264
Camiel, Eric, 249
Camus, Albert, 195, 199

Canadian Broadcasting Corporation, 188, 190, 193
Candy, 149–50
Cannes Film Festival, 130
Carabiniers, Les, 34, 94–98
Caretaker, The, 213, 215
Carey, Macdonald, 263
Carlin, Lynn, 123, 125
Carlino, Lewis John, 196
Carlsen, Henning, 127
Carlyle, Thomas, 132
Carne, Marcel, 45
Carney, Art, 144
Caron, Leslie, 265
Carrière, Jean-Claude, 45
Carroll, Diahann, 263
Carsten, Peter, 88
Casino Royale, 264
Cassavetes, John, 50, 52, 122, 124, 125–26
Cassel, Seymour, 125
Castel, Lou, 78, 179
Castle, John, 201
Chamberlain, Richard, 52, 108, 109
Channing, Carol, 262
Chaplin, Charles, 41, 136
Chaplin, Saul, 156
Charge of the Light Brigade, The, 89–93
Charlie Bubbles, 136–41
Charlot's Review, 157
Charly, 181–82
Chase, Edna Woolman, 111
Chekhov, Anton, 228, 229, 230, 231
Child, Julia, 166
Children of Paradise, 85
Children's Hour, The, 196
China Is Near, 75–83, 178, 179
Chinoise, La, 34, 35, 65–75, 162
Christie, Julie, 108, 109
Citizen Kane, 79, 137, 157
Clark, Petula, 158

Clarke, Arthur C., 53, 58, 59, 62, 63
Clement, Dick, 209
Cleopatra, 243
Clurman, Harold, 210–11, 211–213, 267
Coburn, James, 149
Cochran, C. B., 156
Cocteau, Jean, 248, 252
Comedians, The, 245
Comedy, 142–43
Commare secca, La, 78
Connery, Sean, 81
Contempt, 36, 39, 74
Cooke, Elisha, Jr., 50
Cool Hand Luke, 199, 262
Cooper, Gary, 253
Cooper, Jackie, 254
Coppola, Francis Ford, 251, 252
Corsaro, Frank, 117
Cosby, Bill, 84
Cotten, Joseph, 109
Coutard, Raoul, 38, 67
Coward, Noël, 146, 157
Crauchet, Paul, 120
Crenna, Richard, 264
Crime of Monsieur Lange, The, 162
Culkin, Father John, 248
Curly Top, 254
Curtis, Tony, 183, 184
Cut, 250–51

Dalton, Timothy, 201, 205
Dandy in Aspic, A, 52
Darc, Mireille, 33, 39–40, 42
Dark of the Sun, 88
Darro, Frankie, 254
Dassin, Jules, 83, 84, 85–86
David Copperfield, 228
Davis, Sammy, Jr., 265–66
Day, Doris, 241
Dean, James, 237
De Carlo, Yvonne, 257

Dee, Ruby, 84, 85
De Gaulle, Charles, 258
Delaney, Shelagh, 137, 140
Deneuve, Catherine, 43, 45, 46, 49
Denner, Charles, 162
Dennis, Sandy, 195, 198
Dermithe, Édouard, 78
De Salvo, Albert, 182
Desert Hawk, The, 257
Desperate Journey, 252
Dickens, Charles, 159, 160
Dickey, Bill, 262
Dickinson, Angie, 265
Dirksen, Everett, 142
Dirty Dozen, The, 262
Disney, Walt, 249
Doctor Doolittle, 262
Doctor Faustus, 245
Dr. Strangelove, 53, 57, 58, 61
Doctor Zhivago, 186, 194
Doermer, Christian, 114
Donati, Danilo, 206, 209
Donen, Stanley, 137
Don Giovanni, 132
Donner, Clive, 74
Don't Look Back, 264
Duhamel, Antoine, 35
Duke, Patty, 262
Dullea, Keir, 55, 56, 60, 62, 63, 195
Dunaway, Faye, 111, 112
Dutchman, 202, 204

East Village Other, 102
Edelmann, Heinz, 152, 153
Edge, The, 74
8½, 114
Eisenstein, Sergei, 219, 222
Eisner, Lotte, 258
Eliot, T. S., 31, 204
Elliott, Denholm, 229, 231
Elvira Madigan, 43, 68, 73, 122
Enrico, Robert, 120, 121, 122

Eroticism, 40
Errol, Leon, 142
Evans, Dame Edith, 261
Evans, Maurice, 52, 64
Everything in the Garden, 46

Face of War, A, 98–100
Faces, 122–26
Fahrenheit 451, 35
Fairchild, William, 157
Fallen Idol, The, 160
Far from Vietnam, 73, 103
Farrow, Mia, 50, 52
Fate of a Man, 219
Fellini, Federico, 42, 79, 82, 114, 251
Fetchit, Stepin, 256
Fiddler on the Roof, 227
Fields, W. C., 142, 185, 254
Film fossils, 256–57
Finian's Rainbow, 157–58
Finney, Albert, 136–37, 138, 140
Fires on the Plain, 32
Fisher, Eddie, 243
Fisher, Gerry, 232
Fist in His Pocket, 78, 178–79
Fitzgerald, Geraldine, 117
Fixer, The, 225–27
Flea in Her Ear, A, 85
Fleischer, Richard, 183, 184
Flim Flam Man, The, 250
Flowers for Algernon (Keyes), 181
Flynn, Errol, 250, 252
Fonda, Henry, 183, 184, 218
Fonda, Jane, 150, 151
Fonda, Peter, 236
Ford, John, 38, 84, 85, 259
For Love of Ivy, 87–88
Forty Guns, 163
Fox, The, 194–99
Francks, Don, 158
Franju, Georges, 258
Frank, Gerold, 183

Frankenheimer, John, 225, 226, 227
Fraker, William, 165, 166
Freeman, Al, Jr., 158
Freud, Sigmund, 41
Friedkin, William, 212, 216
Fry, Christopher, 202
Fugitive Kind, The, 137
Fuller, Sam, 163
Funicello, Annette, 236
Funny Thing Happened on the Way to the Forum, A, 108

Garland, Beverly, 177
Garland, Judy, 243
Garland, Timothy, 138
Gégauff, Paul, 41
Geller, Stephen, 176
Genêt, Jean, 46, 47, 48
Germi, Pietro, 80
Gibran, Kahlil, 115
Gielgud, John, 89, 93
Gill, Brendan, 194
Gilliatt, Penelope, 53–57, 94–98, 103–06, 127–30, 179–81, 267
Giraudoux, Jean, 203
Girl Getters, The, 205
Godard, Jean-Luc, 32–33, 34–37, 38, 39, 40, 41, 42, 65–68, 69, 70–73, 74, 75, 76, 79, 94, 96, 97–98, 115, 250
"Golden Pot, The," 131–32
Goldman, James, 200, 202, 203, 204, 205
Gone with the Wind, 216, 221, 261, 264
Gordon, Ruth, 52
Graduate, The, 108, 113, 125, 148, 150, 235–41, 263, 266
Graham, Sheilah, 247
Grant, Cary, 243, 253
Graziosi, Paolo, 80
Great Train Robbery, The, 165
Green, Felix, 102

Green Berets, The, 100, 103–06
Greene, Richard, 257
Greenspun, Roger, 74
Gries, Thomas S., 172, 173
Griffith, D. W., 75, 107
Griffith, Hugh, 227
Guess Who's Coming to Dinner, 206, 262
Guevara, Che, 65
Guinness, Alec, 160
Gunsmoke, 250
"Gym Period, The" (Rilke), 180

Hackett, Joan, 172
Hagen, Uta, 242
Hall, Conrad, 263
Hamlet, 167
Hamsun, Knut, 127
Harburg, E. Y., 158
Hardy, Oliver, 41, 224
Harrington, Kate, 117, 119
Harrington, Stephanie, 263
Harris, Vernon, 160
Harrison, Linda, 64
Harrison, Rex, 265
Hart, William S., 173
Harte, Bret, 173
Hartung, Philip T., 63–64, 87–88, 182–83, 206–08, 216–18, 267
Harvey, Anthony, 200, 202, 204
Hathaway, Henry, 262
Havilland, Olivia de, 264
Hayes, Helen, 117, 203
Head, Edith, 261, 264
Heart Is a Lonely Hunter, The, 223–25
Hecht, Ben, 204
Heckart, Eileen, 185
Heise, Russel, 190
Hemingway, Ernest, 187
Hemmings, David, 90, 91, 93
Henry, Buck, 150
Henry V, 228
Henze, Hans Werner, 180

Hepburn, Audrey, 218, 220, 265
Hepburn, Katharine, 201, 202,
    205, 257, 262
*Here We Go Round the
    Mulberry Bush*, 74
Herlie, Eileen, 231
Heston, Charlton, 63, 64, 172
He Who Must Die, 85
Heywood, Anne, 195
Heywood, John, 147
Hill, Arthur, 242
Hilton, Nicky, 243
Hirsch, Elroy, 262
Hitchcock, Alfred, 146, 162, 163,
    164, 266
Hoffenberg, Mason, 149
Hoffman, Dustin, 235, 236, 237,
    262, 263
Hoffmann, E. T. A., 131
Holbrook, Hal, 175
Holden, William, 255
Hope, Bob, 261, 262, 263, 265
Hopkins, Anthony, 201
Hour of the Wolf, The, 32, 130–
    136
Howard, Leslie, 257
Howard, Trevor, 89, 90, 93
How I Won the War, 93
How to Stuff a Wild Bikini, 173
Hudson, Rock, 265
Hunger, 127–30
Hunter, Kim, 64
Hussey, Olivia, 206, 208
Huston, John, 198

I Call First, 251
If I Had a Million, 253
Illustrated Man, The, 187
I Love You, Alice B. Toklas, 148–
    149
Inadmissible Evidence, 92
In Cold Blood, 196, 263
Informer, The, 84, 85
Inside North Vietnam, 102

Inspector Clouseau, 143, 224
Interlude, 145
In the Heat of the Night, 112,
    186, 198, 250, 262, 263, 265
In the Midst of Life, 120
Invisible Boy, The, 257
It's Always Fair Weather, 137
It's Not Just You, Murray, 251
I Was a Teen-age Werewolf, 173

Jackson, Glenda, 101
Jacobs, Arthur P., 64
Jarry, Alfred, 151
Jeanson, Francis, 75
Jest of God, A (Lawrence), 116,
    118
Jewison, Norman, 112, 186, 250
Joanna, 113–16
Johnson, Van, 255
Jones, Christopher, 174
Jones, Eugene S., 98
Jones, Shirley, 265
Journey to the End of the Night,
    32
Jour se lève, Le, 85
Joyce, James, 36
Judith, 203
Juross, Albert, 94

Kael, Pauline, 32–37, 65–72,
    75–79, 194–99, 267–68
Kanfer, Stefan, 111–12, 149–50,
    185–88, 247–52, 252–57, 268
Karina, Anna, 72, 73, 97
Karloff, Boris, 166
Kauffmann, Stanley, 83–87,
    89–92, 100–03, 152–53,
    178–79, 190–93, 218–21,
    240, 268
Kaye, Simon, 90
Kazan, Lainie, 263
Keaton, Buster, 41, 136, 142
Keith, Brian, 197, 198

Keller, Frank, 165
Kelly, Gene, 137, 265
Kelly, Grace, 265
Kennedy, Edgar, 142
Kennedy, George, 183, 262
Kennedy, Robert F., 110
Kerr, Deborah, 146
Kershner, Irving, 250
Kessel, Joseph, 44, 45, 46
Keyes, Daniel, 181
Kid for Two Farthings, A, 160
Kienholz, Edward, 250
Kienholz on Exhibit, 250
Killing of Sister George, The,
    210–11
King, Allan, 188, 189, 190, 191,
    192, 193
King, Martin Luther, Jr., 83, 261,
    264
King Rat, 186
Kiss Me, Stupid, 147
Kluge, Alexander, 38
Knight, Arthur, 116–17, 148–49,
    157–58, 172–73, 181–82,
    257–60, 268
Koch, Howard, 196
Kramer, Robert, 74
Kramer, Stanley, 84
Kresel, Lee, 217
Kubrick, Stanley, 53, 54, 55, 56,
    57, 58, 59, 60, 61, 62, 63

Ladd, Alan, 255
Lain, Jewell, 257
Lake, Alan, 139
Lang, Fritz, 85
Langlois, Henri, 257–60
Lanovoi, Vasily, 220
Lansbury, Angela, 265
Lassally, Walter, 113, 114
Late show as history, 252–57
La Tour, Georges de, 26
Laughlin, Michael, 113
Laughton, Charles, 253

Laurel, Stan, 41
Laurence, Margaret, 116, 118
Laurents, Arthur, 208
Law and Order, 256
Lawrence, D. H., 195, 196, 197,
    198–99
Lawrence, Gertrude, 156, 157
Lawrence of Arabia, 89, 90, 216
Leacock, Philip, 250
Lean, David, 89, 90, 160
Léaud, Jean-Pierre, 73
Legacy, A (Bedford), 180
Leigh, Vivien, 264
Lemmon, Jack, 144
Leonard, Jack E., 261
Lester, Mark, 160
Lester, Richard, 107–10, 111,
    115, 152
Levin, Ira, 50, 51
Levine, David, 77
Levine, Joseph E., 236, 238
Lewis, Jerry, 248
Lilies of the Field, 181, 256
Lillie, Beatrice, 157
Lincoln, Abbey, 88
Lion in Winter, The, 200–05
Little Caesar, 254
Lloyd, Harold, 41
Locke, Sondra, 224
Lockhart, Calvin, 114
Lockwood, Gary, 60, 62
Lombard, Carole, 243
Long Day's Journey Into Night,
    228
Loved One, The, 186
Lucas, George, 250, 251
Lumet, Sidney, 137, 228, 229,
    230, 231, 232
Luv, 144
Luxemburg, Rosa, 67
Lynch, Alfred, 231

Macbeth, 81
Made in USA, 72

Magee, Patrick, 212, 215, 216
Magic Carpet, The, 257
Magic Flute, The, 132
Magician, The, 131
Magnificent Ambersons, The, 137, 157
Mailer, Norman, 168, 169–71, 196
Malamud, Bernard, 225, 226, 227
Malden, Karl, 257
Malle, Louis, 180
Malone, Dorothy, 256
Malraux, André, 38
Mame, 116
Mann, Daniel, 88
Marat/Sade, 101
Marcello, I'm So Bored, 250
Mark, The, 187
Marker, Chris, 76
Markham, Edwin, 231
Marley, John, 122, 123, 125
Marquand, Christian, 149
Married Woman, The, 33
Martin, Nan, 87
Marty, 115
Marx Brothers, 254
Masculine Feminine, 65, 69, 76
Mase, Marino, 94, 179
Mason, James, 229, 230–31
Massey, Daniel, 157
Matter of Innocence, A, 146
Matthau, Walter, 144–45, 149, 265
Maupassant, Guy de, 229
Mauri, Glauco, 77, 80, 81, 82, 83
Mayer, Louis B., 255
Mayerling, 68
Mayfield, Julian, 84, 85
McCann, Chuck, 224
McCullers, Carson, 195, 198, 199, 223
McDaniel, Hattie, 264
McDowall, Roddy, 64
McEnery, John, 207, 208

McGrath, John, 92
McKuen, Rod, 115
McLaglen, Victor, 85
McLuhan, Marshall, 260
McQueen, Butterfly, 256
McQueen, Steve, 111, 112, 165, 166
Medina, Patricia, 257
Méliès, Georges, 75
Melville, Jean-Pierre, 180
Menjou, Adolphe, 257
Meredith, Lee, 148
Meril, Macha, 47
Merrow, Jane, 201, 205
Metamorphosis (Kafka), 66
Miami and the Siege of Chicago (Mailer), 170
Milius, John, 250
Milk Train Doesn't Stop Here Anymore, The, 246
Miller, Thomas Ellis, 224
Mills, Reginald, 209
Minnelli, Liza, 138, 140
Minnelli, Vincente, 137
Miracle Worker, The, 262
Mollo, John, 90
Molly Bloom, 168
Monroe, Marilyn, 243
Moody, Ron, 160
Moore, Dudley, 146
Moreau, Jeanne, 162, 163, 164
Morgan! 92
Morgenstern, Joseph, 60–63, 115–116, 159–61, 173–74, 176–78, 188–90, 268
Morning Glory, 257
Moross, Jerome, 117
Morris, Desmond, 64
Morris, Oswald, 160
Morrison, Norman, 101
Morse, Robert, 263
Moseley, Peter, 190
Mostel, Zero, 147, 148
Mother Courage, 96

Motion Picture Association of America, 237, 250
Murnau, F. W., 40, 75
Musil, Robert, 179
My Fair Lady, 156

Naked Ape, The (Morris), 64
National Rifle Association, 178
National Society of Film Critics, 263
National Student Association, 250
National Student Film Festival, 250–51
National Velvet, 243
Negatives, 204
Nelson, Ralph, 181, 182
Never the Twain Shall Meet, 257
Newman, Paul, 116, 117, 118, 186
New School for Social Research, 194
New York Film Critics Circle, 266
New York Film Festival, 103, 170
Nichols, Dandy, 213, 215
Nichols, Dudley, 85
Nichols, Mike, 107, 236, 238, 240, 241, 263, 266
Nicklaus, Jack, 111
Niven, David, 146
Nixon, Richard M., 103
Novak, Kim, 162
No Way to Treat a Lady, 185–86
Now Voyager, 261
Nykvist, Sven, 24
Nymph Errant, 156

O'Brien, Pat, 184
O'Connor, Carrol, 87
Odd Couple, The, 143–45
Odd Man Out, 160
O'Flaherty, Liam, 84
O'Kelly, Tim, 166
Old movies, 252–57

Oliver! 159–61
Oliver Twist, 160
Olivier, Laurence, 52
Olson, James, 117, 119
Omnibus, 249
One-Eyed Jacks, 137
O'Neill, Eugene, 228
On the Waterfront, 187
Ophuls, Max, 78
Osborne, John, 229
Oscarsson, Per, 130
O'Shea, Milo, 207
O'Sullivan, Maureen, 257
O'Toole, Peter, 201, 205
Our Gang, 254
Outcast of the Islands, An, 160

Pabst, G. W., 75
Page, Geneviève, 49
Paper Lion, 170
Parker, Chris, 250, 251
Parsons, Estelle, 117, 119, 265
Party, The, 142–43
Pasolini, Pier Paolo, 79
Pattison, Roy, 90
Pawnbroker, The, 186, 228
Peck, Gregory, 255, 265
Perkins, Tony, 176, 177
Persona, 40, 130, 132, 133, 134–135, 136
Peters, Lauri, 87
Pettet, Joanna, 145
Petulia, 52, 107–10
Phaedra, 85
Phantom of the Rue Morgue, 257
Piccoli, Michel, 46
Pierrot le fou, 72
Pinter, Harold, 212, 213–15
Pirates, The, 137
Pitagora, Paola, 78, 179
Place in the Sun, A, 244
Planet of the Apes, 61, 63–64, 93
Plimpton, George, 170, 244

Poitier, Sidney, 84, 87, 88, 187, 256, 265, 266
Polanski, Roman, 50, 51, 52
Poll, Martin, 200
Pollard, Michael J., 262
Porter, Cole, 156
Possessed, The, 68
Potts, Nell, 116
Presley, Elvis, 236, 237
Pretty Poison, 176–78
Prévert, Jacques, 204
Private Lives, 157
Privilege, 174
Producers, The, 66, 147–48
Prudence and the Pill, 145–46
Purvis, Harry, 256

Quaid, David, 176
Quai des brumes, 85
Question, The, 179

Rachel, Rachel, 116–19
Radd, Ronald, 231
Radziwill, Lee, 244
Rafferty, Max, 174
Raksin, David, 172
Randolph, John, 177
Rashomon, 187
Rattigan, Terrence, 137
Raye, Martha, 263
Reade Organization, Walter, 217
Reading, movies and, 194–95, 199
Reagan, Ronald, 256, 261, 264
Rebel Without a Cause, 255
Red Desert, 122
Redgrave, Vanessa, 89–90, 229, 231
Redwoods, The, 264
Reed, Carol, 159, 160
Reed, Oliver, 160
Reflections in a Golden Eye, 194, 195, 196, 197

Reid, Beryl, 211
Remick, Lee, 185
Renoir, Jean, 136, 162, 163, 164, 193
Rescher, Gayne, 117
Resnais, Alain, 180
Reynolds, Debbie, 243
Richardson, Tony, 90, 91, 92–93, 115
Ride the High Country, 172
Rilke, Rainer Maria, 180
Ring of the Nibelungs, 220
Robertson, Cliff, 181, 182
Rocco, 209
Rolland, Romain, 41
Romeo and Juliet, 92, 206–09
Rooney, Mickey, 243, 247, 254
Rosemary's Baby, 49–52
Ross, Katharine, 262, 263, 265
Rota, Nino, 42, 209
Roubeix, François, 121
Rouch, Jean, 76
Rowlands, Gena, 123, 125
Rules of the Game, The, 162
Russell, Bing, 257
Russians Are Coming, The, 112
Ryan, Thomas C., 224
Rydell, Mark, 198

Saidy, Fred, 158
Saint, Eva Marie, 264
St. Jacques, Raymond, 85
Saint Joan, 203
Sandpiper, The, 244
Sarne, Michael, 113, 114, 115
Sarris, Andrew, 37–42, 43–49, 49–52, 72–75, 79–83, 122–25, 136–39, 162–64, 261–66, 268
Sartre, Jean-Paul, 67, 179
Saudek, Robert, 249
Savelyeva, Ludmila, 218
Scarface, 254
Schaffner, Franklin J., 64

Schickel, Richard, 98–100, 107–109, 118–19, 134–36, 139–41, 221–22, 223–25, 225–27, 268

Schifrin, Lalo, 198

Schlesinger, Arthur, Jr., 125–26, 147–48, 156–57, 202–03, 227, 228–29, 268

Schlöndorff, Volker, 179, 180, 181

Schoendoerffer, Pierre, 102

Scorsese, Marty, 251

Scott, George C., 108, 109

Sea Gull, The, 228–32

Searchers, The, 38

Secombe, Harry, 160

Secret Ceremony, The, 204

Segal, George, 185–86

Sellers, Peter, 142, 143, 148

Semple, Lorenzo, Jr., 176, 177

Serling, Rod, 64

Seven Descents of Myrtle, The, 265

Seventh Seal, The, 32

Shakespeare, William, 206, 208, 209, 229

Shame, 23–32

Shane, 172

Shankar, Ravi, 182

Sharif, Omar, 194

Shaw, George Bernard, 203

Shaw, Robert, 212, 214, 215, 216

Shawn, Dick, 148

Sheed, Wilfrid, 31–32, 109–10, 110–11, 142–47, 154–55, 174–175, 183–85, 213–15, 242–47, 268

Sheeler, Charles, 117

Sheratsky, Rodney, 249, 250

Shimkus, Joanna, 122

Shoot the Piano Player, 70

Sidney, Sylvia, 220

Siegel, Donald, 73

Signoret, Simone, 229, 230

Singin' in the Rain, 137

Silence, The, 31

Silliphant, Stirling, 181

Silvera, Frank, 85

Simon, John, 23–29, 92–93, 120–122, 130–34, 150–51, 153–54, 203–05, 208–09, 229–32, 268

Simon, Paul, 237

Simon of the Desert, 45

Skater-Dater, 176

Skobtseva, Irina, 220

Slocombe, Douglas, 200

Smart Money, 254

Smight, Jack, 185

Smiles of a Summer Night, 24

Smith, C. Aubrey, 257

Smith, Pete, 143

Sommer, Elke, 264

Sons and Lovers, 90

Sons of Katie Elder, The, 262

Sordi, Alberto, 82

Sorel, Jean, 46, 47

Sound of Music, The, 156, 237

Southern, Terry, 149, 150

Specter of the Rose, The, 204

Stamp, Terrence, 145

Stanislavski, Konstantin, 166

Stanwyck, Barbara, 117, 253

Star! 156–57

Starr, Ringo, 149

Steel, June, 250

Steele, Tommy, 158

Steiger, Rod, 185, 186–88, 255, 265, 266

Steiner, Max, 261

Stéphane, Nicole, 78

Stephens, Robert, 207

Stern, Stewart, 117, 118

Steller, James, 74

Stevens, George, 259

Stewart, James, 162, 253

Stormy Weather, 256

Stranger, The (Camus), 195, 199

Student movie-makers, 247–52

Suicide Battalion, 257

Sullivan, Ed, 155
Summer Place, A, 261
Sunrise, 75
Surina, Daniela, 80
Surmâle, Le, 151
Sutherland, Donald, 114, 115
Sydow, Max von, 29, 32, 135

Tabu, 75
Tafler, Sydney, 212, 216
Taming of the Shrew, The, 209, 244, 245
Targets, 166–67
Tarzan the Ape Man, 257
Taste of Honey, A, 137
Tattoli, Elda, 77, 80, 82
Taurog, Norman, 248
Taylor, Elizabeth, 197, 198, 242–247
Taylor, Rod, 88
Taylor-Young, Leigh, 148
Tell Me Lies, 100–01, 103
Terry, Nigel, 201
Third Man, The, 160
Thirty Is a Dangerous Age, Cynthia, 146
This Angry Age, 209
Thom, Robert, 174
Thomas, Dylan, 187
Thomas Crown Affair, The, 110–112
Thoreau, Henry David, 126
Thoroughly Modern Millie, 262
Thulin, Ingrid, 136
THX 1138 4EB, 250, 251
Tihonov, Vyacheslav, 218, 220
Titicut Follies, 193
Todd, Mike, 244
Tolstoy, Leo, 217, 222, 229
Tom Jones, 91, 113, 138, 261
Topkapi, 85
Tracy, Spencer, 262
Trauner, Alexandre, 85
Trip, The, 173

Truffaut, François, 35, 70, 81, 162–63, 164, 258, 259
Trumbo, Dalton, 227
Turman, Lawrence, 176
Two or Three Things I Know About Her, 72
2001: A Space Odyssey, 53–63

Ugly American, The, 137
Ullmann, Liv, 29, 40
Un Chien Andalou, 39
Up Tight, 83–87
US, 100, 103

Vadim, Roger, 150, 151
Valley of the Dolls, 262
Van Fleet, Jo, 149
Varsi, Diane, 174
Verdi, Giuseppe, 79, 81
Vidor, King, 218, 248, 259
Viet Rock, 103
Viol, Le, 40
Violence, 110–11
VIP's, The, 245
Viridiana, 45
Visconti, Luchino, 195, 209
Vlady, Marina, 72

Waite, Genevieve, 114, 115
Walker, David, 90
Wallis, Shani, 160
War and Peace, 91, 216–22
Warhol, Andy, 38, 218
Warner, David, 92, 227, 229, 231
Warrendale, 188–93
Waterloo, 187
Watkins, David, 90, 93
Wayne, David, 158
Wayne, John, 100, 103, 105, 106
Webb, Charles, 240
Weekend, 32–42
Weissmuller, Johnny, 257
Weld, Tuesday, 176, 177
Welles, Orson, 136, 137

Werner, Oskar, 145
West, Mae, 254
Westmoreland, General William, 263
West Side Story, 157, 207, 208
Wexler, Haskell, 263
What's New Pussycat? 147
White, Onna, 159, 160
Whitehead, Peter, 100
Whitelaw, Billie, 137, 138, 139, 140
White Sheik, The, 82
Whiting, Leonard, 206, 208
Who's Afraid of Virginia Woolf? 200
Why Are We in Vietnam? (Mailer), 196
Wiazemsky, Anne, 68–69, 73, 75
Widdoes, Kathleen, 231
Wifstrand, Naima, 131
Wild, Jack, 160
Wild Angels, The, 173
Wilder, Billy, 147, 252
Wilder, Gene, 66, 148
Wilding, Michael, 244
Wild in the Streets, 173–75
Wild 90, 168–70
Williams, Tennessee, 246

Williamson, Nicol, 92
Will Penny, 172–73
Wilson, 228
Wilson, Earl, 247
Wilson, Michael, 64
Winchell, Walter, 246
Winters, Shelley, 175
Winwood, Estelle, 147
Wise, Robert, 156, 157, 266
Wittgenstein, Ludwig, 40
Woman Is a Woman, A, 74
Wood, Charles, 90, 93
Wood, Natalie, 264
Woodham-Smith, Cecil, 89
Woodward, Joanne, 116, 117, 118

Yanne, Jean, 33, 39
Yates, Peter, 165, 166
Yellow Submarine, 152–53
York, Michael, 207
York, Susannah, 211
You Are What You Eat, 154–55
Young Törless, 179–81

Zahava, Boris, 218
Zeffirelli, Franco, 206, 208, 209
Zinnemann, Fred, 259
Zita, 120–22